# RESEARCH METHODOLOGY IN LIBRARY SCIENCE

# RESEARCH METHODOLOGY IN LIBRARY SCIENCE

**Dr. P. BALASUBRAMANIAN**
M.A., M.L.I.Sc., M.Phil., PGDCA, PGDPR, Ph.D.
Deputy Librarian
Manonmaniam Sundaranar University
Tirunelveli (T.N.)

**Dr. A. BALADHANDAYUTHAM**
B.Sc., M.A., M.L.I.Sc., M.Phil., (Ph.D.)
Lecturer
Department of Library and Information Science
Directorate of Distance Education
Madurai Kamaraj University
Madurai (T.N.)

**DEEP & DEEP PUBLICATIONS PVT. LTD.**
F-159, Rajouri Garden, New Delhi - 110 027

# Preface

We are extremely happy to place before the readers, the first edition on *"Research Methodology in Library Science"*. The main aim of this book is to facilitate, easy understanding of the matter at one reading without any tediousness. This book is written in accordance with the syllabus prescribed by the Indian Universities for the M.L.I.Sc. and M.Phil. Scholars and also University Grant Commission NET/SLET Examination Syllabus in Library Science for Unit of Research Methodology. This book is written in a simple language and the chapters are arranged logically. More emphasis is given for greater clarity and understanding of the concepts, methods and its application in business. An attempt has been made to cover the interest of the students of Library and Information Science. This book is presented in a lucid manner.

Authors hope that this book will be appreciated by the students as well as researchers. Suggestions to improve and enhance the value of this book are most welcome. We also thank all those well wishers who have contributed to the enrichment of the contents of this book. Authors thank the publishers for their valuable and sincere efforts taken by them in bringing out this book in a very short time.

DR. P. BALASUBRAMANIAN
DR. A. BALADHANDAYUTHAM

# Acknowledgements

Dr. P. Balasubramanian and A. Baladhandayutham would like to thank the Chairman Prof. B. Stephen, M.Sc., M.Ed., D.S.M., Mrs. A. Roselet Bai, M.Sc., M.Ed., correspondent, the Directors Prof. S. Anand, M.E., (Ph.D.), Prof. S. Allwin, M.E., M.B.A., (Ph.D.) and staff members, both teaching and non-teaching members of the Infant Jesus College of Engineering, Keelavallanadu, Tuticorin, Tamilnadu.

We also thank Prof. Subbash Chandra Ghosh, the Principal of Infant Jesus College of Engineering and Prof. Dr. A. Rangasamy, Department of Management Studies for their help and guidance.

We would like to thank Mrs. T. Mangayarkarasi, Assistant Professor, Department of English, Manonmaniam Sundaranar University, Tirunelveli for her help.

We also thank Dr. S. Nadarajan, Professor and Head, Anna University, Tirunelveli, for his valuable suggestions and help.

Our sincere thanks to Dr. G. Jegadeesan, Assistant Professor, Department of Labour Studies, Directorate of Distance Education, Madurai Kamaraj University, for his valuable suggestions and encouragements.

We would also like to thank M/s. Deep & Deep Publication (P) Ltd., New Delhi, for their help in bringing out this book in a short period.

DR. P. BALASUBRAMANIAN
DR. A. BALADHANDAYUTHAM

# 1

# Introduction to Research

## MEANING OF RESEARCH

A systematic search for an answer to a question or a solution to a problem is called research. It is a purposive investigation. It is an organized enquiry. It aims to get explanations to unexplained phenomenon. Redman and Mory defined research as a "systematized effort to gain new knowledge". D. Slesinger and M. Stephenson defined research as, "manipulation of things, concepts, or symbols for the purpose of generalizing to extend, correct or verify knowledge whether that knowledge aids in construction of a theory or in the practice of an art.

P.M. Cook outlines the term "Research" in a popular way to him, Research is an honest, exhaustive, intelligent searching for facts and their meanings or implications, with reference to a problem.

According to Dr. S.R. Ranganathan, the father of Indian Librarianship, the term:

> "Research" represents a critical and exhaustive investigation to discover new facts, to interpret them in the light of known ideas, theories and laws, to revive the current laws and theories in the light of the newly discovered facts to apply the conclusions to practical purpose.

Research is essentially a systematic enquiry seeking facts through objective, verifiable methods in order to discover the relationship among them and to deduce from them broad principles or laws. It comprises of:

- Collecting, organizing and evaluating data,
- Defining and redefining problems, and
- Formulating hypotheses or suggested solutions.

Research is often defined as scientific thinking. It is man's unending search for truth, which has brought him to the stage of using scientific thinking as a main source of evidence.

As a research is a scientific investigation or inquiry, it is essential to study what exactly is meant by Science and Scientific investigation.

As such the term research refers to the systematic method consisting of enunciating the problem, formulating a hypothesis, collecting the facts, analyzing the facts and reaching certain conclusions either in the form of solutions towards the concerned problem or in certain generalizations for some theoretical formulation.

## CHARACTERISTICS OF RESEARCH

1. It is a systematic and critical investigation into a phenomenon.
2. It is not a mere compilation but a purposive one.
3. It adopts scientific method.
4. It emphasizes the development of generalisation, principles and theories.
5. A research is directed towards the solution of a problem.
6. It is based upon experience or empirical evidence.
7. Research demands accurate observation and description.
8. Research involves gathering new data from primary sources or using existing data for a new purpose.
9. Research activities are characterized by carefully designed procedures and applying rigorous analysis.
10. Research requires necessary skill to carry out investigation, search the related literature and to understand and analyze the data gathered.
11. Research strives to be objective and logical, applying every possible test to validate the procedures employed, the data collected and the conclusions drawn.
12. Research requires courage.
13. Research is characterized by patient and unhurried activity.
14. Research is carefully recorded and reported.
15. Research follows a specific plan of procedure.
16. Research accepts certain critical assumptions. These assumptions are underlying theories or ideas about how the world works.
17. Research requires the collection and interpretation of data in attempting to resolve the problem that initiated the research.

## CRITERIA FOR GOOD RESEARCH

One expects scientific research to satisfy the following criteria:

1. The purpose of research should be well-defined and common concepts to be used.
2. The research procedure used should be described in detail to permit another researcher to repeat the research for further advancement.
3. The design of the research should be well planned to get fruitful result.
4. The researcher should report with complete frankness.
5. The analysis of data should be sufficiently adequate to reveal its significance and appropriate methods of analysis should be used. The validity and reliability of the data should be checked carefully.
6. Conclusions should be confined to those justified by the data of the research and limited to those for which the data provide an adequate basis.
7. Good research should be systematic.
8. The research is guided by the rules of logical reasoning and the logical process of induction and detection are of great value in carrying out research.

## OBJECTIVES OF RESEARCH

The objectives or the purposes of the research are as follows:

### 1. Development of Knowledge

Every science tries to collect a systematized body of knowledge about the subject matter. Social research is organized to acquire further knowledge about the social facts and social phenomenon.

### 2. Scientific Study of Social Life

In social research, the researcher studies the social changes, structure and process. He studies in detail, human behaviour and collects data about various aspects of the social life of man and formulates laws in this regard.

### 3. Welfare of Humanity

Every researcher studies with a higher aim, which invariably is, 'welfare of community'. The welfare of the community by the results of the investigation may be improved.

### 4.. Clarification of Facts

Business research aims to clarify facts. To develop a series of clear-cut concepts and to examine the old concepts.

### 5. Prediction

The main objective of many researches is to make it possible, to predict the behaviour of business under specified conditions and the importance of business for the benefit of the society.

**6.** Research unravels the mysteries on nature.

**7.** The research establishes generalizations and general laws and contributes to theory building in various fields of knowledge.

**8.** Research verifies the existing fact and theory and these help in improving the knowledge of the society.

**9.** Research aids planning and thus contributes for national development.

**10.** Research aims to analyse the inter-relationship between variables and to derive casual relations.

**11.** General laws developed through research may enable us to make reliable prediction of events yet to happen.

**12.** Applied Research aims at finding solutions to problems.

**13.** The cost benefit evaluation studies of projects like irrigation projects throw out valuable lesson for improving the projects of similar nature subsequently.

**14.** To test the hypothesis of casual relationship between variables.

**15.** To write the report based upon the findings of the research.

**16.** Research also aims at developing new tools, concepts and theories for a better study of unknown phenomena.

**17.** Research aids planning and thus contributes to national development.

## TYPES OF RESEARCH

The basic types of research are as follows:

### 1. Descriptive Research

Descriptive research includes surveys and fact-finding enquiries of different kinds. The major purpose of descriptive research is description of the state affairs, as it exists at present. It reports the characteristics of a particular individual situation or group and also the frequency of occurrence of an event like, the frequency of accidents in a particular area.

### 2. Applied Research

Applied research aims at finding a solution for an immediate problem facing a society or an industrial/business organization. For example, a researcher undertake to study the causes of chigunkunia fever in a particular area is applied research. Applied research is pragmatic; its purposes are more specific and are generally directed at solving practical problems or at a discovery of new knowledge that can be utilized immediately in actual real work situations. Studies in librarianship fall in the category of applied research.

### 3. Quantitative Vs. Qualitative

Quantitative research is based on the measurement of quantity or amount. It is applicable to phenomena that can be expressed in terms of quantity. Qualitative research, on the other hand, is concerned with qualitative phenomenon, i.e., phenomena relating to or involving quality or kind.

### 4. Conceptual *Vs.* Empirical

Conceptual research is that related to some abstract idea(s) or theory. Philosophers and thinkers to develop new concepts or to reinterpret existing ones generally use it. On the other hand, empirical research relies on experience or observation.

### 5. Historical Research

Historical research is the induction of principles through research to the past and social forces, which have shaped the present. Its aim is to apply reflective thinking to unsolved social problems by discovering past trends of events, facts and attitudes, and by tracing lines of development in human thought and action.

Historical research for its successful implementation depends highly on the sources of information, which include:

- Oral history records.
- News papers.
- Annual reports.
- Manuscripts.

Historical method in Library and Information Science can be applied to write the biography of a person (e.g. Ranganathan, Melvil Dewey) or in the development of a Library during a particular period (e.g. Library of Congress, National Library of Calcutta), or to record the history of libraries in a country, or history of development of library technique (e.g. Library Classification, Cataloguing and Indexing), etc.

### 6. Formulative or Exploratory Research

An exploratory study/research is one, which has the purpose of formulating a problem for more precise investigation or for developing hypotheses. Besides, this study may, however, have other functions as follows:

(1) Clarifying concepts;
(2) Increasing investigator's familiarity with the phenomenon they wish to investigate in a subsequent, more highly structured study, with the setting in which they have plan to carry out such a study;
(3) Establishing priorities for further research; and

(4) Providing a census of problems regarded as urgent by people working in a given field of social relations.

### Categories of Exploratory Research

The purpose, rather than the technique, of the research determines whether a study is exploratory, descriptive, or causal. A manager may choose from three general categories of exploratory research:

### Experience Surveys

Concepts may be discussed with top executives and knowledgeable managers who have had personal experience in the field. This constitutes an informal experience survey. The business manager rather than the research department may conduct such a study. The purpose of such a study is to help formulate the problem and clarify concepts rather than to develop conclusive evidence.

### Secondary Data Analysis

A quick and economical source of background information is trade literature in the public library. Searching through such material is exploratory research with secondary data; research rarely begins without such an analysis. Business managers can conduct an informal situation analysis using secondary data and experience surveys.

### Case Study Method

The purpose of a case study is to obtain information from one, or a few, situations similar to the researcher's situation. A case study has no set procedures, but often requires the cooperation of the party whose history is being studied.

### Pilot Studies

The term "pilot studies" is used as a collective to group together a number of diverse research techniques all of which are conducted on a small scale. Thus, a pilot study is a research project, which generates primary data from consumers, or other subjects of ultimate concern.

### Focus Group Interviews

These interviews are free-flowing interviews with a small group of people. They have a flexible format and can discuss anything from brand to a product itself. The group typically consists of six to ten participants and a moderator. The moderator's role is to introduce a topic and to encourage the group to discuss it among themselves. There are four primary advantages of the focus group: (1) it allows people to discuss their true feelings and convictions, (2) it is relatively fast, (3) it is easy to execute and very flexible, and (4) it is inexpensive.

## 7. Experimental Research

The experiment is the basic tool of the physical sciences for tracing cause and effect relationships and for verifying inferences. Its application in the social science is still in its infancy. Experimental studies have their purposes to test a hypothesis of a casual relationship between variables. The three main features of the experiment and quantitative measurement of results appear to be applicable and relevant at least in some social sciences and in some fields. The three broad types of experiments are:

(1) The natural or uncontrolled one as in astronomy, made up mostly of observation;
(2) The laboratory type as in physics, chemistry and psychology, in which the scientists reproduce the situation he want to observe and in which he manipulates one or more of the conditions; and
(3) The field experiment—the best suited to social sciences—which is a theoretically-oriented project in which the investigator manipulates one independent variable in some real social setting.

## 8. Other Types of Research

All other types of research are variations of one or more of the above stated approaches, based on either the purpose of research, or the time required to accomplish research, or the environment in which research is done, or on the basis of some other similar factor.

## BASIC RESEARCH AND APPLIED RESEARCH

There are two types of research:

**A.** *Basic or pure research* attempts to expand the limits of knowledge. It does not directly involve the solution to a particular problem. Basic research findings cannot be immediately implemented. It is conducted to verify the acceptability of a given theory or to discover more about a certain concept. Basic research is not concerned with solving any practical problem or policy. On the contrary it is concerned with designing the tools of analysis and with discovering universal laws and theories.

Examples for Basic Research in Library and Information Science are: .

(a) Use of periodicals in a University Library, and
(b) Impact of Library on faculty improvement programme.

**B.** *Applied research* is conducted when a decision must be made about a specific real-life problem. Applied research is undertaken to answer questions about specific problems or to make decision about a particular course of action. For example, an organisation contemplated a paperless office and a networking system for the companies personal computers, may conduct a research to learn the amount of time its employees spent at personal computer in an average week.

*Quasi-experimental research* is to test cause and effect by observing how subjects react to phenomena. It is, therefore, at least in intent, a quantitative approach. However, in quasi-experimental research full control is not possible because one or more of the three characteristics of true experimental research is missing. In educational research, it is rarely possible to control all the variables. This, of course, means that confidence in assertions of causality must be weaker than in the classic experiment.

There are many different procedures that are used in quasi-experimental research. Two of the most common are:

### *Using a Non-equivalent Control Group*

In this model the researcher does not randomly assign subjects to a control or experimental group. Rather an experimental group is chosen and a similar group is selected as the 'non-equivalent' control group. For example, someone researching into the effects of using peer-assessment might compare two groups of students on similar courses, one where peer-assessment is used and one where it is not.

The key differences between this model and that of the classic experiment is that subjects are not randomly assigned to each group and the researcher is, usually, unable to control all random variables. The basic weakness of the method is the lack of certainty about the exact degree of similarity between the experimental and control groups and the possibility of 'contamination' by other variables, e.g. the quality of the teaching might be better in one group that in the other.

### *Making a Series of Observations on a Single Group Before and After the Experimental Change*

In this model, the researcher makes a series of observations ('pre-tests') on a group of subjects to establish an existing pattern. S/he then makes the experimental change and, again, observes the behaviour of the group over time (in a series of 'post-tests'). If there is a consistent and measurable change, it is considered reasonable to infer causality.

For example, suppose a group of students fail to use the Harvard Referencing System correctly after three coursework assessment episodes. Suppose in response, that the teacher then devotes three hours of teaching time to a workshop on the use of the Harvard System. If, in each of the next three assessment episodes the number of students failing to use Harvard correctly diminishes, then it is reasonable to suppose that the workshop had a positive effect.

Both types of research employ the scientific method, the analysis and interpretation of empirical evidence (facts from observation or experimentation), to confirm or disprove prior conceptions.

## APPROACHES TO RESEARCH

The above description of the types of research brings to light the fact that there are two basic approaches to research, viz., quantitative approach and the qualitative approach. The former involves the generation of data in quantitative form, which can be subjected to rigorous quantitative analysis in a formal and rigid fashion. This approach can be further classified in to inferential, experimental and simulation approaches to research. The purpose of inferential approach to research is to form a database from which to infer characteristics or relationships of population. This usually means survey research where a sample of population is studied (questioned or observed) to determine its characteristics, and it is then inferred that the population has the same characteristics. Experimental approach is characterized by much greater control over the research environment and in this case some variables are manipulated to observe their effect on other variables. Simulation approach involves the construction of an artificial environment within which relevant information and data can be generated. This permits an observation of the dynamic behaviour of a system (or its sub-system) under controlled conditions.

Simulation approach can also be useful in building models for understanding future conditions. Qualitative approach to research is concerned with subjective assessment of altitudes, opinions and behavior. Research in such a situation is a function of researcher's insights and impressions. Such an approach to research generates results either in non-quantitative form or in the form, which are not subjected to rigorous quantitative analysis. Generally, the techniques of focus group interviews, projective techniques and depth interviews are used. All these are explained at length in chapters that follow.

## RESEARCH AND SCIENTIFIC METHOD

The two terms, research and scientific method, are closely related. Research, as we have already stated, can be termed as "an inquiry into the nature of, the reasons for, and the consequences of any particular set of circumstances, whether these circumstances are experimentally controlled or recorded just as that occur. Further, research implies the researcher is interested in more than particular results; he is interested in the repeatability of the results and in their extension to more complicated and general situations". On the other hand, the philosophy common to all research methods and techniques, although they may vary considerably from one science to another, is usually given the name of scientific method. In this context, Karl Pearson writes, "The scientific method is one and same in the branches (of science) and that method is the method of all logically trained minds.... The unity of all sciences consists alone in its methods, not its material; the man who classifies facts of any kind whatever, who sees their mutual relation and describes their sequences, is applying the Scientific Method and is a man of science."

Scientific method is a pursuit of truth as determined by logical considerations. This ideal of science is to achieve a systematic interrelation of facts. Scientific method attempts to achieve "this ideal by experimentation, observation, logical arguments from accepted postulates and a combination of these three in varying proportions." In scientific method, logic aids in formulating propositions explicitly and accurately so that their possible alternatives become clear. Further, logic develops the consequences of such alternatives, and when these are compared with observable phenomena, it becomes possible for the researcher or the scientist to state which alternative is most in harmony with the observed facts.

## LIMITATIONS OF RESEARCH

(1) *Problem of finding good investigators:* No research can be a success unless the investigator is sincere.
(2) *Dependence on others:* Dependence on others poses another problem. A researcher cannot do every thing by himself. He is required to employ the investigators. Similarly, he is to collect information from others who may not be prepared to give information and least willing to co-operate.
(3) *Problem of analysing data:* when the data has been collected, the problem of social researcher does not end. Findings of researcher would always depend on the interpretation of data. Usually, it is seen that data is analysed by the analyzer in such a way that suits his convenience and attitudes.

## THE HALLMARKS OF SCIENTIFIC RESEARCH

The hallmarks of scientific research may be listed as follows:

### 1. Purposiveness

The manager should start the research with a definite aim or purpose. This will be beneficial in many ways. For example, when we study about labour, we will have more information with regard to reduction of turn over, reduction of absenteeism and increased performance level, all of which would definitely benefit the organisation. The research thus has a purposive focus.

### 2. Rigor

A good theoretical base and a sound methodological design would add rigor to purposive study. Rigor means carefulness. Scrupulousness, and the degree of exactness in research investigations. This factor enables the researcher to collect the right kind of information from the appropriate sample with a minimum degree of buyers. This facilitates suitable analysis of the data gathered. Rigor in research design also makes possible the achievement of the other six hallmarks of scientific research.

**3. Testability**

After taking a random selection of samples, the manager or the researcher develops certain hypothesis. A hypothesis is one, which can be tested when the data are collected. For example, a correlation analysis would indicate whether the hypothesis is substantiated or not. In addition to this, there are other tests like chi-square test, t-test, f-test, and so on. Scientific research is thus lends itself to testing logically developed hypothesis to see whether or not the data supports. Testability thus becomes another hallmark of scientific research.

**4. Replicability**

The results of the test of hypothesis should be supported again and yet again when the same type of research is repeated in other similar circumstances. To the extent that this thus happen, we will gain confidence in the scientific nature of our research. To sum up our hypothesis would not have been supported merely by chance but of reflective of the true state of affairs in the population. Replicability is thus another hallmark of scientific research.

**5. Precision and Confidence**

In management research, we are able to draw definite conclusion on the basis of the results of data analysis. We are unable to study the universe of items, events, or population we are interested in, and have to base our findings on a sample that we draw from the universe. Precision refers to the closeness of the findings to reality based on a sample. Precision reflects the degree of accuracy of the results on the basis of the sample, to what really exists in the universe. You may recall the term confidence interval in the statistics, which is what is referred to here as precision. Confidence refers to the probability that our estimations are correct. That is, it is not merely enough to be precise, but it is also important that we can confidently claim that 95% of the item of our results would be true and there is only a 5% chance of our being wrong. This is also known as confidence level. The narrower the limits within which we can estimate the range of our predictions and the greater the confidence we have in our research results, then our scientific findings will be more useful.

**6. Objectivity**

The conclusions drawn through the interpretation of the results of data analysis should be objective. That is, it should be based on the facts of the findings derived from the actual data, and not on our own subjective or emotional values. More damages can be sustained by organisations that implement non-data-based or misleading conclusions drawn from the research. If the interpretations are more objective, then research investigations become meaningful. Though researchers must start with some initial subjective values and believes, their interpretation of data should be clear. In order to be more precise, the managers should be particularly sensitive to this aspect. Objectivity is thus another hallmark of scientific investigation

### 7. Generalisability

It refers to the scope of applicability of the research findings in one of the organizational setting to other settings. Wider the range of applicability, more useful information may reach the users. For a wider generalisability, the research sampling design has to be logically developed and number of other details in the data collection methods need to be followed carefully. However, we have to bear the cost in our mind. Most applied research is generally confined to research within the particular organisation or settings. Though such a limited applicability does not necessarily decrease its scientific value.

### 8. Parsimony

Simplicity in explains in the phenomena, generalizing solutions for the problems is always referred. The achievement of meaningful and parsimonious rather than an elaborate and cumbersome model becomes a critical issue in research. Economy in research model is achieved when we use lesser number of variables. Parsimony can be introduces with a good understanding of a problem and the important factors that influence the problem. Such a conceptual theoretical model can be realized through structured and unstructured interview with the concerned people and a detailed literature review of the previous research work in the particular problem area.

## THE BUILDING BLOCKS OF SCIENCE IN RESEARCH

The building blocks of scientific enquiry include the process of initially observing phenomenon, identifying the problem, constructing a theory as to what might be happening, developing hypothesis, determining aspects of research design, collecting data, analyzing the data and interpreting the research. One of the primary methods of scientific investigation is the hypothetical deductive method.

### Deduction

Answers to issues can be found either by the process of deduction or the process of induction, or by a combination of the two. Deduction is the process by which we arrive at reasonable conclusions by logical generalization of a known fact. For example, we know that, all high performers are highly proficient in their jobs. If Robert is a high performer, we can conclude that, Robert is highly proficient in his job.

### Induction

It is a process where we observe certain phenomena and on this basis, we arrive at conclusions. In other words, in induction, we logically establish a general proposition based on observed facts. For example, the production process or the prime features of factories. Therefore, we conclude that, factories exist for production purposes. Both the deductive and inductive processes are applied in scientific applications.

Theories based on deduction and induction helps us to understand, explain and predict business phenomena. When research is designed to test some specific hypothesized outcomes, the investigator begins with the theory concept. Then, the hypothesis is generated. The results of the study help the researcher to deduce or conclude. This method of starting with theoretical framework, formulating hypothesis and logically deducing from the results is known as hypothetico deductive method.

## SIGNIFICANCE OF BUILDING BLOCKS

1. A sales manager might observe that customers are perhaps not satisfied as they used to be. Therefore, to know the customer satisfaction and the decline he may opt for observation. This process of observation around us will tell the happenings. Now we may decide whether to follow applied research or basic research.
2. Then the manager is to determine whether there is a real problem and it seriousness. For this, he may arrange for initial data gathering. He may talk to few customers and know their feelings and opinions about the products and service.
3. Integration of information obtained through interviews help the manager that the problem thus exists. It will help the manager to formulate conceptual models of all the factors contributing to the problem.
4. From the theoretical framework, several hypotheses can be generated and can be tested to determine whether the data support them.
5. Concepts are then operationally defined so that they can be measured.
6. A research design is set-up to decide on how to collect further data, analyse and interpret them, and finally to provide an answer to the problem. The drawing of from logical analysis and inference that purports to be conclusive is called deduction. Thus, the building blocks of science provide the geneses for the hypothetical deductive method of scientific research.

## THE NEED FOR A THEORETICAL FRAMEWORK

After conducting the interviews, completing a literature survey, and defining the problem, one is ready to develop a theoretical framework. A theoretical framework is a conceptual model of how one theorizes or makes logical sense of the relationships among the several factors that have been identified as important to the problem. This theory flows logically from the documentation of previous research in the problem area. The theoretical framework discusses the interrelationships among the variables that are deemed to be integral to the dynamics of the situation being investigated. Developing such a conceptual framework helps us to postulate or hypothesize and test certain relationships and thus to improve our understanding of the dynamics of the situation.

From the theoretical framework, then, testable hypotheses can be developed to examine whether the theory formulated is valid or not. Since the theoretical framework offers the conceptual foundation to proceed with the research, and since a theoretical framework is none other than identifying the network of relationships among the variables considered important to the study of any given problem situation, it is essential to understand what a variable means and what the different types of variables are.

### Goals of Theory

Prediction and understanding are the two purposes of theory. Accomplishing the first goal allows the theorist to predict the behavior or characteristics of one phenomenon from the knowledge of another phenomenon's characteristics. The ability to anticipate future conditions in the environment or in an organization may be extremely valuable, yet prediction alone may not satisfy the scientific researcher's goals. Understanding is desired. In most situations, of course, prediction and understanding go hand in hand, but to predict phenomena, we must have an explanation of why variables behave as they do.

### The Meaning of Theory

A theory is a coherent set of general propositions, used as principles of explanation of the apparent relationships of certain observed phenomena. Before a proposition can be explained, the nature of theoretical concepts must be understood.

### Concepts

Theory development is essentially a process of describing phenomena at increasingly higher levels of abstraction. A concept (or construct) is a generalized idea about a class of objects, occurrences, or purposes. Concepts are our building blocks and some examples of organizational theory concepts might be "leadership," "productivity," and "morale." Concepts abstract reality. That is, concepts are expressed in words that refer to various events or objects. Concepts, however, may vary in degree of abstraction. The abstraction ladder indicates that it is possible to discuss concepts at various levels of abstraction. The basic or scientific business researcher operates at two levels: the abstract level of concepts (and propositions) and the empirical level of observation and manipulation of objects and events

Researchers are concerned with the observable world, or what we will loosely term "reality." Theorists translate their conceptualization of reality into abstract ideas. Thus, theory deals with abstraction. Things are not the essence of theory, ideas are: Only when we begin to explain how concepts relate to other concepts do we begin to construct theories.

### Nature of Propositions

Concepts are basic units of theory development. However, theories require that the relationship among concepts be understood. Propositions are statements concerned with the relationships among concepts. A theory is an abstraction from observed reality. Concepts are at one level of abstraction. Investigating propositions requires that we increase our level of thinking.

### An Example of a Theory

Two concepts—(1) the "perceived desirability of movement" to another job, and (2) the "perceived ease of movement" from the present job—are expected to be the primary determinants of "intentions to quit." This is a proposition. The concept "intentions to quit" is expected to be a necessary condition before the actual "voluntary turnover behaviour" occurs. This is a second proposition that links concepts together in this theory.

### Verifying Theory

In most scientific theory there are alternative theories to explain certain classes of phenomena. To determine which is the better theory, researchers gather empirical data or evidence to verify theories.

One task of science is to determine if a given theoretical proposition is false or if there are inconsistencies between competing theories—theories are made to be tested.

Business research gathers facts to verify theories. However, the researcher must understand the difference between facts and theories. Facts are the world's data. Theories are structures of ideas that explain and interpret facts. Facts do not go away when scientists debate rival theories to explain them.

### Overview of the Scientific Method

Seven operations may be viewed as the steps involved in the application of the scientific theory:

A. Assessment of relevant existing knowledge
B. Formulation of concepts and propositions

C. Statement of hypotheses
D. Design the research to test the hypotheses
E. Acquisition of meaningful empirical data
F. Analysis and evaluation of data
G. Provide explanation and state new problems raised by the research

## Practical Value of Theories

Theories allow us to generalize beyond individual facts or isolated situations. Theories provide a framework that can guide managerial strategy by providing insights into general rules of behaviour. A good theory allows us to generalize beyond individual facts so that general patterns may be predicted and understood.

## Components of Theoretical Framework

A good theoretical framework identifies and labels the important variables in the situation that are relevant to the problem defined. It logically describes the inter connections among these variables. The relationships among he independent variables, the dependent variables and if applicable, the moderating and intervening variables are elaborated. Any interrelationships among the independent variables themselves, or among the dependent variables themselves (in case there are two or more dependent variables), if any, should also be clearly spelled out and adequately explained.

The elaboration of the variables in the theoretical framework thus addresses the issues of why or how we expect certain relationships to exist, and the nature and direction of the relationships among the variables of interest.

It may be noted that we have used the terms theoretical framework and model interchangeably. There are differences of opinion as to what a model actually represents. Some describe models as simulations; others view a model as a representation of relationships between and among concepts. In sum, there are five basic features that should be incorporated in any theoretical framework:

1. The variables considered relevant to the study should be clearly identified ad labeled in the discussions.
2. The discussions should state how two or more variables are related to one another.
3. If the nature and direction of the relationships can be theorized on the basis of the findings of previous research, then there should be an indication in the discussions as to whether the relationships would be positive or negative.
4. There should be a clear explanation of why we would expect these relationships to exist.

5. A schematic diagram of the theoretical framework should be given so that the reader can see and easily comprehend the theorized relationships.

## RESEARCH PROCESS

Before entering on the details of Research Methodology, it is essential to give a brief overview of the research process. It consists of series of actions and steps necessary to effectively carried out research and the desired result.

One should remember that the various steps involved in the research process are not mutually exclusive. They do not necessarily follow each other in a specific order. The following are the steps in research process.

### 1. Formulating the Research Problem

At the very beginning the researcher must single out the problems he wants to study. Initially the problem may be stated in a general way. Then the formulation of a general topic into a specific research problem should be his first step in a scientific enquiry. The researcher should examine all available literature to become familiar with selected problem. Care must be taken to verify the objectivity and validity of the background facts concerning the problem.

### 2. Extensive Survey of Literature

The researcher should undertake a detailed survey of literature connected with the problem. He or she may refer journals published and unpublished bibliographies, conference proceedings, government reports, books, survey findings. In this process he should remember that one source would lead to another. The earlier studies if any, which are similar to the study, should be carefully studied. A good library will be of great help to the researcher at this stage.

### 3. Development of Working Hypothesis

The researcher should state in clear terms the hypothesis, which is a tentative assumption made in order to test its logical consequences. Hypothesis should be very specific and limited, as it has to be tested. It also indicates the type of data required and the method of collecting the data.

### 4. Preparing the Research Design

The researcher should prepare a research design in which the conceptual structure of the research would be mentioned. In the design, the means of obtaining the information, time available for research, cost involved and the objective of the research are mentioned.

### 5. Determining Sample Design

The researcher must decide the way of selecting the sample from the universe popularly known as the sample design. It is decided before any data are actually collected. The important sample designs are, simple random sampling, deliberate sampling, systematic sampling, stratified sampling, quota sampling, cluster sampling, multi-stage sampling, and sequential sampling.

### 6. Collecting the Data

In dealing the real life problem, it is often found that, data at hand are inadequate and hence, it is necessary to collect data. There are several ways of collecting appropriate data, which is decided, by cost, time, and other resources at the disposal of the researcher. Primary data can be collected either through experiment or through survey. But in case of survey, any one or more of the following ways can collect the data: that is, by observation, through personal interviews, through telephone interviews, by mailing of questionnaires, through schedules.

### 7. Execution of the Project

It is an important step in research process. If the execution of the projects proceeds on correct line, the data to be collected would be adequate and dependable. The execution should be systematic and in time. The fieldwork for data collection should be in a systematic manner and steps should be taken to get the co-operation of the respondents.

### 8. Analysis of Data

After the data have been collected, the researcher turns to the task of analysing them. He should classify the raw data into some purposeful and usable categories. At this stage, coding is done through which the categories of data are transformed into symbols that may be tabulated and counted. Editing is the procedure that improves the quality of data for coding. Tabulation is a part of the technical procedure wherein the classified data are put in the form of tables. Analysis of work after tabulation is generally based on a computation of various percentages, coefficients, etc. by applying various well-defined statistical formulae.

### 9. Hypothesis Testing

After analysing the data, the researcher is in a position to test the hypothesis if any, he had formulated earlier. Statistician has developed various tests such as Chi-square test, T-test, F-test for the purpose. The test to be used depends upon the nature and object of research enquiry. Hypothesis testing will result in either accepting the hypothesis or in rejecting it.

### 10. Generalisation and Interpretation

If a hypothesis is tested and upheld several times, it may be possible for the researcher to arrive at generalization. If the researcher had no hypothesis to start with, he might seek to explain his findings on the basis of some theory. It is known as interpretation. The process of interpretation may create new questions, which in turn may lead to further researches.

### 11. Preparation of the Report or the Thesis

Finally, the researcher has to prepare the report what he has done. It should be written in a concise and objective style in simple language avoiding vague terms and expressions. The lay out of the report should be as follows:

*Preliminary pages:* It includes title, date, acknowledgement, and forward. Then there should be a table of contents, list of tables, list of graphs, chart if any in the report.

*Main text:* It should include an introduction, summary of findings, main report and conclusion.

*The end matter:* It includes bibliography, i.e. list of books, journals, reports, etc.

## RESEARCH PROBLEM

The first and the foremost step is selecting and properly defining a research problem. This saves the researchers time and his efforts are directed towards a particular direction. For the selection of the problem to be analysed, we have so many sources from which we can select the suitable, needy, and possible topic.

The term problem is derived from the Greek word "proballein" which means anything thrown forward; a question proposed for solution; a matter stated for examination. The word 'Topic' is a synonym to the term 'Problem'.

"Research *problem is a statement that can be investigated and define its nature and scope."*

R.S. Woodworth defines a problem as "a situation for which we have no ready and successful response by instinct or by previously acquired habit". A problem is a situation for which there is no ready solution available but it is required to search for the same. There may be many problems. All the problems cannot be solved, nor do they deserve to be solved for that matter. In brief problem means the state of situation for which one has to find a proper solution adopting scientific means.

### Components of Research Problem

The formulation of a problem depends upon the knowledge of the components of a problem. A researcher should identify five components of a problem.

There must be an individual or group, which has the problem;

The researchers should have some objectives, goals, ends, and desires;

The researchers must have various alternative means of obtaining or achieving the ends and objectives. For this purpose he may use even simple instruments, mathematical formula, scientific devises, etc.;

The researcher must be able to decide which course of action is better and efficient and practical; there must be one or more environments to which the problem pertains.

## Sources of Research Problems

The research problems may be selected from the following sources:

1. Theory of one's interest;
2. Daily problems;
3. Technological changes;
4. Unexplored areas;
5. Discussions with experts and authorities including the supervisor or research advisor; and
6. Theories in social sciences.

### *1. Theory of One's Interest*

A researcher may select a problem for investigation from a given theory in which he has considerable interest. In such situations, the researcher must have a detailed knowledge of that theory and should be sufficiently capable of exploring unexplained aspects. The assumptions of that theory may also be taken as the problem to be analysed.

### *2. Daily Problems*

Research problem can also be selected on the basis of current experience of a researcher. A research problem may be identified from the burning problems of the time. The researcher can keep a diary and note down the ideas that comes to him. In the course of his daily work, like reading, conversation with his colleagues and businessman, some idea may flash in his mind. He can immediately note it down and then discuss with others who have enough experience in the same area.

### *3. Technological Changes*

Technological changes in a fast changing society are constantly bringing forth new problems and new opportunities for research. What is the impact of a changed technology on the existing socio-economic set up, always interests the researcher and tempts him to undertake such studies.

### *4. Unexplored Areas*

Research problems can be both abstract and applied interest. These may also be selected from those areas, which have not been explored so far; such areas may be theoretical or empirical in nature. A good starting point either for selecting or for learning about a topic is some one who is well acquainted with the topic.

### 5. Discussions with Experts and Authorities Including the Supervisor or Research Advisor

Trade and professional associations, chambers of commerce, executives and researchers are all important source of information. Much, valuable information consists of information obtained through experience. Sorted information and conclusions based on experience are often the only source of information on topics.

### *Study of Current Literature*

There are a lot of professional journals in social sciences. A researcher should read such journals, the master's thesis, dissertations, etc. In government organisations they may publish report about their activities, achievements, etc. By a careful study and analysis of such literature, the researcher can find problems, which require answers.

### 6. Theories in Social Sciences

There are a lot of theories in social sciences, for example, the Modiglioni Miller approach, in Maslow's theory of motivation. Walter's model on dividend policy, etc. The researcher may select a problem for investigation from a given theory in which he has considerable interest. In appropriate situations the researchers must have through knowledge of such theories. Some unexplained aspects and assumptions of the theory could be considered for identifying a research problem.

### *Selecting the Problem*

The research problem undertaken for study must be carefully selected. The task is a difficult one, although it may not appear to be so. Help may be taken from a research guide in this connection. Nevertheless, every researcher must find out his own salvation for research problems cannot be borrowed. A problem must spring from the researcher's mind like a plant springing from its own seed. However, a researcher in selecting a research problem or a subject for research may observe the following points:

1. Subject which is overdone should not be normally chosen, for it will be a difficult task to throw any new light in such a case;
2. Controversial subject should not become the choice of an average researcher;

   Too narrow or too vague problems should be avoided;
3. The subject selected for research should be familiar and feasible so that the related research material or sources of research are within one's reach. Even then it is quite difficult to supply definitive ideas concerning how a researcher should obtain ideas for his research. For this purpose, a researcher should contact an expert or a professor in the University who is already engaged in research;

4. The importance of the subject, the qualifications and the training of a researcher, the costs involved, the time factor are few other criteria that must also be considered in selecting a problem. In other words, before the final selection of a problem is done, a researcher must ask himself the following questions:

   a. Whether he is well equipped in terms of his background to carry out the research?
   b. Whether the study falls within the budget he can afford?
   c. Whether the necessary cooperation can be obtained from those who must participate in research as subjects? If the answer to all these questions are in the affirmative, one may become sure so far as the practicability of the study is concerned.
   d. The selection of a problem must be preceded by a preliminary study. This may not be necessary when the problem requires the conduct of a research closely similar to one that has already been done. But when the field of inquiry is relatively new and does not have available a set of well-developed techniques, a brief feasibility study must always be undertaken.

## RESEARCH DESIGN

Now-a-day there is an increasing tendency on the part of students and teachers to do research. The section of a research topic is the first and foremost problem, that the prospective researchers. As soon as the problem is selected, one hastily leaps forward with the work of collection of data or writing the plan for the thesis or dissertation and even some times writing the initial, introductory chapters in the thesis or dissertation. This shows that the researcher is not devoting considerable time in thinking about his future work. The smooth sailing in the field of research is possible only when the researcher thinks considerably about problem. He should think about the way in which he should proceed in attaining his objective in his research work.

### Meaning of Research Design

The researcher makes a plan of his study before he undertakes his research work. This will enable the researcher to save time and resources. Such a plan of study or blue print for study is called a Research Design or Research Strategy. A researcher attempting to solve his problem should necessarily prepare a plan, which will help him to attain his ultimate motto. This plan is nothing but a research design. A research design or model indicates a plan of action to be carried out in connection with a proposed research work. It provides only a guideline for the researcher to enable him to keep track of his actions and to know that he is moving in the right direction in order to achieve his goal.

According to Claire Seltiz *et. al.*, Research Design is a catalogue of the various phases and facts relating to the formulation of a research effort. It is the arrangement of conditions for collection and analysis of data in a manner that aims to combine relevance to the research purpose with economy in procedure.

Paline V. Young outlines the Research Design, "A research design is the logical and systematic planning and directing a piece of research".

According to Vimal Shah, "The research design is the plan of study and as such it is planned in every study uncontrolled as well as controlled and subjective as well as objective".

Prof. Miller, "The planned sequence of the entire process involved in conducting a research study".

Accordingly, research design is "a general model for the conduct of a scientific inquiry". Fred N. Kerlinger defines research as "*the plan, structure,* and *strategy* of investigation conceived so as to obtain answers to research question and to control variance". By *'plan'* he means the overall scheme or design of research. By *'structure'* he refers to the outline, the scheme and design of the operation of the variables. In *'strategy'*, he has included the methods to be used to gather and analyse data.

The preparation of the research design appropriate for a particular research problem involves usually the consideration of the following factors:

1. The means of obtaining information;
2. The availability and skill of the researcher and his staff, if any;
3. Explanation of the way in which selected means of obtaining information will be organised and the reasoning leading to the selection; and
4. The time available for research;

The cost factor relating to research, i.e., the finance available for the purpose.

## Need for Research Design

Research design is needed because it facilitates the smooth sailing of the various research operations, thereby making research as efficient as possible yielding maximal information with minimal expenditure of effort, time and money. Just as for better, economical and attractive construction of a house, we need a blueprint (or what is commonly called the map of the house) well thought out and prepared by an expert architect, similarly we need a research design or a plan in advance of data collection and analysis for our research project.

Preparation of the research design should be done with great care as any error in it may upset the entire project. Research design, in fact, has a great bearing on the reliability of the results arrived at and as such constitutes the firm foundation of the entire edifice of the research work.

Thoughtlessness in designing the research project may result in rendering the research exercise futile. It is, therefore, imperative that an efficient and appropriate design must be prepared before starting research operations. The design helps the researcher to organise his ideas in a form whereby it will be possible for him to look for flaws and inadequacies.

## Features of a Good Design

A good design is often characterized by adjectives like flexible, appropriate, efficient, economical and so on. Generally, the design, which minimizes bias and maximizes the reliability of the data collected and analysed is considered a good design. The design that gives the smallest experimental error is supposed to be the best design in many investigations. One single design cannot serve the purpose of all types of research problems. A research design appropriate for a particular research problem, usually involves the consideration of the following factors:

1. The means of obtaining information;
2. The availability and skills of the researcher and his staff, if any;
3. The objective of the problem to be studied;
4. The nature of the problem to be studied; and
5. The availability of time and money for the research work.

If the research study happens to be an exploratory or a formulative one, wherein the major emphasis is on discovery of ideas and insights, the research design most appropriate must be flexible. Accuracy becomes a major consideration and a research design, which minimizes bias and maximizes the reliability of the evidence collected, is considered a good design.

Studies involving the testing of a hypothesis of a causal relationship between variables require a design, which will permit inferences about causality in addition to the minimization of bias and maximization of reliability. Besides, the availability of time, money, skills of the research staff and the means of obtaining the information must be given due weightage while working out of the relevant details of the research design such as experimental design, survey design, sample design and the like.

## Advantages of Research Design

The preparation of research design has the following advantages:

(a) It saves a lot of researcher's time;
(b) It directs him to prepare himself for executing the various activities systematically;
(c) It enables resource planning procurement in right time;

(d) It betters documentation of the activities while the project is in progress;
(e) It ensures project time schedule;
(f) It instills and builds up confidence in the researcher; and
(g) It provides satisfaction and sense of success from the beginning to the completion of every stage of the project.

## Preparation of the Design

Planning involves deciding things before hand. Therefore, the preparation of a research design or plan involves a careful consideration of the following questions and making appropriate decisions on them:

1. What is the study about?
2. What is the study made?
3. What is its scope?
4. What are the objectives of the study?
5. What are the propositions to be tested?
6. What are the major concepts to be defined operationally?
7. On the basis of what criteria or measurements are the operational definitions to be made?
8. When or in what area will the study be conducted?
9. What is the reference period of the study?
10. What methodology is to be used?
11. What kinds of data are needed?
12. What are the sources of data?
13. What is the universe from which the sample has to be drawn?
14. What is the sample size?
15. What sampling techniques can be used?
16. What methods are to be adopted for collection of data?
17. What tools are to be used for collecting data?
18. How are the data to be processed?
19. What techniques of analysis are to be adopted?
20. To what target audience is reporting of the finding meant?
21. What is the type of report to be prepared?
22. What is the duration of time required for each stage of the reseach work?
23. What is the cost involved?

Keeping in views of the above stated design decisions, one may split the overall research design into the following parts:

(a) The sampling design which deals with the method of selecting items to be observed for the given study;
(b) The observational design which related to the conditions under which the observations are to be made;
(c) The statistical design which is concerned with the questions of

how many items are to be observed and how the information and data gathered are to be analysed; and

(d) The operational design, which deals with the techniques by which the procedures specified in the sampling, statistical and observational designs can be carried out.

## Major Steps in Preparing a Research Design

Statement of Research problem is an essential step in preparing a model.

1. *Review of earlier literature:* Reviewing of the literature on the area of research is a preliminary step before attempting to plan the study. It is essential to review all the relevant material connected with the problem chosen.
2. *Sources of information to be tapped:* The sources of information to be tapped vary with the interest of the researcher and the type of his study. The sources are divided into documentary and field sources. These sources are either primary or secondary. Primary source of information include data gathered at first hand, (i.e. the responsibility for their compilation and promulgation remaining under the same authority) and summaries gathered from primary sources. Census reports may be cited as an example for the former type and statistics based on Census reports may be the example for the latter type.
3. *Development of bibliography:* As soon as the consultation of available source is begun, the development of bibliography preferably with annotations should be undertaken.
4. *Nature of study:* The next step in formulating research design is to ascertain the nature of study, whether it is statistical study, case study or a comparative study or an experimental study or a combination of these and other types, should be decided.
5. *Objectives of study:* The objectives of the research study should be compiled in clear-cut terms. The objectives, of course, differ with the nature of studies and goals to be attained. Some research studies aim to gather descriptive data, or explanatory data.
6. *Socio-cultural context of study:* If the problem under investigation relates to human beings, then it is necessary to ascertain the socio-cultural behaviour pattern of the persons.
7. *Geographical areas to be covered:* Tt is essential to determine the geographical area to be covered in connection with the research study.
8. *Periods of time to be covered or time dimension of the study:* In the case of historical studies, it is necessary to determine the period to be encompassed so that exploration of the problem will be made easier and clear.

9. *The basis for selecting the data:* The factors of time and cost are usually important considerations in social research. It is more economical and efficient to base studies on samples rather than to study the universe. Instead of studying every case, which might be included in an investigation logically, only a small portion is selected for analysis. Great care is to be taken in drawing the sample from the universe.
10. *Techniques of study:* The next stage in the preparation of a research design is the determination of suitable techniques for collecting the necessary data. Here also the techniques that are normally used will differ on the basis of the nature of study. If the study requires close attention of the researcher, the observation method will be used.
11. *Establish the reliability and validity of test instruments:* It is necessary in empirical studies to establish the reliability and validity of test instruments. This is, do tests provide consistent measurements and do tests in fact measure what is claimed for them?
12. *Chapter Scheme:* The preparation of a chapter outline is last step in planning the thesis/dissertation and it is a useful first step in writing the rough drafts. Some of the headings may need to be changed as the investigation progresses. The final form is determined by the nature of the study itself and by the conventions. The number of chapters that the study contains and name of each chapter must be mentioned.

## HYPOTHESIS

Hypothesis is usually considered as the principal instrument in research. In social science, where direct knowledge of population parameter(s) is rare, hypothesis testing is the often-used strategy for deciding whether a sample data offer such support for a hypothesis that generalization cam is made. Thus, hypothesis testing enables us to make probability statements about population parameter(s).

## MEANING

A hypothesis may be defined as a proposition or a set of propositions set forth as an explanation for the occurrence of some specified group of phenomena either asserted merely as a provisional conjecture to guide some investigation or accepted as highly probable in the light of established facts. Quite often a research hypothesis is a predictive statement, capable of being tested by scientific methods.

"Students who receive counseling will show a greater increase in creativity than students not receiving counseling" or "the automobile A is performing as well as automobile B." These are hypothesis capable of being objectively verified and tested.

## DEFINITION OF HYPOTHESIS

In the words of George A. Lundgergs, "A hypothesis is a tentative generalization, the validity of which remains to be tested. In it's most elementary stage the hypothesis may be very hunch, guess, imaginative data, which becomes the basis for action or investigation".

Goode and Hatt have defined it as "a proposition, which can be put to test to determine validity".

Rummel and Balline say, "A hypothesis is a statement capable of being tested and thereby verified or rejected".

### Need for Hypothesis

While a hypothesis is useful, it is not always indispensable. In physical sciences, the hypothesis is most often necessary but in social sciences useful facts may be discovered, organised and presented purposefully even without a hypothesis other than the one, which might incidentally be suggested in the course of the investigation. Thus, it is desirable to have hypothesis/hypotheses.

## CHARACTERISTICS OF HYPOTHESIS

Hypothesis must possess the following characteristics:

(a) Hypothesis should be clear and precise. If the hypothesis is not clear and precise, the inferences drawn on its basis cannot be taken as reliable.
(b) Hypothesis should be capable of being tested. Quite often the research programme fails owing to its incapability of being subject to testing for validity.
(c) Hypothesis should state relationship between variables, if it happens to be a relational hypothesis.
(d) Hypothesis should be limited in scope and must be specific. This is because a simpler hypothesis generally would be easier to test for the research.
(e) Hypothesis should be stated in most simple terms so that the same is easily understandable by all concerned.
(f) It should be consistent with most known facts i.e., it must be consistent with a substantial body of established facts.
(g) Hypothesis should be amenable to testing within a reasonable time. One should not use even an excellent hypothesis, if the same cannot be tested in reasonable time.
(h) A hypothesis should state the facts that gave rise to the necessity of looking for an explanation.

## UTILITY OF HYPOTHESIS

The utility or importance of hypothesis for social research are as follows:

(a) Hypothesis provides guidance to proceed on certain definite lines. Hypothesis helps the investigator in knowing the direction in which he should proceed. In the absence of hypothesis the researcher is like a sailor on an un chartered vessel without compass or rudder.

(b) Hypothesis helps in selecting pertinent factors. Once the investigator is able to get the direction with the help of hypothesis, he is able to eliminate the irrelevant facts and concentrate only on relevant and pertinent facts. Pauline Y. Young has rightly remarked: "The use of hypothesis prevents a blind search and indiscriminate gathering of masses of data which may later prove irrelevant to the problem under study".

(c) Hypothesis helps in drawing specific conclusions. If hypothesis is rightly drawn scientifically formulated it helps the researcher not only to proceed in his study on right lines but also to draw conclusions. Goode and Hatt have aptly said, "without hypothesis the research is unfocussed, a random empirical wandering. The results cannot be stated/studied as facts with clear meaning. Hypothesis is necessary link between theory and investigations, which lead to discovery of addition to knowledge".

Thus, hypothesis is the integral part of scientific research, and without the former the latter shall neither be valuable nor possible. To sum up, hypothesis is the foundation of scientific social research.

## NULL HYPOTHESIS

When a hypothesis is stated negatively, it is called null hypothesis. The object of this hypothesis is to avoid the personal bias of the investigator in the matter of collection of data. A null hypothesis is used to collect additional support for the known hypothesis. For example, the age of the entrepreneur does not have any relationship with the level of satisfaction provided by small industries service institute. If this hypothesis is proved, then we may come to a conclusion that the age of the entrepreneur does not influence the level of satisfaction. On the other hand, if this null hypothesis is not proved, then we may conclude that the age of the entrepreneur and the level of satisfaction are related.

## HYPOTHESIS DEVELOPMENT

Once we have identified the important variables in a situation and established the relationships among them through logical reasoning in the theoretical framework, we are in a position to test whether the relationships that have been theorized do in fact hold true. By testing these relationships scientifically through appropriate statistical analyses, or through negative case analysis in qualitative research (described later in the chapter) we are able to obtain reliable information on what kinds of relationships exist among the variables operating in the problem situation. The result of these tests offers us some clues as to what could be changed in the situation to solve the problem. Formulating such testable statements is called hypotheses development.

If the pilots are given adequate training to handle midair crowded situations, air-safety violations will be reduced.

The above is a testable statement. By measuring the extent of training given to the various pilots and the number of safety violations committed by them over a period of time, we can statistically examine the relationship between these two variables to see if there is a significant negative correlation between the two. If we do find this to be the case, then the hypotheses is substantiated. That is, giving more training to pilots in handling crowded space in midair will reduce safety violations. If a significant negative correlation is not found, then the hypotheses would not have been substantiated. By convention in the social sciences, to call a relationship "statistically significant", we should be confident that 95 times out of 100 the observed relationship will hold true. There would be only a 5% chance that the relationship would not be detected.

## Statement of Hypotheses: Formats

### *If-then Statements*

A hypothesis is a testable statement of the relationship among variables. Hypotheses can also test whether there are differences between two groups (or among several groups) with respect to any variable or variables. To examine whether or not the conjectured relationships or differences exist, these hypotheses can be set either as propositions or in the form of if-then statements. The two formats can be in the following two examples:

Example 1: Employees who are more healthy will take sick leave less frequently.

Example 2: If employees are more healthy, then they will take sick leave less frequently.

Hypotheses: The nature of the difference between two groups on a variable (more than/less than) is postulated.

Example 3: The greater the stress experienced in the job, the lower the job satisfaction of employees.

Example 4: Women are more motivated than men.

On the other hand, non-directional hypotheses are those that do postulate a relationship of difference, but offer no indication of the direction of these relationships or differences. In other words, though it may be conjectured that there would be a significant relationship would be positive or negative.

Example 5: There is a relationship between age and job satisfaction.
Example 6: There is a difference between the work ethic values of American and Asian employees.

Non-directional hypotheses are formulated either because the relationship or differences have never been previously explored and hence there is no basis for indicating the direction, or because there have been conflicting findings in previous research studies on the variables. In some studies a positive relationship might have been found, while in others a negative relationship might have been traced. Hence, the current researcher might only be able to hypothesize that there would be a significant relationship, but the direction may not be clear.

### Null and Alternate Hypotheses

The null hypothesis is a proposition that states a definite, exact relationship between two variables. That is, it states that the population correlation between two variables is equal to zero or that the difference in the means or two groups in the population is equal to zero (or some definite number). In general, the null statement is expressed as no (significant) relationship between two variables or no (significant) difference between two groups.

In setting up the null hypothesis, we are stating that there is no difference between what we might find in the population characteristics (i.e., the total group we are interested in knowing something about) and the sample we are studying (i.e., a limited number representative of the total population or group that we have chosen to study). Since we do not know the true state of affairs in the population, all we can do is to draw inferences based on what we find in our sample. What we imply through the null hypothesis is that any differences found between two sample groups or any relationship found between two variables based on our sample is simply due to random sampling fluctuations and not due to any "true" differences between the two population groups (say, men and women), or relationships between two variables (say, sales and profits). The null hypothesis is thus formulated so that it can be tested for possible rejection. If we reject the null hypothesis, then all permissible alternative hypotheses relating to the particular relationship tested could be supported.

### Hypothesis Testing with Qualitative Research: Negative Case Analysis

Hypotheses can also be tested with qualitative data. For example, let us say that a researcher has developed a theoretical frame work after extensive interviews, that unethical practices by employees are a function of their inability to discriminate between right and wrong, or due to a dire need for more money, or the organisations indifference to such practices. To test the hypothesis that these three factors are the primary ones that influence unethical practices, the researcher would look for data that would refute the hypothesis. When even a single case does not support the hypothesis, the theory would be revised. Let us say that the researcher finds one case where an individual is deliberately engaged in the unethical practice of accepting kickbacks (despite the fact that he was knowledgeable enough to discriminate right from wrong, was not in need of money, and knew that the organisation would not be indifferent to his behaviour), simply because he wanted to "get back" at the system, which "would not listen to his advice". This new discovery through disconfirmation of the original hypothesis, known as the negative case method, enable the researcher to revise the theory and the hypothesis.

## STATISTICAL TESTING PROCEDURE

Testing for statistical significance follows a well-defined pattern. The following are the stages:

(1) *State the null hypothesis*

It is always followed to frame a null hypothesis by the researchers.

(2) *Choose the statistical test:* An appropriate statistical test has to be selected. There are at least four criteria while selecting a test. One is the power efficiency of the test. A more powerful test with provides the same level of significance with a small sample than a less powerful test. The other factor is the method of sampling, nature of the population, and the type of measurement of scale used. Some tests are adequate only when the sequences are paired. Other types are appropriate only when the population has certain characteristics.

(3) *Select the desired level of significance:* The choice of the level of significance should be made before we collect the data. The most common level is .05 although .01 is also widely used. The exact level to be determined is decided by how much risk one is willing to accept.

(4) *Compute the difference value:* After the data are collected use the formula for the appropriate significance test to obtain the calculated value.

*Obtain the critical test value*: After we calculated the t, $x^2$ or other measure we must lookup the critical value in the appropriate table for that distribution. The critical value is the criterion that decides the accept or reject criteria.

(5) *Interpret the test:* For most of the tests if the calculated value is larger than the critical value, we reject the null hypothesis and conclude that the alternative hypothesis is accepted. If the critical value is larger, we conclude we have failed to reject the null hypothesis.

## TESTING OF HYPOTHESIS

Testing the hypothesis means subjecting it to some sort of empirical scrutiny to determine if it is supported or refuted by what the researcher observes.

There are two fairly important means of testing hypothesis:

(a) The study of hypothesis for logical consistency; and
(b) The study of hypothesis for agreement with fact.

The study of hypothesis for logical consistency is phase of thinking. It consists of checking the logical character of the reasoning by which the consequences of hypotheses are deduced for verification. In the second place the study of hypothesis for logical consistency involves checking it for agreement with the already known laws of nature. It must not conflict with the highest and simplest laws of good thinking and it must not disagree with those principles of science which are considered valid beyond reasonable doubt.

## PROCEDURE FOR HYPOTHESIS TESTING

The various steps involved in hypothesis testing are stated below:

### 1. Making a Formal Statement

The step consists in making a formal statement of the null hypothesis and also of the alternative hypothesis. This means that hypotheses should be clearly stated, considering the nature of the research problem. The formulation of hypotheses is an important step which must be accomplished with due care in accordance with the object and nature of the problem under consideration.

### 2. Selecting a Significance Level

The hypotheses are tested on a pre-determined level of significance and as such the same should be specified. Generally, in practice, either 5% level or 1% level is adopted for the purpose. The factors that affect the level of significance are: (a) the magnitude of the difference between sample means; (b) the size of the samples; (c) the variability of measurements within samples; and (d) whether the hypothesis is directional or non-directional.

### 3. Deciding the Distribution to Use

After deciding the level of significance, the next step in hypothesis testing is to determine the appropriate sampling distribution. The choice generally remains between normal distribution and the t-distribution.

### 4. Selecting a Random Sample and Computing an Appropriate Value

Another step is to select a random sample and compute an appropriate value from the sample data concerning the test statistic utilizing the relevant distribution.

### 5. Calculation of the Probability

One has to calculate the probability that the sample result would diverge as widely as it has from expectations, if the null hypothesis were in fact true.

### 6. Comparing the Probability

Yet another step consists in comparing the probability thus calculated with the specified value for á, the significance level. If the calculated probability is equal to or smaller than the á value in case of one-tailed test (and á/2 in case of two-tailed test), then reject, the null hypothesis (i.e., accept the alternative hypothesis), but if the calculated probability is greater, then accept the null hypothesis. In case we reject $H_0$, we run a risk of (almost the level of significance) committing an error of Type I, but if we accept $H_0$, then we run some risk (the size of which cannot be specified as long as the $H_0$ happens to be vague rather than specific) of committing an error of Type II.

After testing the hypothesis by applying it to already known facts, it may have to be tested by a new appeal to experience. In this new appeal the data are collected, recorded and manipulated according to the conventions of science. If the data already available are adequate, no new appeal to experience will be necessary.

### *Some General Problems in Testing Hypotheses*

Many problems may arise while testing a hypothesis.

A hypothesis suggested by the observations in a given sample cannot be tested against that sample. The hypothesis must be tested with a new set of observations—

1. Statistical evidence is not positive proof of the truth of the hypothesis. Here, the facts are given a chance to disprove the hypothesis.
2. Statistical evidence by itself is not enough to establish a hypothesis. There must be rational basis for it. The hypothesis must be reasonable and it must be fit logically into the relevant body of established knowledge.

3. A statistically significant correlation co-efficient implies only that two or more variables tend to vary together in a particular direction. It does not always mean that one is the cause of another.
4. The success of a statistical test depends on the availability and reliability of appropriate data.
5. Another problem faced in Economics and other social sciences is the ideological bias of the researcher. This bias tends to tamper with the testing process. The researcher may try to manipulate his analysis in such a way as to prove or disprove the hypothesis according to his interest.

## METHODS OF TESTING HYPOTHESIS

Statisticians have developed several tests of hypothesis, which can be classified as follows:

(a) Parametrec Test
(b) Non-parametric Test

Parametric test usually assume certain properties of the parent population from which we draw samples. Assumptions like observations come from a normal population, sample size is large, assumptions like mean, variance, etc. must hold good before the parametric test can be used.

When the researcher cannot or does not want to make such assumptions, statistical methods for testing the hypothesis are used which are called as non-parametric test. In this test, we need more observations than parametric test.

## IMPORTANT PARAMETRIC TEST

The important Parametric Tests are:

### (a) Z-TEST

It is based on the normal probability distribution and it is used for judging the significance of several statistical measures, particularly, the mean. The relevant test static, "Z" is worked out and compared with its probable value at a specified level of significance. This is a most frequently used test in research studies.

Mean of the population can be tested presuming difference situations such as the population may be normal or other than normal, may be finite or infinite, sample may be small or large, variance of the population may be known or unknown, and the alternative hypothesis may be two sided or one sided. Testing technique will differ in different situations.

### (b) T-TEST

It is based on t-distribution and is considered as appropriate test for judging the significance of a sample mean or for judging the significance of the difference between the means of two samples, in case of small samples, when population variance is not known. In case of two samples are related, we use paired T-Test for judging the significance of the mean difference of the two related samples. For a paired T-test, it is necessary that, the observations in the two samples to be collected in the form of what is called matched pairs. That is, each observation in the one sample must be paired with an observation in the other sample in such a manner that these two observations are some how related.

### (c) $X^2$-TEST

It is based on Chi-Square distribution and as a Parametric Test; it is used for comparing a sample variance to a theoretical population variance.

### (d) F-TEST

It is based on frequency distribution and it is used to compare the variance of two independent samples. This test is also used in the context of analysis of variance (ANOVA) for judging the significance of more than two sample means at one and the same time. It is also used for judging the significance of multi-correlation coefficients.

Hypothesis Testing of correlation coefficients: We may be interested in knowing whether the correlation coefficient that we calculate on the basis of sample data is indicative of significance correlation. For this purpose we may use T-Test or F-Test depending upon the type of correlation coefficient.

We shall now learn a technique known as analysis of variance to test for the significance of the difference between more than two sample means and to make inferences about whether our samples are drawn from the populations having the same mean. The "analysis of variance" procedure or "F-test" is used in such problems where we want to test for the significance of the difference between more than two sample means. In fact, the technique of analysis of variance is one of the most powerful of statistical methods developed by R.A. Fisher.

The analysis of variance originated in agrarian research and its language is thus loaded with such agricultural terms as blocks (referring to land) and treatments (referring to populations or samples, which are differentiated in terms of varieties of seeds, fertilizers or cultivation methods). Today, analysis of variance finds application in every type of experimental design, in natural sciences as well as social sciences and has become a very broad and technical subject. The methods of analysis of variance are a fundamental part of planned research and the design of experiment; comparative studies are essential in judging the effects of new technology, procedures and policies. Though analysis of variance can be used in a number of ways, in this chapter, an attempt would be made to illustrate some business applications of this highly useful tool.

## COMPUTATION OF ANALYSIS OF VARIANCE

The null hypothesis taken while applying of variance technique is that the means of different samples do not differ significantly. The procedure followed in the analysis of variance would be explained separately for:

(1) One-way classification, and
(2) Two-way classification.

Irrespective of the type of classification, the analysis of variance is a technique of partitioning the total sum of squared deviations of all sample values from the grand mean and is divided into two parts – sum of squares between the samples and sum of squares within the samples. Individual observations in the same treatment samples, however, can differ from each other only because of chance variation, since each individual within the group receives exactly the same treatment.

### One-way Classification Model

The term one-factor analysis of variance refers to the fact that a single variable or factor of interest is controlled and its effect on the elementary units is observed. In other words, in one-way classification the data are classified according to only one criterion. Suppose we have independent samples of $n_1, n_2, \ldots, n_k$ observations from k populations. The population means are denoted by by $\mu_1, \mu_2, \ldots, \mu_k$. The one-way analysis of variance is designed to test the null hypothesis:

H0: $\mu_1 = \mu_2 = \ldots = \mu_k$

i.e., the arithmetic means of the population from which the k samples are randomly drawn are equal to one another.

Calculate the F-ratio as follows:

F* = Variance between the samples/Variance within the samples.

F is always computed with the variance between the sample means as the numerator and the variance within the sample means as the denominator. The denominator is computed by combining the variance within the k samples into single measures.

Compare the calculated value of F with the table value of F for the given degrees of freedom at a certain critical level (generally we take 5% level of significance). If the calculated value of the f is greater than the table value of f, it indicates that the difference in sample means is significant, that is, it could not have arisen due to fluctuations of random sampling or, in other words, the samples do not come from the same population. On the other hand, if the calculated value of f is less than the table value, the difference is not significant and hence could have arisen due to fluctuations of random sampling.

### Two-way Classification

In a one-factor analysis of variance explained above the treatments constitute the different level of a single factor, which is controlled in one experiment. There are, however, many situations in which the response variable of interest may be affected by more than one factor. For example, sales of Maxfactor cosmetics, in addition to being affected by the point of sale display, might also be affected by the price charge, the size and/or location of the store or the number of competitive products sold by the store. Similarly, petrol mileage may be affected by the type of car driven, the way it is driven, the road conditions and other factors in addition to the brand of petrol used.

When it is believed that two independent factors might have an effect on the response variable of interest, it is possible to design the test so that an analysis of variance can be used to test for the effects of the two factors simultaneously. Such a test is called two-factor analysis of variance. Thus, with the two-factor analysis of variance, we can test two sets of hypothesis with the same data at the same time.

We can plan and experiment in such a ways to study the effects of two factors in the same experiment. For each factor, there will be a number of classes or levels.

The procedure for analysis of variance is somewhat different than the one followed while dealing with problems of one-way classification.

## NON-PARAMETRIC TEST

Important Non-parametric or Distribution-free Tests:

Tests of Hypotheses with 'order statistics" or non-parametric statistics' or 'distribution-free' statistics are known as non-parametric or distribution-free tests. The following distribution-free tests are important and generally used:

(a) Test of a hypothesis concerning some single value for the given data (such as one-sample sign test).
(b) Test of a hypothesis concerning no difference among two or more sets of data (such as two-sample sign test, Fisher-Irwin test, Rank sum test, etc.).
(c) Test of a hypothesis of a relationship between variables (such as Rank correlation, Kendall's coefficient of concordance and other tests for dependence).
(d) Test of a hypothesis concerning variation in the given data i.e., test analogous to ANOVA viz., Kruskal-Wallis test.

(e) Tests of randomness of a sample based on the theory of runs viz., one sample runs test.

(f) Test of hypothesis to determine if categorical data shows dependence or if two classifications are independent viz., the chi-square test.

## SIGN TEST

The sign test is one of the easiest non- parametric tests. Its name come from the fact that it is based on the direction of the plus or minus signs of observations in a sample and not on the numerical magnitudes.

## FISHER-IRWIN TEST

Fisher-Irwin test is a distribution-free test used in testing a hypothesis concerning no difference between two sets of data. It is employed to determine whether one can reasonably assume, for example, that two supposedly different treatments are in fact different in terms of the results they produce. Suppose the management of a business unit has designed a new training programme, which is now ready, and as such it wishes to test its performance against that of the old training programme.

## MCNEMER TEST

McNemer test is one of the important nonparametric tests often used when the data happen to be nominal and relate to two related samples. As such this test is especially useful with before-after measurement of the same subjects. The experiment is designed for the use of this test in such a way that the subjects initially are divided into equal groups as to their favourable and unfavourable views about, say, any system. After some treatment, the same numbers of subjects are asked to express their views about the given system whether they favour it or not. Through McNemer test we in fact try to judge the significance of any observed change in views of the same subjects before and after the treatment by setting up a table.

## WILCOXON MATCHED-PAIRS TEST (OR SIGNED RANK TEST)

In various research situations in the context of two-related samples, we can use an important nonparametric test viz., Wilcoxon matched-pairs test. While applying this test, we first find the differences (di) between each pair of values and assign rank to the differences from the smallest to the largest without regard to sign. The actual signs of each difference are then put to corresponding ranks and the test statistic T is calculated which happens to be the smaller of the two sums viz., the sum of the negative ranks and the sum of the positive ranks.

## RANK SUM TESTS

Rank Sum Tests are a whole family of test, but we shall describe only two such tests commonly used namely, U-Test and H-Test. U-Test is popularly known as Wilcoxon-mann-Whitney test whereas H-Test is also known as Kruskal-Wallis Test.

### U-TEST

This is a very popular test amongst the Rank Sum Tests. This test is used to determine whether two independent samples have been drawn from the same population. It uses more information than Sign-test. This test applies under very general conditions and requires only the populations sampled are continuous. However, in practice, even the violation this assumption does not affect the results very much. In applying U-Test we take the null hypothesis that the two samples come from identical populations. If this hypothesis is true, we can come to a conclusion that, the values of the two samples are more or less the same. Under the alternative hypothesis, the means of the two populations are not equal and if this is so, then most of the smaller ranks will go to the value of one sample while most of the higher ranks will go to those of the other sample.

### H-TEST

This test is conducted in a way similar to the U-Test described above. This test is used to test the null hypothesis that "K" independent random samples come from identical universes against the alternative hypothesis that the means of these universes are not equal. It does not require the assumption that the samples come from normal population.

## ONE SAMPLE RUNS TEST

It is a test used to judge the randomness of a sample on the basis of the order in which the observations are taken. There are many applications in which it is difficult to decide whether the sample used is a random one or not. This is particularly true when we have little or no control over the selection of the data. For Example, if we want to predict retail stores sales volume for a given month, we have no choice but to use past sales data and perhaps prevailing conditions in general.

## SPEARMAN'S RANK CORRELATION

When the data are not available to use in numerical form for doing correlation analysis but when the information is sufficient to rank the data as first, second, third, and so forth, we quite often use the rank correlation method and work out the coefficient of that exists between the two sets of ranks. In other words, it is a measure of association that is based on the ranks of the observations and not on the numerical values of the data. It was developed by famous statistician Charles Spearman in the early 1900s and as such it is also known as Spearman's rank correlation coefficient.

## KENDALL'S COEFFICIENT OF CONCORDANCE

Kendall's coefficient of concordance, represented by the symbol W, is an important nonparametric measure of relationship. It is used for determining the degree of association among several (k) sets of ranking of N objects or individuals. When there are only two sets of rankings of N objects, we generally work out Spearman's coefficient of correlation, but Kendall's coefficient of concordance (W) is considered an appropriate measure of studying the degree of association among three or more sets of rankings.

## THE HYPOTHETICO-DEDUCTIVE METHOD

The seven-step process in the hypothetico-deductive method.

The seven steps involved in the hypothetico-deductive method of research stem from the building blocks discussed above, and are listed and discussed below:

1. Observation
2. Preliminary information gathering
3. Theory formulation
4. Hypothesizing
5. Further scientific data collection
6. Data analysis
7. Deduction

### 1. Observation

Observation is the first stage, in which one senses that certain changes are occurring, or that some new behaviors, attitudes, and feelings are surfacing in one's environment (i.e., the workplace). When the observed phenomena are seen to have potentially important consequences, one would proceed to the next step.

### 2. Preliminary Information Gathering

Preliminary information gathering involves the seeking of information in depth is observed. This could be done by talking informally to several people in the work setting or to clients, or to other relevant sources, thereby gathering information on what is happening and why. Through these unstructured interviews, one gets an idea or a "feel" for what is transpiring in the situation. A mass of information would have been collected through the interviews and library search.

### 3. Theory formulation

Theory formulation, the next step, is an attempt to integrate all the information in a logical manner, so that the factors responsible for the problem can be conceptualized and tested. The theoretical framework formulated is often guided by experience and intuition. In this step the critical variables are examined as to their contribution or influence in explaining why the problem occurs and how it can be solved.

### 4. Hypothesizing

Hypothesizing is the next logical step after theory formulation. From the theorized network of associations among the variables, certain testable hypotheses or educated conjectures can be generated. Hypothesis testing is called deductive research. Sometimes, hypotheses that were not originally formulated do get generated through the process of induction. That is, after the data are obtained, some creative insights occur, and based on these, new hypotheses could get generated to be tested later.

### 5. Further Scientific Data Collection

After the development of the hypotheses, data with respect to each variable in the hypotheses need to be obtained. In other words, further scientific data collection is needed to test the hypotheses that are generated in the study.

### 6. Data analysis

In the data analysis step, the data gathered are statistically analysed to see if the hypotheses that were generated have been supported. Other hypotheses could be tested through appropriate statistical analysis. Analyses of both quantitative and qualitative data can be done to determine if certain conjectures are substantiated. Qualitative data refer to information gathered in a narrative form through interviews and observations.

### 7. Deduction

Deduction is the process of arriving at conclusions by interpreting the meaning of the results of the data analysis. Based on these deductions, the researcher would make recommendations on how the "customer dissatisfaction" problem could be solved.

## QUESTIONS

1. What do you understand by research?
2. Describe the hallmarks of scientific research.
3. What are the objectives of business research?
4. What are the limitations of research?
5. What is the need for a clear theoretical background?
6. Describe the significance of building blocks?
7. What do you understand by deduction and induction?
8. What are the components of theoretical framework?
9. Explain the significance of a good research.
10. What are the types of research?
11. What is action research? Describe the specific situation where action research is warranted.
12. What are the categories of exploratory research?
13. What are the major sources of research problems?
14. What are the major steps in preparing a research design?
15. What are the types of exploratory research?
16. Evaluate case study method.
17. Describe the meaning and uses of descriptive study.
18. Explain the steps in the exploratory study.
19. What are the contents of a good design?
20. What are the advantages that can be claimed by a good design?
21. What is the purpose of literature survey?
22. How would you describe the research process?
23. What are the steps in research process?
24. Describe the various sources of research problem.
25. What are the hallmarks of scientific research?
26. Describe the scope of research.
27. Explain the process of deduction and induction, giving an example of each.
28. What do you mean by hypothesis? What are the characteristics of a good hypothesis?
29. What are the types of hypothesis?
30. Describe the sources of hypothesis.
31. Describe the procedure for hypothesis testing.
32. Many problems may arise while testing a hypothesis. What are the difficulties?
33. Describe various parametric test applied in hypothesis testing.
34. Describe various non-parametric test applied in hypothesis testing.
35. Generate a set of testable hypothesis based on the theoretical framework.
36. Describe the stages involved in statistical testing procedure.
37. What are the seven-step process in the hypothetico—deductive method?

38. What are the uses of hypothesis in research?
39. What do you mean by Null and Alternate Hypotheses?
40. What is the need for a theoretical framework?
41. Explain the procedure for the analysis of variance.
42. What do you mean by rank correlation?
43. Write a brief note on Cross-sectional and longitudinal studies.
44. Describe briefly the process of research.

# 2

# Experimental Design

## MEANING OF EXPERIMENTS

Experiments are studies involving intervention by the researcher beyond that required for measurement. The usual intervention is to manipulate some variable in a setting and observe how it affects the subjects being studied (e.g. People or physical entities). The researcher manipulates the independent or explanatory variable and then observes whether the hypothesized dependent variable is affected by the intervention.

An example of such an intervention is the study of bystanders and thieves. In this experiment, students were asked to come to an office where they had an opportunity to see a fellow student steal some money from a receptionists' desk. A confederate of the experimenter, of course, did the stealing. The major hypothesis concerned whether people observing a theft would be more likely to report it (1) if they observed the crime alone, or (2) if they were in the company or someone else.

There is at least one independent variable (IV) and one dependent variable (DV) in a casual relationship. We hypothesize that in some way the IV "causes" the DV to occur. The independent or explanatory variable in our example was the state of either being alone when observing the theft or being in the company of another person. The dependent variable was whether the subjects reported observing the crime. The results suggested that bystanders were more likely to report the theft if they observed it alone rather than in another person's company.

Beyond the correlation of independent and dependent variables, the time order of the occurrence of the variables must be considered. The dependent variable should not precede the independent variable. They may occur almost simultaneously, or the independent variable should occur before the dependent variable.

The important support for the conclusion comes when researchers are confident that other extraneous variables did not influence the dependent variable. To ensure that these other variables are not the source of influence, researchers control their ability to confound the planned comparison.

## Advantages of Experimental Design

(1) The foremost advantage is the researcher's ability to manipulate the independent variables. Consequently the probability that changes in the dependant variables are a function of that manipulation increases.
(2) The contamination from extraneous variables can be controlled more effectively than in other design.
(3) Experimental variables can be isolated and their impact over time can be evaluated.
(4) Flexibility in data collection to adjust variables and conditions that evoke extremes not evoked.
(5) Repeating an experiment with different subject groups and conditions leads to the discovery of average effect of independent variables across people, situation and times.
(6) Naturally occurring events can be used by the researcher and this can be used as a source of intervention in the every day life.

## Disadvantages of Experimental Design

1. The artificial laboratory is one of the main disadvantages.
2. Generalisation from non-probability samples can create problems in spite of random assignment.
3. Despite the low cost of experimentation many application of experimentation exceeds the budgeted cost allotted.
4. Experimentation is most effectively targeted at the problems of the present of immediate future.
5. Management research is often concerned with the study of people. There are limits to the types of manipulations and control that are ethical.

## Precautions to be taken while Using Experimental Design

Before using experimental designs in research studies, it is essential to consider whether they are necessary at all, and if so, at what level of sophistication. This is because experimental designs call for special efforts and varying degrees of interference with the natural flow of activities.

1. Is it really necessary to identify casual relationships?
2. If it is important to trace the casual relationships, which of the

two, internal validity or external validity, is needed more, or are both needed? If only internal validity is important, a carefully designed lab experiment would be the answer; if generalizability is the more important criterion, then a field experiment would be called for; if both are equally important, then a lab study should be first undertaken, followed by a field experiment.

3. Is cost an important factor in the study? If so, would a less rather than more advanced experimental design do?

The managers may not be interested to know the cause-and-effect relationship. But a good knowledge of experimental design could foster some pilot studies to be undertaken to examine various factors, which lead to positive outcomes. Marketing managers would be able to use to study the effect of sales on advertisements, sales promotion, pricing and the like. Awareness of the usefulness of simulation as a research tool can also result in creative results in the management area.

### Problems in Experimental Design

Following are the problems inherent in the form of research design:

1. *The problem of recognizing the variable:* It is not easy to locate and recognize the potential variables under study. They may not be apparent always and the nature and the time occurrences may be uncertain.
2. *Control of variables:* The control of variables may imply the actual manipulation or changing of the values of the variables. Since the manipulation is usually confined to the experimental variable. The two groups are equated by Precision matching, matching by frequency distribution, matching by using random.
3. *Unclear casual relationship:* The casual relationship is often confused. That is why the scientists avoid term 'cause' altogether and say simply that one event leads to another.
4. *The element of time and confusing results:* The social phenomenon affects the social behaviour in the experimental design.
5. *Qualitativeness:* The classical design is stated in simplest form and for this the classical design is presented in an all or nothing form. The quantity aspects are not considered.

## CONDUCTING EXPERIMENT

Although the experiment is a premier scientific methodology for establishing causation, resourcefulness and creativeness of the researcher are needed to make the experiment live up to the potential. There are seven activities that must be performed by the researcher to make the experiment successful:

1. Select relevant variable.
2. Specify the level(s) of the treatment.
3. Control the experimental environment.
4. Choose the experimental design.
5. Select and assign the subjects.
6. Analyse the data.
7. Pilot-test, revises, and test.

### 1. Select relevant variable

The researcher's task is to translate an amorphous problem into the question or hypothesis that best states the objectives of the research. Depending on the complexity of the problem, investigative questions and additional hypothesis can be created to address specific facets of the study or data that need to be gathered. The researcher's challenges at this step are to Select variables that are the best operational representations of the original concepts.

Determine how many variables to test. Select or design appropriate measures for them.

### 2. Specifying the Levels of Treatment

The treatment levels of the independent variable are the distinctions the researcher makes between different aspects of the treatment condition. For example, if salary is hypothesized to have an effect on employees exercising stock purchase options, it might be divided into high, middle and low ranges to represent three levels of the independent variable.

The levels assigned to an independent variable should be based on simplicity and common sense. Similarly, if the benefits module is placed in the first and second minutes of the presentation, observable differences may not occur because the levels are too close together. Thus, in the first trial, the researcher is likely to position the midpoint of the benefits module the same interval from the end of the introduction as from the end of the conclusion.

### 3. Controlling the Experimental Environment

At this stage, we are principally concerned with environmental control, holding constant the physical environment of the experiment. The introduction of the experiment to the subjects and the instructions would likely be videotaped for consistency. The arrangement of the room, the time of administration, the experimenter's contact with the subjects, and so forth, must all be consistent across each administration of the experiment.

Other forms of control involve subject's and experimenters. When subjects do not know if they are receiving the experimental treatment.

### 4. Choosing the Experimental Design

Experimental designs are unique to the experimental method. They serve as positional and statistical plans to designate relationships between experimental treatments and the experimenter's observations or measurement points in the temporal scheme of the study. In the conduct of the experiment, the researchers apply their knowledge to select one design that is best suited to the goals of the research. Judicious selection of the design improves the probability that the observed change in the dependent variable was caused by the manipulation of the independent variable and not by another factor. It simultaneously strengthens the generalisability of results beyond the experimental setting.

### 5. Selecting and Assigning Subjects

The subjects selected for the experiment should be representative of the population to which the researcher wishes to generalize the study's results. This may seem self-evident, but we have witnessed several decades of experimentation with college sophomores that contradict that assumption.

The procedure for random sampling of experimental subjects is similar to survey. He prepares a sampling frame and then assigns subjects for the experiment to groups using random techniques. Random assignment to the groups is required to make the groups as comparable as possible with respect to dependent variables. When it is not possible to randomly assign subjects to groups, the matching concept may be used. It employs non probability quota sampling approach. The objective of matching is to have experimental and control subject on every characteristic used in research.

Some authorities suggest a quota matrix as the most efficient means of visualising the matching process. Under this method one-third of the subjects from each cell of the matrix would be assigned to each of the three groups. If matching does not alleviate the assignment problem, a combination of random, matching and increasing the sample size would be used.

### 6. Analyzing the Data

Researchers have several measurements and instrument options with experiments. Among them are, Observational techniques and coding schemes, Paper and pencil tests, Self-report instruments with open-ended and closed ended questions, Scaling techniques (likert scales, semantic differentials, etc.). Physiologic measures (galvanic skin response, EKG, voice pitch analysis, eye dilation)

## EXPERIMENTAL RESEARCH DESIGNS

Experimental designs vary in their power to control contamination of the relationship between independent and dependent variables. The most accepted designs are based on this characteristic of control.

1. Pre-experiments.
2. True experiments.
3. Field experiments.

## 1. Pre-Experimental Design

All three pre experimental designs are weak in their scientific measurement power that is, they fail to control adequately the various threats to internal liquidity. This is especially true on the one- shot case study.

*One-Shot Case Study:* This may be represented as follow:

| X | O |
|---|---|
| Treatment or manipulation of independent variable | Observation or measurement of dependent variable. |

For example, an employee education campaign about the company's financial condition without a prior measurement of employee knowledge. Results would reveal only how much the employees know after the education campaign, but there is no way to judge the effectiveness of the campaign. The lack of pre test and control group makes this design inadequate for establishing casual relationship.

*One-Group Pretest-Post-Test Design:* while applying this design in the previous example, which meets the various threats to internal validity better than the one-shot case study, but it is still a weak design.

| O | X | O |
|---|---|---|
| Pre-test | Manipulation | Post-test |

*Static group Comparison:* This design provides for two groups. One of which receives the experimental stimulus while the other serves as a control. In a field setting, imagine this scenario. A forest fire or other natural disaster is the experimental treatment, and psychological trauma (or property loss) suffered by the residents is the measured outcome. A pretest before the forest fire would be possible, but not on a large scale (as in the California fires). Moreover, timing of the pretest would be problematic. The control group, receiving the post-test would consist of residents whose property was spared.

| X | O1 |
|---|---|
| | O2 |

The addition of a comparison group creates a substantial improvement over the other two designs. However it runs with a weakness that there is no way to be certain that the two groups are equivalent.

## 2. True Experimental Designs

The major deficiency of the pre-experimental designs is that they fail to provide comparison groups that truly equivalent. The way to achieve equivalence is through matching and random assignment. With randomly assigned groups, we can employ tests of statistical significance of the observed differences.

It is common to show an X for the test stimulus and a blank for the existene of a control situation. This is an oversimplification of what really occurs. More precisely, there is an X1 and X2 and sometimes more. The X1 identifies one specific variable while X2 is another independent variable that has been chosen, often arbitrarily.

### *Pretest-Post-Test Control Group Design*

This design consists of a control group to the one-group pretest-post-test design and assigning the subjects to either of the groups by a random procedure (R) the diagram is:

| | | | |
|---|---|---|---|
| R | O1 | X | O2 |
| R | O3 | X | O4 |

The effect of the experimental variable is,

E—(O2—O1)—(O4—O3)

In this design, the seven major internal validity problems are dealt with fairly well, although there is still some difficulties. Local history may occur in one group and not the other.

Maturation, testing, and regression are handled well because one would expect them to be felt equally in experimental and control groups.

The record of the design is not as good on external validity; however, there is a chance for a reactive effect from testing. This might be a substantial influence in attitude change studies where pretests introduce unusual topics and content.

### *Post–Test–Only Control Group Design*

In this design, the pre-test measurements are omitted. Pre-tests are well established in classical research design but are not really necessary when it is possible to randomize. The design is:

| | | |
|---|---|---|
| R | X | O1 |
| R | | O2 |

The experimental effect is measured by the difference between O1 and O2. The simplicity of this design makes it more attractive than the pretest-post-test control group design. Internal validity threats from history, maturation, selection and statistical regression are adequately controlled by random assignment. Since the subjects are measured only once, the threats of testing and instrumentation are reduced, but different mortality rates between experimental and control groups continue to be a potential problem. The design reduces the external validity problem of testing interaction effect, although other problems remain.

Factor is widely used to denote an independent variable. Factors are divided into treatment levels, which represent various sub-groups. A factor may have two or more levels such as : (1) male and female; (2) large, medium, and small; or (3) no training, brief training and extended training. These levels should be operationally defined.

Active Factors are those the experimenter can manipulate by causing a subject to receive one level or another.

In blocking factor the experimenter can identify and classify the subject on an existing level. Gender, age, customer status are organizational rank are some of the examples.

### Completely Randomnized Design

The basic form of a true experiment is a completely randomnized design. This will be useful in complex designs as well as in knowing the differences in prices.

### Randomnized Block design

When here is a single major extraneous variable, the randomnized Block design is used. Random assignment is still the basic way to produce equivalence among treatment groups, but something more may be needed. The sample studied may be small which is risky and another reason for blocking is to learn whether treatment brings different results among various groups of subjects.

*Latin Square Design:* Latin square design may be used when there are two major extraneous factors. For example, assume we decide to block on the size of store and on customer income. It is convenient to consider these two blocking factors as forming the rows and columns of a table. Each factor is divided into three levels to provide nine groups of stores, each representing a unique combination of the two blocking variables. Treatments are then randomly assigned to these cells so that a given treatment appears only once in each row and column. Because of this restriction, a Latin square must have the same number of rows, columns and treatments. The design looks like the table given on the next page.

| *Store* | *Customer income* | | |
|---|---|---|---|
| | *High* | *Medium* | *Low* |
| Large | $X_2$ | X | $X_1$ |
| Medium | $X_2$ | $X_3$ | $X_1$ |
| Small | $X_1$ | $X_2$ | $X_3$ |

Treatments can be assigned by using a table of random numbers to set the order of treatment in the first row. For example, the pattern may be 3, 1, 2 as shown above. Following this, the other two cells of the first column are filled similarly, and the remaining treatments as assigned to meet the restriction that there can be no more than one treatment type in each row and column.

The experiment is carried out, sales results are gathered, and the average treatment effect is calculated. From this, we can determine the main effect of the various price spreads on the sales of company and national brands. With cost information, we discover which price differential produces the greatest margin.

### *Limitation of the Latin Square*

A limitation of the Latin square is that, we must assume there is no interaction between treatments and blocking factors.

We cannot determine the interrelationships among store size, customer income, and price.

There is no exposure of all combinations of treatments, store sizes, and customer income groups.

*Factorial Design* : One commonly held misconception about experiments is that the researcher can manipulate only one variable at a time. This is not true; with factorial designs, you can deal with more than one treatment simultaneously. Consider again the pricing experiment. The president of the chain might also be instead in finding the effect of pasting unit prices on the shelf to aid shopper decision-making. The accompanying table can be used to design an experiment that includes both the price differentials and the unit pricing.

| *Unit Price Information* | *Price Spread* | | |
|---|---|---|---|
| | *7 Cents* | *12 Cents* | *17 Cents* |
| Yes | $X_1 Y_1$ | $X_1 Y_2$ | $X_1 Y_3$ |
| No | $X_2 Y_1$ | $X_2 Y_2$ | $X_2 Y_3$ |

This is known as a 2 X 3 factorial design in which we use two factors: one with two levels and one with three levels of intensity. The version shown here is completely randomized, with the stores being randomly assigned to one of six treatment combinations. With such a design, it is possible to estimate the main effects of each of the two independent variables and the interactions between them. The results can help to answer the following questions:

What are the sales effects of the different price spreads between company and national brands?

What are the sales effects of using unit-price marking on the shelves?

What are the sales-effect interrelations between price spread and the presence of unit-price information?

### 3. Field Experiments: Quasi- or Semi-Experiments

Under field conditions, we often cannot control enough of the extraneous variables or the experimental treatment to use a true experimental design. Because the stimulus condition occurs in a natural environment, a field experiment is required.

A modern version of the bystander and thief field experiment, involves the use of electronic article surveillance to prevent shrinkage due to shoplifting.

This study was not possible with a control group, a pretest, or randomization of customers, but the information gained was essential and justified a compromise of true experimental designs. We use the pre-experimental designs previously discussed or quasi-experiments to deal with such conditions. In a quasi-experiment, we often cannot know when or to whom to expose the experimental treatment. Usually, however, we can decide when and whom to measure. A quasi-experiment is inferior to a true experimental design but is usually superior to pre-experimental designs.

*Non-equivalent Control Group Design:* This is a strong and widely used quasi-experimental design. It differs from the pre-test-post-test-control group design, because the test and control groups are not randomly assigned. The design is diagrammed as follows:

| O1 | X | O2 |
|---|---|---|
| O3 | | O4 |

There are two varieties. One is the intact equivalent design, in which the membership of the experimental and control groups is naturally assembled.

The second variation, the self-selected experimental group design, is weaker because volunteers are recruited to form the experimental group, while non-volunteer subjects are used for control. Such a design is likely when subjects believe it would be in heir interest to be a subject in an experiment—say, an experimental training program.

Comparison of pretest results (O1—O3) is one indicator of the degree of equivalence between test and control groups. If the pretest results are significantly different, there is a real question about the groups' comparability. On the other hand, if pretest observations are similar between groups' there is more reason to believe internal validity of the experiment is good.

*Separate Sample Pre-test-Post-test Design:* This design is most applicable when we cannot know when and to whom to introduce the treatment but we can decide when and whom to measure. The basic design is :

| R | O1 | (X) | |
|---|---|---|---|
| R | | X | $O_2$ |

X is irrelevant to the purpose of study but is shown to suggest that the experimenter cannot control the treatment. This is not a strong design because several threats to internal validity are not handled adequately. History can confound the results but can overcome by repeating the study in other settings. It is better method than true experiments in external validity. It is because of the fact that the samples are drawn from the population to which we wish to generalize the findings.

## Group Time Series Design

A Time Series Design introduces repeated observations before and after the treatment and allows subjects to act as their own control. The single treatment group design has before and after measurements as the only controls. There is also a multiple design with two or more comparison groups as well as the repeated measurements in each treatment group.

The time series format is especially useful where regular records are kept. It is a good way to study unplanned events. The internal validity problem for this design is history. To reduce this risk, we keep a record of possible extraneous factors during the experiment and attempt to adjust the results to reflect their influences.

# INTERNAL AND EXTERNAL VALIDITY

## *Validity*

Validity refers to the extend to which a test measures what we actually wish to measure. Many forms of Validity are mentioned in the literature, and the number goes as we expand the concern for more scientific management. This text analyses both internal and external validity.

## *Meaning of Validity*

It is the extend to which differences found with measuring tool reflect true difference among the respondents tested. The measurement tool must be sensitive. The difficulty in validity testing is that one does not know what the true differences are? One cannot discover validity without directly confirming knowledge. At the same time the problem of relevant evidence also arises. What is relevant depends upon the nature of research problem and the researcher's judgment. One widely accepted.

## Major Forms of Validity

- Content Validity
- Criterion-related Validity
- Construct Validity

## External Validity

Internal validity factors cause confusion about whether the experimental treatment (X) or extraneous factors are the source of observation differences. In contrast, external validity is concerned with the interaction of the experimental treatment with other factors and the resulting impact on the ability to generalize to (and across) times, settings or persons. Among the major threats to external validity are the following interactive possibilities.

The Reactivity of testing on X. The reactive effect refers to sensitizing subjects via a pretest so they respond to the experimental stimulus (X) in a different way. A before-measurement of a subject's knowledge about the ecology programs of a company will often sensitize the subject to various experimental communication efforts that might be made about the company. This before-measurement effect can be particularly significant in experiments where the IV is a change in attitude.

Interaction of selection and X. The process by which test subjects are selected for an experiment may be a threat to external validity. The population from which one select subjects may not be the same as the population to which one wishes to generalize results.

## Other Reactive Factors

The experimental settings may be having a biased settings effect on the subject's response to X. An artificial setting can obviously produce results that are not representative of larger population. Suppose the workers who are paid the incentive pay are moved to a different work area to separate them from the control group. These can create a strong reactive condition.

Problems of internal validity can be solved by a careful design of experiments. This is not possible in the case of external validity. External validity is largely a matter of generalization, is an inductive process of extrapolating beyond the data collected. In generalizing we estimate the factors that can be ignored and that will interact with experimental variable.

## Identifying Threats to Internal Validity

Let us examine each of the possible seven threats to internal validity in the context of the following scenario.

An organizational consultant wanted to demonstrate to the president of a company, through an experimental design, that the democratic style of leadership best enhances the morale of employees. She set-up three experimental groups and one control group for the purpose and assigned members to each of the groups randomly. The three experimental groups were headed by an autocratic leader, a democratic leader, and a *laissez-faire* leader respectively.

The members in the three experimental groups were administered a pretest. Since the control group was not exposed to any treatment, they were not given a pretest. As the experiment progressed, two members in the democratic treatment group got quite excited and started moving around to the other members saying that the participative atmosphere was "great" and "performance was bound to be high in the group". Two members from each of the autocratic and *laissez-faire* groups left after the first hour saying they had to go and could no longer participate in the experiment. After 2 hours of activities, a posttest was administered to all the participants, including the control group members, on the same lines as the pretest. Each type of validity has specific threats we need to guard against.

## Internal Validity

Among the many threats to internal validity, we consider the following seven:

- History
- Maturation
- Testing
- Instrumentation
- Selection
- Statistical regression
- Experimental mortality

### 1. *History Effects*

The action of the two members in the participative group by way of unexpectedly moving around in an excited manner and remarking that participative leadership is "great" and the "performance is bound to be high in this group" might have boosted the morale of all the members in the group. During the time that an experiment is taking place, some events may occur that confuse the relationship being studied. In many experimental designs, we take a control measurement (O1) of the dependent variable before introducing the manipulation (X). After the manipulation, we take an after-measurement (O2) of the dependent variable. Then the difference between O1 and O2 is the change that the manipulation has caused.

### 2. *Maturation*

Changes also may occur within the subject that are a function of the passage of time and are not specific to any particular event. These are of special concern when the study covers a long time, but they may also be factors in tests that are as short as an hour or two. A subject can become hungry, bored or tired in a short time, and this condition can affect response results. It is doubtful that maturation will have any effects on morale in this situation, since the passage of time, in itself, may not have anything much to do with increase or decrease in morale.

### 3. *Testing*

The pretests are likely to have sensitized the respondents to the posttest. Thus, testing effects would exist. However, if all the groups had been given both the pre- and the post-tests, the testing effects across all groups would have been taken care of (i.e., nullified) and the post-tests of each of the experimental groups could have been compared with that of the control group to detect the effects of the treatment.

### 4. *Instrumentation*

This threat to internal validity results from changes between observations in either the measuring instrument or the observer. Using different questions at each measurement is an obvious source of potential trouble, but using different observers or interviewers also threatens validity. There can even be an instrumentation problem if the same observer is used for all measurements. Observer experience, boredom, fatigue and anticipation of results can all distort the results of separate observations.

Since the same questionnaire has measured morale both before and after the treatment for all members, we do not expect instrumentation bias.

### 5. *Selection Bias*

An important threat to internal validity is the differential selection of subjects for experimental and control groups. Validity considerations require that the groups be equivalent in every respect. If subjects are randomly assigned to experimental and control groups, this selection problem can be largely overcome. Additionally, matching the members of the groups on key factors can enhance the equivalence of the groups. Since members have been randomly assigned to all groups, we do not expect selection bias to exist.

### 6. *Statistical Regression*

This factor operates when groups have been selected by their extreme scores. Suppose we measure the output of all workers in a department for a few days before an experiment and then conduct the experiment with only those workers whose productivity scores are in the top 25 percent and bottom 25 percent. Though not specifically stated, we can assume that all the members participating in the experiment were selected randomly from a normally distributed population; in which case, the issue of statistical regression contaminating the experiment does not arise.

### 7. *Mortality*

Since members dropped out of two experimental groups, the effects of mortality could affect internal validity. This occurs when the composition of the study groups changes during the test. Attrition is especially likely in the experimental group and with each dropout, the group changes. Because members of the control group are not affected by the testing situations, they are likely to withdraw.

All the threats mentioned to this point are generally, but not always, dealt with adequately in experiments by random assignment. However, five additional threats to internal validity are independent of whether or not one randomizes. The first three have the effect of equalizing experimental and control groups.

### Review of Factors Affecting Internal and External Validity

At least seven contaminating factors exists that might affect the internal validity and experimental designs. These are the effects of history, maturation, testing, instrumentation, selection, statistical regression, and mortality. It is, however, possible to reduce the biases by enhancing the level of sophistication of the experimental design. Whereas some of the more sophisticated designs, discussed below, would help increase the internal validity of the experimental results, they could also become expensive and time consuming.

Threats to external validity can be combated by creating experimental conditions that are as close as possible to the situations to which the results of the experiment are to be generalized.

## SCALES AND MEASUREMENT OF VARIABLES

### Scales

In research we quite often face measurement problem, especially when the concepts to be measured are complex and abstract and we do not possess the standardized measurement tools. Alternatively, we can say that while measuring attitudes and opinions, we face the problem of their valid measurement. A researcher may face similar problem, of course in a lesser degree, while measuring physical or institutional concepts.

### Meaning of Scaling

Scaling describes the procedures of assigning numbers to various degrees of opinion, attitude and other concepts. This can be done in two ways viz., (i) making a judgment about some characteristic of an individual and then placing him directly on a scale that has been defined in terms of that characteristic, and (ii) constructing questionnaire in such a way that the score of individual's responses assigns him a place on a scale. It may be stated here that a scale is a continuum, consisting of the highest point( in terms of some characteristic e.g., preference, favourableness, etc.) and the lowest point along with several intermediate points between these two extreme points. Hence the term 'scaling' is applied to the procedures for attempting to determine quantitative measures of subjective abstract concepts. Scaling has been defined as a "procedure for the assignment of numbers (or other symbols) to a property of objects in order to impart some of the characteristics of numbers to the properties in question.

*Definition:* Scaling is a, "Procedure for the assignment of numbers (or other symbols) to a property of objects in order to impart some of the characteristics of the numbers to the properties in question".

## Scale Classification Bases

The number assigning procedures or the scaling procedures may be broadly classified on one or more of the following bases:

(a) Subject orientation;
(b) Response form;
(c) Degree of subjectivity;
(d) Scale properties;
(e) Number of dimensions; and
(f) Scale construction techniques. We take up each of these separately.

### (a) Subject Orientation

Under it a scale may be designed to measure characteristics of the respondent who completes it or to judge the stimulus object, which is presented to the respondent. The importance in the objective to measure the attitudinal differences among people. With the second study objective you might have the same data but in this case you are truly interested to know the satisfaction level of the people with regard to a Government scheme.

### (b) Response Form

Under this we may classify the scales as categorical and comparative. Categorical scales are also known as rating scales. These scales are used when a respondent scores some object without direct reference to other objects. Under comparative scales, which are also known as ranking scales, the respondent is asked to compare two or more objects. In this sense the respondent may state that one object is superior to the other. Measurement scales are of three types. They are rating, ranking and categorization. A rating scale is used when respondents score an object without making a comparison of another object or attitude. Ranking scales are used when the participant makes a comparison objects. Categorization asks respondents to put themselves in groups or categories.

### (c) Degree of Subjectivity

With this basis the scale data may be based on whether we measure subjective personal preferences or simply make non-preference judgments.

### (d) Scale Properties

Considering scale properties, one may classify the scales as nominal, ordinal, interval and ratio scales.

### (e) Number of Dimensions

In respect of this basis, scales can be classified as 'one-dimensional' and 'multi-dimensional' scales. Under the former we measure only one attribute of the respondent or object; whereas multi-dimensional scaling recognizes that an object might be described better by using the concept of an attribute space of 'n' dimensions, rather than a single dimension continuum.

### (f) Techniques of Constructing a Scale

Following are the five main techniques by which scales can be developed:

1. *Arbitrary Approach*
   It is presumed that such scales measure the concepts for which they have been designed. But the researcher has no advanced evidence of a particular scales validity or reliability.
2. *Consensus Approach*
   Here a panel of judges evaluate the items chosen for inclusion in the instrument in terms of whether they are relevant to the topic area.
3. *Item Analysis Approach*
   Under it a number of individual items are developed in to a test, which is given to a group of respondents. After administering the test, the total scores are calculated for every one. Individual items are then analysed to determine which items discriminate between persons or objects with high total scores and those with low scores.
4. *Cumulative Scales*
   These are chosen on the basis of their conforming to some ranking of items with ascending and descending discriminating power.
5. *Factor Scales*
   This may be constructed on the basis of inter correlations of items, which indicate that a common factor accounts for the relationship between items. This relationship is typically measured through factor analysis method.

## Characteristics of a Good Scale

The following are the essential characteristics of a good scale:

### *Reliability*

The scale must be reliable in the sense that it must give the same measurement or result in similar conditions. In case a scale gives different measurements, on being applied to the same of highly similar phenomena, its reliability is doubtful.

### *Validity*

The validity of scale lies in the fact that it measures in some demonstrable way, what 'it claims to measure'. The test of validity of a scale is an extremely complicated task and it is difficult to give a satisfactory criteria of the phenomena being measured and also no objective measurement of the validity of a scale have yet been evolved. 'Logical test of validity is generally used for this purpose and a scale is said to be valid if the measurements given by it stands to real'.

### *Simplicity*

The scale should be simple and easy enough to be understood by a common man.

### *Universality*

A good scale should be widely applicable. The most notable characteristic of physical scales is their universal acceptance, whereas, one of the limitations of scale is limited applicability. But the point bearing upon this limited applicability be cleared at this stage in the social phenomena is not 'so homogeneous as the physical phenomena'.

### *Practicability*

A good scale should be practicable and this implies that factors which are considered for the construction of the scale must be such as to be measured and gathered. If in a study, the intangible behaviour of 'traits' are included in the scale, it would be difficult to introduce the scale as these cannot be measured.

### *Based on Norms*

A scale should be based on accepted norms since for all purposes of comparisons the researcher will use norms with which the measurement is to be compared. Proper weight age scale should have proper weight age for each factor included in the scale.

## IMPORTANT SCALING TECHNIQUES

### 1. Rating Scales

The rating scale involves qualitative description of a limited number of aspects of a thing or of traits of a person. When we use rating scales (or categorical scales), we judge an object in absolute terms against some specified criteria; we judge properties of objects without reference to other similar objects. These ratings may be in such forms as "like-dislike", "above average, average, below average", or other classifications with some more categories such as "like very much-like somewhat-neutral-dislike somewhat-dislike very much"; "excellent-good-average-below average-poor", "always-often-occasionally-rarely-never", and so on. Rating scale may be either a graphic rating scale or an itemized rating scale.

(a) *The Graphic rating scale* is quite simple and is commonly used in practice. Under it the various points are usually put along the line to form a continuum and the rater indicates his rating by simply making a mark (such as a 'tick' mark) at the appropriate point on a line that runs from one extreme to the other. Scale-points with brief descriptions may be indicated along the line, their function being to assist the rater in performing his job.

(b) *The Itemized rating scale* (also known as numerical scale) presents a series of statements from which a respondent selects one as best reflecting his evaluation. These statements are ordered progressively in terms of more or less of some property.

## 2. Method of Paired Comparisons

Under it the respondent can express his attitude by making a choice between two objects, say; between a new flavour of soft drink and an established brand of drink. But when there are ore than two stimuli to judge, the number of judgments required in a paired comparison is given by the formula:

$$N = n\,(n-1)/2$$

where, N = number of judgments.
n = number of stimuli or objects to be judged.

Thus, paired-comparison data may be treated in several ways. If there is substantial consistency, we will find that if X is preferred to Y, and Y to Z, then X will consistently be preferred to Z. If this is true, we may take the total number of preferences among the comparisons as the score for that stimulus.

## 3. Method of Rank Order

Under this method of comparative scaling, the respondents are asked to rank their choices. This method is easier and faster than the method of paired comparisons stated above. For example, with 10 items it takes 45 pair comparisons to complete the task, whereas the method of rank order simply requires ranking of 10 items only. The problem of transitivity (such as A prefers to B, B to C, but C prefers to A) is also not there in case we adopt method of rank order. Then there may be the problem of respondents becoming careless in assigning ranks particularly when there are many (usually more than 10) items.

## 4. Differential Scales (or Thurstone-type Scales)

The name of L.L. Thurstone is associated with differential scales, which have been developed using consensus scale approach. Under such an approach the selection of items is made by a panel of judges who evaluate the items in terms of whether they are relevant to the topic area and unambiguous in implication. The detailed procedure is as under:

The researcher gathers a large number of statements, usually twenty or more, that express various points of view toward a group, institution, idea, or practice (i.e., statements belonging to the topic area).

These statements are then submitted to a panel of judges, each of who arranges them in eleven groups or piles ranging from one extreme to another in position. Each of the judges is requested to place generally in the first pile the statements which he thinks are most unfavourable to the issue, in the second pile to place those statements which he thinks are next most unfavourble and he goes on doing so in this manner till in the eleventh pile he puts the statements which he considers to be the most favourable.

This sorting by each judge yields a composite position for each of the items. In case of marked disagreement between the judges in assigning a position to an item, that item is discarded.

For items that are retained, each is given its median scale value between one and eleven as established by the panel. A final selection of statements is then made. For this purpose a sample of statements, shoes median scores are spread evenly from one extreme to the other is taken. The statements so selected, constitute the final scale to be administered to respondents.

## 5. Summated Scales (or Likert-type Scales)

Summated scales are developed by utilizing the item analysis approach wherein a particular item is evaluated on the basis of how well it discriminates between those persons whose total score is high ant those whose score is low. Thus, summated scales consist of a number of statements, which express a favourable or unfavourable attitude towards the given object to which the respondent is asked to react. The respondent indicated his agreement or disagreement with each statement in the instrument. Each response is given a numerical score, indicating its favourableness or unfavourableness, and the scores are totaled to measure the respondent's attitude. For example, when asked to express opinion whether one considers his job quite pleasant, the respondent may respond in any one of the following ways: (i) strongly agree, (ii) agree, (iii) undecided, (iv) disagree, (v) strongly disagree.

We find that these five points constitute the scale. At one extreme of the scale there is strong agreement with the given statement and at the other, strong disagreement, and between them lie intermediate points. Each Point on the scale carries a score. Response indicating the least favourable degree of job satisfaction is given the least score (say 1) and the most favourable is given the highest score (say 5). These score-values are normally not printed on the instrument but are shown here just to indicate the scoring pattern. The Likert scaling technique, thus, assigns a scale value to each of the five responses. The same thing is done in respect of each and every statement in the instrument. If the instrument consists of, say 30 statements, the following score values would be revealing:

$30 \times 5 = 150$ most favourable response possible.
$30 \times 3 = 90$ A neutral attitude.
$30 \times 1 = 30$ most unfavourable attitude.

The scores for any individual would fall between 30 and 150. If the score happens to be above 90, it shows favourable opinion to the given point of view, a score of below 90 would mean unfavourabvle opinion and a score of exactly 90 would be suggestive of a neutral attitude.

*Advantages:* The Likert-type scale has several advantages—

(a) It is relatively easy to construct the Likert-type scale in comparison to Thurstone-type scale.
(b) Likert-type scale is considered more reliable.
(c) Each statement, included in the Likert-type scale, is given an empirical test for discriminating ability.
(d) Likert-type scale can easily be used in respondent-centered and stimulus-centered studies i.e., through it we can study how responses differ between people and how responses differ between stimuli.
(e) Likert-type scale takes much less time to construct, it is frequently used by the students of opinion research studies that there is high degree of correlation between Likert-type scale and Thurstone-type scale.

### Limitations

One important limitation is that, with this scale, we can simply examine whether respondents are more or less favourable to a topic, but we cannot tell positions indicated on the scale are equally spaced. The interval between 'strongly agree' and 'agree' may not be equal to the interval between "agree" and "undecided".

One further disadvantage is that often the total score of an individual respondent has little clear meaning since a given total score can be secured by a variety of answer patterns. There "remains a possibility that people may answer according to what they think they should feel rather than how they do feel".

### 6. Cumulative Scale

Cumulative scales or Louis Guttman's scalogram analysis, like other scales, consists of series of statements to which a respondent expresses his agreement or disagreement. The special feature of this type of scale is that statements in it form a cumulative series. This, in other words, means that the statements are related to one another in such a way that an individual, show replies favourably to say item No. 3, also replies favourably to items No. 2 and 1, and one who replies favourably to item No. 4 also replies favourably to items No. 3, 2 and 1, and so on.

**Response Pattern in Scalogram Analysis**

| *Item Number* | | | | *Respondent Score* |
|---|---|---|---|---|
| 4 | 3 | 2 | 1 | |
| X | X | X | X | 4 |
| — | X | X | X | 3 |
| — | — | X | X | 2 |
| — | — | — | X | 1 |
| — | — | — | X | 0 |

X = Agree, — Disagree

A score of 4 means that the respondent is in agreement with all the statements which is indicative of the most favourable attitude. But a score of 3 would mean that the respondent is not agreeable to item 4, but he agrees with all others. In the same way one can interpret other values of the respondent's scores. This pattern reveals that the universe of content is scalable.

## 7. Factor Scales

Factor scales are developed through factor analysis or on the basis of intercorrelations of items indicate that a common factor accounts for the relationship between items. Factor scales are particularly "useful in uncovering latent attitude dimensions and approach scaling through the concept of multiple-dimension attribute space." More specifically the two problems viz., how to deal appropriately with the universe of content, which is multi-dimensional, and how to uncover underlying (latent) dimensions which have not been identified, are dealt with through factor scales. An important factor scale based on factor analysis is Semantic Differential (S.D.) and the other one is Multidimensional Scaling. We give below brief accounts of these factor scales.

## 8. Semantic Differential Scale

Semantic differential scale or S.D. scale developed by Charles E. Osgood (1957) is an attempt to measure the psychological meanings of an object to an individual. This scale is based on the presumption that an object can have different dimensions of connotative meanings, which can be located in multi-dimensional property space.

*Procedure:* Various steps involved in developing semantic Differential Scale are as follows:

First of all the concepts to be studied are selected. The concepts are usually chosen by personal judgment, keeping in view the nature of the problem.

The next step is to select the scales bearing in mind the criterion of factor composition and the criterion of scale's relevance to the concepts being judged (it is common practice to use at least three scales for each factor with the help of which an average factor score has to be worked out). One more criterion to be kept in view is that scales should be stable across subjects and concepts.

Then a panel of judges is used to rate the various stimuli (or objects) on the various selected scales and the responses of all judges would then be combined to determine the composite scaling.

### *Advantages*

1. It produces interval date.
2. It is an easy way to secure attitudes from a large sample.
3. These may be measured in both direction and intensity.
4. The total set of responses provides a comprehensive picture.
5. It is a standardized technique that is easily repeated.

### 9. Multi-dimensional Scaling

Multidimensional scaling (MDS) is relatively more complicated scaling device, but with this sort of scaling one scaling one can scale objects, individual or both with a minimum of information. Multi-dimensional scaling (or MDS) can be characterized as a set of procedures for portraying perceptual or affective dimensions of substantive interest. It "provides useful methodology for portraying subjective judgments of diverse kinds." MDS is used when all the variables in a study are to be analyzed simultaneously and all such variables happen to be independent. The underlying assumption in MDS is that people "perceive a set of objects as being more or less similar to one another on a number of dimensions (usually uncorrelated with one another) instead of only one." Through MDS techniques one can represent geometrically the locations and interrelationships among a set of points.

### 10. Numerical Scale

Numerical scales have equal intervals that separate their numeric scale points. The verbal anchors serve as the labels for the extreme points. Numerical scales are often 5-point scales, but may have 7 or 10 points. The respondent writes a number from the scale next to each item. If numerous questions about employee performance were included in the example, the scale would provide both an absolute measure of importance and a relative measure of importance and a relative measure (ranking) of the various items rated. The scales' linearity, simplicity, and production of ordinal or interval data make it popular for managers and researchers.

### 11. The Multiple Rating List Scale

The multiple rating list scale is similar to the numerical scale but differs in two ways: 1. It accepts a circled response from the rater, and 2. The layout allows visualization of the results. The advantage is that a mental map of the respondent's evaluations is evident to both the rater and the researcher. This scale produces interval data. A scale that helps the researcher discover proportions is the fixed sum scale.

### 12. The Stapel Scale

The staple scale is used as an alternative to the semantic differential, especially when it is difficult to find bipolar adjectives that match the investigative question. The scale is composed of he work identifying the image dimension and a set of 10 response categories for each of the three attributes. Fewer response categories are sometimes used. Respondents select a plus number for the characteristic that describes the named company. The more accurate the description, the larger is the positive number. Similarly, the less accurate the description, the larger is the negative number chosen. Ratings range from +5 to –5, very accurate to very inaccurate. Like the semantic differential, stapel scales usually produce interval data.

## ERRORS TO AVOID WITH RATING SCALES

The value of rating scales for measurement purposes depends on the assumption that a person can and will make good judgments. Before accepting respondents' ratings, we should consider their tendencies to make errors of three types:

1. Leniency;
2. Central tendency; and
3. Halo effect.

### Leniency

The error of leniency occurs when a respondent is either an "easy rater" or a "hard rater". The latter is an error of negative leniency. Raters are inclined to score people higher whom they know well and with whom they are ego involved. There is also the opposite—where acquaintances are rated lower because one is aware of the tendency toward positive leniency and attempts to counteract it.

### Central Tendency

Raters are reluctant to give extreme judgments, and this fact accounts for the error of central tendency. This is most often seen when the rater does not know the object or property being rated. To counteract this type of error try the following:

Adjust the strength of descriptive adjectives.
Space the intermediate descriptive phrases farther apart.
Provide smaller differences in meaning between the steps near the ends of the scale that between the steps near the center.
Use more points in the scale.

### Halo

The halo effect is the systematic bias that the rater introduces by carrying over a generalized impression of the subject from one rating to another.

## SAMPLE RATING SCALES (VARIOUS MODELS)

### Single Category Scale (Dichotomous Data, Nominal)

I plan to purchase a desktop computer

Yes ☐
No ☐

### Multiple Choices Single Responses Scale

What Newspaper do you Read most often for Stock Market Movements?

The Hindu ☐
Financial Express ☐
Economic Times ☐
Others ☐

### Multiple Choice Multiple Response Scale

What are the sources you have consulted when designing your new home?

Online planning ☐
Magazines ☐
independent builder? ☐
Developer's models ☐
Designer ☐
Architect ☐
Others ☐

### Likert Scales Summated Rating

Internet is useful than libraries ☐
Strongly agree ☐
Agree ☐
Neither agrees nor disagrees ☐
Disagree ☐
Strongly disagree ☐

### Semantic Differential Scale

Lands end catalog
Fast ——: ——: ——: ——: ——: ——: ——: Slow
High quality ——: ——: ——: ——: ——: ——: ——: Low quality
Numerical scale data
Extremely favourable 5 4 3 2 1 Extremely unfavourable
Employees cooperation in teams ————
Employees knowledge of task ————
Employees planning effectiveness ————

### Graphic Rating Scale

How likely do you recommend complete care to others (place an X at the position along the line that best reflects your judgment).

Very likely /————————————————————/Very unlikely

/————————————————————/

(alternative with graphic)

## STABILITY MEASURES

### Goodness of Measures

Now that we have seen how to operationally define variables and apply different scaling techniques, it is important to make sure that the instrument that we develop to measure a particular concept is indeed accurately measuring the variables, and that in fact, we are actually measuring the concept that we set out to measure. This ensures that in operationally defining perceptual and attitudinal variables, we have not overlooked some important dimensions and elements or included some irrelevant ones. The scales developed could often be imperfect, and errors are prone to occur in the measurement of attitudinal variables. We need to assess the "goodness" of the measures developed. That is, we need to be reasonably sure that the instruments we use in our research do indeed measure the variables they are supposed to, and that they measure them accurately.

### Item Analysis

Item analysis is done to see if the items in the instrument belong there or not. Each item is examined for its ability to discriminate between those subjects whose total scores are high, and those with low scores. In item analysis, the means between the high score and the low-score group are tested to detect significant differences through the *t*-values. The items with a high *t*-value (test which is able to identify the highly discriminating items in the instrument) are then included in the instrument. Thereafter, tests for the reliability of the instrument are done and the validity of the measure is established.

Very briefly, reliability tests how consistently a measuring instrument measures whatever concept it is measuring. Validity tests how well an instrument that is developed measures the particular concept it is intended to measure.

### Reliability

The reliability of a measure indicates the extent to which it is without bias (error-free) and hence ensures consistent measurement across time and across the various items in the instrument.

### Stability of Measures

The stability of a measure to remain the same over time—despite uncontrollable testing conditions or the state of the respondents themselves—is indicative of its stability and low vulnerability to changes in the situation this attests to its "goodness" because the concept is stably measured, no matter when it is done. Two tests of stability are test-re-test reliability and parallel-form reliability.

### Test-Re-test Reliability

The reliability coefficient obtained with a repetition of the same measure on a second occasion is called test-re-test reliability. That is, when a questionnaire containing some items that are supposed to measure a concept is administered to a set of respondents now, and again to the same respondents, say several weeks to 6 months later, then the correlation between the scores obtained at the two different times from one and the same set of respondents is called the test-re-test coefficient.

### Parallel-form Reliability

When responses on two comparable sets of measures tapping the same construct are highly correlated, we have parallel-form reliability. Both forms have similar items and the same response format, the only changes being the wordings and the order or sequence of the questions.

### Internal Consistency of Measures

The internal consistency of measures is indicative of the homogeneity of the items in the measure that tap the construct. The items should "hang together as a set", and be capable of independently measuring the same concept so that the respondents attach the same overall meaning to each of the items.

### Inter-item Consistency Reliability

This is a test of the consistency of respondents' answers to all the items in a measure. To the degree that items are independent measures of the same concept, they will be correlated with one another.

### Split-half Reliability

Split-half reliability reflects the correlations between two halves of an instrument. The estimates would vary depending on how the items in the measure are split into two halves. Split-half reliabilities could be higher than Cronbach's alpha only in the circumstance of three being more than one underlying response dimension tapped by the measure and when certain other conditions are met.

It is important to note that reliability is a necessary but not sufficient condition of the test of goodness of a measure. For example, one could very reliably measure a concept establishing high stability and consistency, but it may not be the concept that one had set out to measure. Validity ensures the ability of a scale to measure the intended concept. We will now discuss the concept of validity in measurement of stability.

### Content Validity

Content validity ensures that the measure includes an adequate and representative set of items that tap the concept. The more the scale items represent the domain or universe of the concept being measured, the greater the content validity. To put it differently, content validity is a function of how well the dimensions and elements o a concept have been delineated.

*Face validity:* It is considered by some as a basic and a very minimum index of content validity. Face validity indicates that the items that are intended to measure a concept, do on the face of it look they measure the concept.

*Criterion-related Validity:* It is established when the measure differentiates individuals on a criterion it is expected to predict. This can be done by establishing concurrent validity or predictive validity, as explained below.

*Concurrent Validity:* It is established when the scale discriminates individuals who are known to be different; that is, they should score differently on the instrument.

*Construct Validity:* It testifies to how well the results obtained from the use of the measure fit the theories around which the test is designed. This is assessed through convergent and discriminant validity, which are explained below.

*Convergent Validity:* It is established when the scores obtained with two, different instruments measuring the same concept are highly correlated.

*Discriminant Validity:* It is established when, based on theory, two variables are predicted to be uncorrelated, and the scores obtained by measuring them are indeed empirically found to be so.

Validity can thus be established in different ways. Published measures for various concepts usually report the kinds of validity that have been established for the instrument, so that the user or reader can judge the "goodness" of the measure.

## Types of Validity

| *Validity* | *Description* |
|---|---|
| Content validity | Doe the measure adequately measure the concept? |
| Face validity | Do "experts" validate that the instrument measures what its name suggests it measures? |
| Criterion-related validity | Does the measure differentiate in a manner that helps to predict a criterion variable? |
| Concurrent validity | Does the measure differentiate in a manner that helps to predict a criterion variable currently? |
| Predictive validity | Does the measure differentiate individuals in a manner as to help predict a future criterion? |
| Construct validity | Does the instrument tap the concept as theorized? |
| Convergent validity | Do two instruments measuring the concept correlate highly? |
| Discriminant validity | Does the measure have a low correlation with a variable that is supposed to be unrelated to this variable? |

## QUESTIONS

1. What do you understand by variables?
2. What are the types of variables?
3. What do you understand by experimental design?
4. What are the advantages of experimental design?
5. What are the precautions to be taken while using experimental design?
6. What are the problems to be faced by the researcher while using experimental design?
7. Describe the seven activities to be performed to do successful experiment?
8. What are the types of experimental design?
9. What do you understand by factor?
10. What do you mean by Latin Square Design?
11. What do you understand by Factorial Design?
12. What do you mean by Field Experiments?
13. What do you understand by validity? What are the forms of it?
14. What is internal validity? Elucidate the threats to the internal validity.
15. What is external validity? Describe the factors that affect the external validity?
16. What is meant by scales?
17. What are the uses of scales used in business research?
18. Briefly explain the characteristics of a good scale.
19. What are the bases of scaling?
20. What do you understand by rating scale? Also enumerate the types of rating scales.
21. Explain the concepts in Likert types scale. Explain the merits and draw backs of this method.
22. Briefly explain about the cumulative scale.
23. What do you mean by reliability?
24. What is Test-Re-test Reliability?
25. What do you understand by construct validity?
26. What is meant by descriminate validity?
27. What do you understand by face validity?
28. What is meant by Predictive validity? What are its applications in business research?
29. What do you understand by internal consistency measures?
30. What is meant by stability of measures?

# 3

# Data Collection Methods

## INTRODUCTION

The task of data collection begins after a research problem has been defined and research design/plan chalked out. While deciding about the method of data collection to be used for study, the researcher should keep in mind two types of data to be used in the research. Any research needs adequate data. Data serve like the base or the raw materials for analysis. Without an analysis of factual data inferences cannot be drawn. Data form the basis for testing the hypotheses formulated in a study. Data also provide facts and figures required for constructing measurement scales and tables, which are analysed with statistical techniques. The scientific process of measurement, analysis, testing and inferences depend on the availability of relevant data

## TYPES OF DATA

### Primary Data and Secondary Data

The primary data are those, which are collected afresh and for the first time. The secondary data, on the other hand, are those which have already been collected by someone else and which have already been passed through statistical process. The methods of collecting primary and secondary data differ since primary data are to be originally collected, while in the case of secondary data the nature of data collection work is merely that of compilation.

| Primary | Secondary |
|---|---|
| Direct personal interview | Published and unpublished sources: |
| Indirect personal interview | Government publications |
| Information from correspondents | Publications of international bodies |
| Mailed Questionnaires | Semi-official publications |
| | Reports of Committes and Commissions |
| Questionnaires filled by enumerators | Private publications; |
| | (a) Journals and newspapers |
| | (b) Research institutions |
| | (c) Professional Trade |

The most common methods for collecting primary data are Observation, Interview, and Questionnaire.

## OBSERVATION METHOD

The observation method is the most commonly used method especially in studies relating to behavioural sciences. Under this method, the information is sought by way of investigator's own direct observation without asking from the respondents. The main advantages of this method are as follows:

1. The subjective bias is eliminated, if observation is done accurately.
2. The information obtained under this method related to what is currently happening.
3. This method is independent of respondents' willingness to respond.
4. This method is particularly suitable to those who are not capable of giving verbal reports.

## INTERVIEW METHOD

The interview method of collecting data involves presentation of oral-verbal stimuli and reply in terms of oral-verbal responses. This method can be used through personal interviews and, if possible, through telephone interviews.

### Personal Interviews

Personal interview method requires a person known as the interviewer asking questions generally in a face-to-face contact to the other person or persons. This sort of interview may be in the form of direct personal investigation or it may be an indirect oral investigation. In the case of direct personal investigation the interviewer has to collect the information personally from the sources concerned. Most of the commissions and committees appointed by government to carry on investigations make use of this method. The method of collecting information through personal interviews is usually carried out in a structured way. As such we call the interviews as structured interviews. Such interviews involve the use of a set of pre-determined questions. Thus, the interviewer in a structures interview follows a rigid procedure laid down, asking questions in a form and order prescribed.

## QUESTIONNAIRES

Questionnaire is one among the survey methods and it is a most common and widely used device for data collection. It is a primary data collection method by asking questions to elicit answer from the units of study known as, respondents. The important step in this method is to take care in the design of questions. The questions should be specific and relevant to the formulated hypothesis and direct to the purpose of research.

Questionnaire is a tool to collect data from diverse large and widely scattered population groups. Goode and Hatt state "Questionnaire refers to a device for securing answers to questions by using a form which the respondent fills himself".

### Types of Questionnaire

Questionnaire technique falls into two types, namely;

(a) Personally distributed, and
(b) Mailed questionnaire.

Distributing and collecting back filled in Questionnaire personally is known as personally distributed Questionnaire and sending the Questionnaire by mail is known as mailed Questionnaire. The investigator will have to attach a self-addressed, sufficiently stamped envelope for the respondent to return the filled in Questionnaire back.

Now-a-days Web-based questionnaires are rapidly gaining popularity as the Internet and World-Wide Web usage increases. The advantages of web page surveys are:

a. Web-based questionnaires are very fast.
b. It is possible to get (a) large number of responses (e.g. several thousand responses).
c. The order of the questions (and even the number and type of questions) can be changed according to the respondents' answers.
d. The questionnaire can use multimedia content (e.g. sounds, videos etc.), colours, fonts, and different formatting options.

Although the Internet is gaining popularity, it is still far from being universal. Therefore, Web-based questionnaires may not reflect the whole population. Also, Web-based questionnaires could lead to a biased sample because there is often no control over the respondents. People with a varying spectrum of background from all over the world can complete the questionnaire. Moreover, some of them may respond to the same questionnaire multiple times.

## Preparation Process

The investigator should identify the various areas in his topic. Write down the questions under each area in simple terms. For example, starting with the biosketch details frequency of library visit, days and hours of visit, duration of, time spent per visit, abstracts, indexes consulted, periodicals consulted, articles obtained, publications based on library information retrieved suggestions, etc.

Next step will be to consult questionnaires, used in the previous/ similar investigations sometimes, one may find more than one source instead of finding whole in a single report. Many a time a pretested questionnaire may be available in whole. An investigator will have to tailor/modify questions in the light of his study and the environment, which may differ even slightly. A few examples should be given to some of the respondents and clarify whether the question are understandable and whether they are able to respond properly. Based, on that experience, one will have to sit and formulate the questions in tune with the identified areas. Some questions will never he answered by all of the respondents, if they are not structures properly.

One more aspect to be taken care of by the respondents will be to look into the arrangement/ordering of the inner segments/areas in a proper, helpful sequence.

## Questions—Types

The questions to be formulated fall into two categories, namely,

(a) Open-end questions, and
(b) Pre-coded questions.

## a. Open end Questions

Name is an example for Open end questions. The respondent will provide an answer to a question without any help from the investigator under this category.

What do you read? And
How often do you visit the library?

Are some more examples? The reader may respond by giving an answer from humpty number of options.

### b. Pre-coded Questions

Preceded questions will give possible answer choice along with the question so that the respondents will tick to choose a suitable answer.

What do you read in the library? (Please Rank)

| | |
|---|---|
| Subject books | Newspapers |
| Periodicals | Magazines |
| Reference books | Novels |

How often do you visit the library?

| | |
|---|---|
| Daily | Weekly |
| Fortnightly | Monthly |

Whenever possible the investigator should resort to precoded questions. Otherwise, the number and variety of answers will make it difficult to tabulate.

### Advantages of Questionnaire

This method is economical comparatively specking, questionnaire method is cheaper in cost and can cover a wider geographical area under study.

It saves time, conditionally, as once the questionnaire is ready it can be distributing simultaneously to users. Users have more liberty in answering the questions. Questionnaire method ensures reliability and accuracy as accuracy as it collects first hand information.

### Limitations

Now-a-days it is very costly as printing cost and postage have gone up.

Many respondents do not react even after wasting two or three copies of the questionnaire. For analysis purpose it is very important to have a large quantum of response. Poor response will lead to incorrect inferences.

All the respondents do not return the filled in questionnaire in time. The relevance of the answers are mostly dependent on the effectiveness of the questions framed. Answers to many of the questions may not be accurate.

### Construction of the Questionnaire

While constructing a questionnaire, the following points should be taken into consideration:

(1) What is expected from the Questionnaire?
(2) Type of questions to be asked: unstructured or structured?
(3) If structured questions are to be included then the type of scale to be used Nominal or Ordinal or Interval or Ratio?

(4) The content of the questions should not be biased or suggestive.
(5) Sequencing of the questions in an orderly pattern.
(6) The first draft should be subjected to pre-testing for modification and establishing reliability and validity.

## Process of Questionnaire Technique

Study of Questionnaire is divided into:

(a) Designing or Making,
(b) Issuing, and
(c) Returning.

While designing attention should be paid to three important matters:

1. Physical appearance of the questionnaire,
2. Contents of the questionnaire, and
3. Subject matter.

## Preliminary Steps

a. Consult colleagues and friends to get their thinking on the problem.
b. Formulation of such a list of areas and questions.
c. Submit this list to experts both in the field of problem and elated fields.
d. Drafting the questionnaire (first page).
e. Pre-testing the questionnaire.
f. Re-examining and revising the questionnaire (second stage).
g. Go to the field for large scale study in order to see how best his major draft seems to fit the subject.
h. Editing and coding the questionnaire responses.

## Factors affecting responses

Different factors are responsible for varying degree of response to the questionnaire as stated below:

1. *Characteristics of the Group:* The response normally differs according to the characteristics of the respondent group. Generally educated people are more responsive as compared to the illiterate people.
2. *Prestige of Sponsoring Body:* If the institution has a good reputation, the percentage of response is very high.
3. *Importance of the Problem:* If the problem under study is important a higher response is expected.
4. *Nature of Questionnaire:* If the get up of the questionnaire is attractive, the respondents feel like responding quickly.

5. *Size of the Questionnaire:* If the questions are small in number the percentage of response is high.

## Characteristics of a Good Questionnaire

A summary of main characteristics of a good questionnaire is given below:

(1) It asks and obtains all the information required for achieving the research objective.
(2) It contains the questions relevant to the study and does not include any irrelevant and unimportant questions.
(3) It contains no open – ended or discussion questions unless they are absolutely necessary.
(4) It does not contain questions which are beyond the memory span of the respondents.
(5) Questions and alternative answers are properly coded.
(6) It contains the questions, which can be answered easily and quickly by the respondents.
(7) Appropriate introduction and instructions are given.
(8) Inter-related questions are properly positioned.
(9) Transition between one section and another is smooth.
(10) The questionnaire is adequately pretested and revised so as to be a satisfactory tool for the particular survey.
(11) Filter questions are used whenever necessary.
(12) Each question is limited to a single idea.
(13) It avoids unwarranted presumptions about the respondents.
(14) Choices to the closed questions are adequate reasonable and logically consistent.
(15) The questions are arranged in a sequential order.
(16) No embarrassing questions are asked to the respondents.

Distinction between schedule and questionnaire:

1. *Methodology:* The schedule is a direct method. Here, the researcher comes in direct contact with the respondent, whereas in the questionnaire method the data are collected indirectly through communications.
2. *Types of Questions:* In the schedule method, the questions that are included are very short. But the questionnaire method consists of rather lengthy questions.
3. *Reliability:* The information that is collected through the schedule method is more reliable. But in questionnaire method the reliability is somewhat doubtful.
4. *Area:* The schedule method covers only a limited area, whereas the questionnaire method covers a wide area.

5. *Clarification of Questions:* In schedule method the investigator can collect the information from uneducated people by clarifying the meaning and purpose of the question and study. But this is impossible in the questionnaire method.
6. *Collection of Information:* Through the schedule method, it is not possible to collect confidential information whereas in questionnaire method, the respondent is free to express the actual fact.
7. *Use in Sampling Method:* Questionnaire method is not useful for sampling unlike the schedule, which is very useful for sampling.
8. *Representativeness:* The data collected through the questionnaires are not completely representative. This problem does not arise in the schedule method.
9. *Structure of Questions:* In the questionnaire method, the questions are made on the basis of the cultural and educational background of the respondents. In a word, it is respondent-oriented. But the schedule method is just opposite to this.

## Electronic Questionnaire Design and Surveys

Online questionnaire surveys are easily designed and administered when microcomputers are hooked up to computer networks. Data disks can also be mailed to respondents, who may use their own personal computers for responding to the questions. These will, of course, be helpful only when the respondents know how to use the computer and feel comfortable responding in this manner.

Several programs are developed to administer questionnaires electronically. As disks are inexpensive, mailing them across the country is no problem either. The PC medium non-response rates may not be any higher than those of the mail questionnaire response. With increase of computer literacy, we can expect electronic questionnaire administration to take on an increasing role in the future.

SPSS (Statistical Package for the Social Sciences) has several software programs for research purposes including: (1) SPSS Data Entry Builder for creating surveys that can be administered over the web, phone, or mail; (2) SPSS Data Entry Enterprise Server for entering the responses; and (3) SPSS 11.0 for data analysis and charts.

It should be pointed out that information obtained from respondents either through interviews or questionnaires, being self-report data, could be biased.

Questionnaires can also be distributed via fax machines. These fax surveys replace the sender's printing and postage costs and are delivered and/or returned faster than traditional mail surveys. Facsimile machines or fax machines have been used as a way for respondents to return questionnaires and as a means to deliver questionnaires. A questionnaire inserted in a magazine may instruct the respondent to clip out the questionnaire and fax it to a certain phone number. In a mail survey, a prepaid postage enveloped places little burden on the respondent. Faxing a questionnaire to a long-distance number requires that the respondent pay for the transmission of the fax. Thus, a disadvantage of fax surveys is that only respondents with fax machines who are willing to exert the "extra" effort return questionnaires. It is likely that people with extreme opinions will be more likely to respond.

### E-mail Surveys

Questionnaires can be distributed via E-mail. E-mail is a relatively new method of communication, and many individuals cannot be accessed by it. However, certain circumstances lend themselves to e-mail surveys, such as internal surveys of employees or satisfaction surveys of retail buyers who regularly deal with the organization via e-mail.

Benefits of E-mail surveys:

- Speed of distribution,
- Cheaper distribution and processing costs,
- Faster turnaround time, and
- More flexibility and less paper chasing.

The speed of e-mail distribution and quick response time can be a major advantage for surveys dealing when time is a crucial factor.

### Internet Surveys

An Internet survey is a self-administered questionnaire posted on a Web site. Respondents provide answers to questions displayed online. Many in the survey research community believe Internet surveys are the way of the future. The advantages are summarized below.

#### A. *Quick and Less Cost*

Internet surveys allow marketers to reach a large audience), to personalize individual messages, and to secure confidential answers in a simple, quick, and very cost-effective manner. These computer-to-computer self-administered questionnaires eliminate the cost of paper, postage, data entry cost, and other administration costs. Once an Internet questionnaire has been developed, the incremental cost of additional respondents is marginal. Surveys can be conducted in less than a week.

#### B. *Visual and Interactive*

Surveys conducted on the Internet can be interactive. The researcher can use more sophisticated lines of questioning based on the respondents' prior answers. The Internet is an excellent medium for the presentation of visual materials.

### C. Respondent Participation and Cooperation

Participation in some Internet surveys occurs when a computer user intentionally navigates to a particular Web site where questions are displayed. In some cases, individuals anticipate a survey at the web site and in other cases it is totally unexpected. In some instances, the visitor cannot venture beyond the survey page without providing information for the organization's "registration" questionnaire.

In many other Internet surveys, respondents are initially contacted via e-mail. Often they are members of consumer panels who have previously indicated their willingness to cooperate.

### D. Representative Samples

The quality of Internet samples may vary substantially. If the survey is merely a sample of those who visit a Web page and voluntarily fill out a questionnaire, the sample is not likely to be representative of the entire United States population because of self-selection error. Scientifically drawn samples from a consumer panel or samples randomly generated in other ways can yield representative samples.

### E. Accurate Real-time Data Capture

The computer-to-computer nature of Internet surveys means each respondent's answers are directly entered into the researcher's computer as soon as the questionnaire is submitted. In addition, the questionnaire software may be programmed to reject improper data entry. Real-time data capture allows for real-time data analysis. Up-to-the-minute sample size counts and tabulation data from an Internet survey can be viewed in real-time.

### F. Callbacks

When the sample is drawn from a consumer panel, re contact to those who have not completed the survey is quick and easy. It is often a simple function of computer software automatically sending an e-mail reminder notification to panel members who did not visit the welcome page. Because computer software can identify the passwords of respondents who only completed a portion of the questionnaire, customized messages can be sent to individuals who terminated the questionnaire with only a few additional questions to answer. Sometimes the e-mails explain that additional incentives are offered for those individuals who comply with the request to finish the questionnaire.

### G. Personalized and Flexible Questioning

Computer-interactive Internet surveys are programmed in much the same way as computer-assisted telephone interviewing surveys. That is, software is available to allow questioning to branch-off into two or more different lines depending on each respondent's answer to filtered questions.

One major advantage of computer-assisted surveys is the computer's ability to sequence questions based on previous responses. The computer can be programmed to skip from question 6 to question 9 if the answer to question 6 is no. Furthermore, responses to previous questions can lead to questions that can be personalized for individual respondents.

Use of a variety of dialog boxes (windows that prompt the respondent to enter information) allows questionnaire designers to be creative and flexible in the way questions are presented.

### H. *Respondent Anonymity*

Respondents are more likely to provide sensitive or embarrassing information when they can remain anonymous. The anonymity of the Internet encourages respondents to provide honest answers to sensitive questions.

### I. *Increasing Response Rates*

A password system that identifies people who, after a pre-determined period of time, have not participated in the survey can send a 'friendly' e-mail reminder asking the non respondents to participate in the survey before the study ends. Follow-ups like this, preliminary notification, interesting early questions, and variations of most other techniques for increasing response rate to mail questionnaires are recommended for Internet surveys.

Unlike mail surveys, Internet surveys do not offer the opportunity to send a physical incentive, such as a dollar bill, to the respondent. Incentives to respond to survey must be in the form of a promise of a future reward such as:

As a token of appreciation for completing this survey, the sponsor of this survey will make a sizable contribution. One important advantage of these systems is to restrict individuals from filling out a questionnaire over and over again.

While some researchers have had success with the promised incentives, academic research about Internet surveys is sparse and few definitive answers about the most effective ways to increase response rates may be given at this moment in time.

## Disadvantage of Internet Surveys

1. Many individuals in the general population cannot access the Internet.
2. All people with Internet access do not access the Internet with the same technological level.
3. Low speed Internet connections (low bandwidth), many individuals cannot quickly download high-resolution graphic files.

4. Many powerful computers or compatible software required to interact.
5. Some individuals have minimal computer skills.
6. *Security Concerns:* Many organizations worry that hackers or competitors may access Web sites researching new product concepts, new advertising campaigns, and other top-secret ideas. Respondents may worry if personal information will remain private. No system can be 100% secure. However, many research suppliers specializing in Internet surveying have developed password protected systems that are very secure.

### Kiosk Surveys

A computer may be installed in a kiosk at a trade show, at professional conference, in an airport, or other high traffic location to administer an interactive survey. Because the respondent chooses to interact directly with an on-site computer, self-selection often is a problem in this type of survey. Computer literate individuals are most likely to complete these interactive questionnaires

### Selecting the Appropriate Survey Research Design

There is no best form of design—each has its advantages and disadvantages. The different criteria—cost, speed, anonymity—may be different for each individual survey.

## PRE-TESTS

To check that questionnaires are understandable and not ambiguous or misleading, it is advisable to carry out a pretest or a screening procedure before administering the surveys. Pretests are trial runs with a group of respondents to iron out fundamental problems in the instructions or design. Screening procedures involve administering the test to a panel of experts to identify errors. The test can also be given to managers to ensure that it provides them with the information they require.

### Best Question Sequence

The order of questions may serve several functions for the researcher. For example, if the respondents' curiosity is not aroused at the outset, they can become disinterested and terminate the interview.

*Order bias:* Order bias results from an alternative answer's position in a set of answers or from the sequencing of questions. Order bias tends to distort survey results. Specific questions tend to influence more general ones. Thus, it is advisable to ask the general questions before the specific questions to obtain the best responses. This technique is known as the funnel technique, and it allows researchers to understand the respondent's frame of reference before asking more specific questions about the respondent's particular level of information and intensity of opinion.

When using attitude scales, there also may be an anchoring effect. That is, the first concept measured tends to become a comparison point from which subsequent evaluations are made. Randomization of these items on a questionnaire helps to minimize this order bias.

Rarely do marketing researchers print alternative question forms to eliminate problems arising from order bias. A more common practice is to pencil X's or check marks on the printed questionnaires to indicate that the interviewer should start a series of repetitive questions at a certain point.

Filter questions minimize the asking of questions that may be inapplicable, and pivot questions may be used to obtain information that the respondent may be reluctant to provide. For example, a respondent is asked, "Is your family income over Rs. 30,000?" If under, ask, "Is it over or under Rs. 10,000?" If over, ask "Is it over or under Rs. 50,000?". The logical orders of questions, which can help, ensure the respondent's cooperation, and can help eliminate any confusion or indecision.

### The Best Layout

The layout and attractiveness of the questionnaire are of crucial importance. In mail questionnaires, often the rate of return can be improved by adding the money that might have been used as an incentive, to improve the attractiveness and quality of the questionnaire. Questionnaires should be designed to appear as short as possible and experienced researchers have found that it pays to carefully phrase the title to be printed on the questionnaire.

The researcher can design the questionnaire to make the interviewee's job of following interconnected questions much easier by utilizing several forms, special instructions, and other tricks of the trade.

## INTERVIEW

### Meaning and Definition

Interview is one of the important and powerful tools for the data collection in social research. It is a direct method of enquiry. According to *C. Williamsemory*, "Personal interviewing is a two-way purposeful conversation initiated by an interviewer to obtain information that is relevant to some research purpose". The person who is interviewing is called as interviewer (interrogator) and the person who is giving interview is called interviewee or respondent or informant. The respondent is asked to provide information in the form of facts, attitudes, opinions and intentions. It should however be noted that an interview is not the same as conversation or inquiry or investigation. It is essentially an interactional process. Only through interview, varied types of data can be gathered intensively and extensively.

In the words of *Pauline V. Young*, 'Personal interview' is an effective, informal verbal and non-verbal conversation, initiated for specific purpose and focused on certain planned content areas.

*Goode and Hatt* also remark that interviewing is fundamentally a process of social interaction. Personal interview is also known as "door-step" interview because the interviewer calls on the respondent at the house of the latter with a schedule in his hands to collect material personally from him.

*Moser and Kalton* feel that the term 'door-step interview' is in fact inappropriate, since many organizations train their interviewers to ask to enter the respondent's home and to conduct their interview indoors.

## Objectives of the Interview

The interview is conducted in order to exchange ideas, data and experiences. It elicits information pertaining to a wide range of data, in which the interviewer may wish to rehearse his past and define his present and convince his future possibilities. The objectives are:

(i) Interview method helps to achieve the objectives of the study as the distance between the investigator and respondent is very much reduced.
(ii) It helps to ascertain attitudes or trends in brief.

The most important types of interviews are face-to-face interviews and telephone interviews. In face-to-face interviews, the interviewer works directly with the respondent. Unlike questionnaires, the interviewer has the opportunity to monitor the user and ask follow-up questions. However, face-to-face interviews are rather time consuming due to some factors such as warming up time for the respondent, irrelevant conversations, etc. On the other hand, telephone interviews enable a researcher to gather information rapidly. Like face-to-face interviews, they allow for some personal contact between the interviewer and the user. But they also have some major disadvantages. For example, people often don't like the intrusion of a call to their homes, and telephone interviews have to be relatively short or people may feel imposed upon.

Mainly, there are three methods that are used in designing the interviews. Unstructured interviewing methods are used during the earlier stages of usability evaluation. The objective of the interviewer at this stage is to gather as much information as possible concerning the user's experience and on their expectations of the system. Semi-structured interviews are used when the interviewer has a better understanding of system requirements. Therefore, a more focused interview design can be used to focus on the points of interest. However, there can still be a degree of flexibility to allow the user to expand on an answer. Finally, structured interviewing has a specific, predetermined agenda with specific questions to guide and direct the interview. The interviewer, in this design, has a fully developed product and prepares questions to measure the user's reactions to that product.

Regardless of the interview method chosen, there are some issues that must be considered during the design of an interview from the very beginning to the very end. The first issue to consider is training of the interviewer, which is very important because the interviewer controls everything in an interview. Another important point is that s(he) should clarify any confusion that the users may have, and should answer the users' questions clearly and honestly. The interviewer has the advantage of observing the users and acting accordingly. S(he) should control the mood of the interview by his/her behaviours, voice tone, etc.

Interviews can be considered to be similar to ethnographic methods. Both are data-gathering techniques involving user participation and both may be flexible. On the other hand, there are significant differences as well. Ethnographic methods, originated from anthropology, are qualitative data gathering methods, which require long-term observation of a group of people in their natural environments. However, traditional ethnographic methods usually have long time requirements to be used in this field.

### The Interview Process

Interviews must be conducted in more formal and relaxed manner. Interviewer must get himself well prepared to ask relevant questions, before the actual process of interview begins. Skilled interviewers carefully frame their questions well in advance.

The following are some tips for conducting a successful interview:

(1) Fix an appointment with the interviewee,
(2) Inform him/her about the mechanical gadgets to be used by you. Such as video camera, tape recorder, etc.
(3) Prepare questions to be asked in advance.
(4) Be courteous and put friendly questions at the beginning of the interview.
(5) Don't use suggestive questions.
(6) Don't dispute with the respondent or express your emotions.
(7) Express thankfulness at the end of the interview.

### Types of Interview

#### 1. *Classification According to Formality*

(a) *Formal Interview:* In this type of interview, the interviewer presents a set of well-defined questions
(b) *Informal Interview:* In contrast with the formal interview, the interviewer has full freedom to make suitable alterations in the questions to suit a particular situation.

## 2. Classification According to the Number

(a) *Personal Interview:* In personal interview, a single individual is interviewed. It helps to establish close personal contacts between the interviewer and the interviewee and by its means detailed knowledge about intimate and personal aspects of the individual can be had.

(b) *Group Interview:* As the name makes it plain the group interview is the opposite of the personal, because in it 2 or more persons are interviewees. The first is aimed at probing into the inner life and feelings of an individual; the group interview is suited for routine information.

## 3. Classification According to Purpose

(a) *Diagnostic interview:* This type of interviewers, try to understand the cause or causes of a malady. In clinical psychology and psychoanalysis, the preliminary interviews are held with a purpose to grasp the nature and cause of the disease.

(b) *Treatment Interview:* If the cause of the psychological malady is diagnosed as non-physical further interviews are held to bring to fore-conscious of the patient that his malady is due to this or that mental complex or faulty styles of life. These interviews are christened "Treatment Interview".

(c) *Research Interviews:* These interviews are held to gather information pertaining to certain problem. The questions to be asked to gather the desired information are predetermined and by asking them of the informants the data is collected.

(d) *Interview to Fulfil Curiosity:* These interviews, as the name implies, are held to satisfy some questions lurking in the mind of the scientists.

## 4. Classification According to the Period of Contact

(a) *Short Contact Interview:* For filling up schedules etc., a single sitting of small duration suffices. Therefore, in researches of this type short-contact interview suffices.

(b) *Prolonged contact Interview:* In contrast with research by schedule, the case history method requires prolonged interviews. In these, establishment of close personal relations between the interviewee and the interviewer is very likely.

## 5. Classification According to Subject Matter

(a) *Qualitative Interview:* The qualitative interviews are about complex and non-quantifiable subject matter.

(b) *Quantitative Interview:* The quantitative interviews are those in which certain set facts are gathered about a large number of persons. The census interviews are its examples.

(c) *Mixed Interview:* In certain interviews both types of data—the routine and specialize—is sort some of it is quantifiable while some is not.

### 6. Classification According to Role

(a) *Non-Directive Interview:* This is also known as unstructured interview. This is a type of interview in which the interviewer exercises no control, provides no direction and has no brief or predetermined set of questions to ask. The interviewer merely engages the interviewee in talk and encourages him to tell about his experiences and feelings.

(b) *Focused Interview:* This type of interview takes place when the interviewees are specialized concrete situation. This type of interview is possible in these concrete circumstances, which have been analysed before hand, that is, prior to the beginning of the interview. This interview is done on the basis of an interview guide. In an interview of this type the inner feelings and emotional attitudes of the interviews *vis-à-vis* a given problem or situation are given particular attention.

(c) *Repeated Interview:* This type of interview is eminently suited to trace the development of processes and to determine the factors or attitudes which are behind a given behaviour pattern or situation.

## Basic Guidelines to Good Interviewing

*Have Thorough Knowledge of the Subject Matter:* The interviewer should have a complete knowledge of the theoretical aspect of the interview.

*Determine Who is to be Interviewed (Selection of the Respondents):* For the success of any research project it is essential to know who can be most helpful, who know most about the problem and are likely to cooperate. Taking these factors into account, a selection of the respondents should be made. It is neither possible nor desirable to interview each and every member of a group.

Have knowledge of the daily routine of the interviewee to know the time and place. It is of crucial significance that an interviewer makes right initial approach to the interviewee. In this connection the most important thing is that the interviewee should be approached at a time when he is free and relaxed.

## Principles of Good Interviewing

This section presents the principles of good interviewing as put together by one of the nation's top business research organizations, Yankelovich Partners. These principles have been divided into two categories: (1) the basics—the interviewing point of view, and (2) required practices—standard inquiry premises and procedures.

A. *The basics:* Interviewing is a skilled occupation. The basic qualities of a good interviewer are as follows:

1. Integrity and honesty.
2. Patience and tact.
3. Attention to accuracy and detail: a good rule of thumb is not to record an answer unless you fully understand it yourself. Probe for clarification and rich, full answers and record all answers verbatim.
4. Exhibit a real interest in the inquiry at hand, but keep your own opinions to yourself.
5. Be a good listener.
6. Keep inquiry and respondent's answers confidential.
7. Respect others' rights. There is a "happy medium" path to pursue in obtaining this information. On the one hand is failure to get it all; and on the other hand is unnecessary coercion.

B. *Required practices:* There are the practical rules of business research inquiry, to be followed and used without exception—

1. Complete the number of interviews according to the sampling plan assigned to you.
2. Follow directions provided. Lack of uniformity in procedure can only spell disaster for later analysis.
3. Make every effort to keep schedule.
4. Keep control of each interview you do. It is up to you to determine the "pace" of a particular interview, keeping several points in mind:

   (a) There is an established average length of interview from the time you start to talk to the respondent to the time you finish.
   (b) It's important to "get the whole story" from the respondent and also to write it all down in the respondent's own words, but it's equally important to keep the interview to the subject at hand.
   (c) The researcher must avoid offending the respondent by being too talkative.

5. Complete the questionnaires sent to you meticulously. This means:

   (a) Follow exactly all instructions that appear directly on the questionnaire.

(b) Ask the questions from the first to the last in the exact numerical order.
(c) Ask each question exactly as it is written.
(d) Never leave the answer to a question blank. If none of the answer categories provided proves suitable, write in what the respondent said, in his or her own words.
(e) Use all the "props" provided to aid both interviewers and respondents.

6. Check out each questionnaire you have completed. If you find something you have done wrong or have omitted, correct it.
7. Check out your sample execution and quota assigned against the total number of questionnaires you have completed.
8. Clear up any questions with the research agency.

## Limitation of the Interview Techniques

1. *Uneconomical:* The transportation cost and the time required to cover addresses in a large area as also possibility of non-availability or 'not at home', may make the interview method uneconomical and often unfeasible.
2. *Emotionalism:* The interview is liable to cease being objective and becoming emotional. In the current of emotionalism all objectivity is swept aside.
3. *Personal Bias:* Because of the personal bias the data may be distorted, resulting in wrong generalizations. In spite of the best efforts the personal bias cannot be totally eliminated in this method.

# SCHEDULE

## Meaning of Schedule

Schedule and questionnaire are the most important tools used in social research. The schedule is the form containing some questions or blank tables which are to be filled by the research workers after getting information from the informants. The schedule may thus contain two types of questions: (i) direct questions, (ii) form of a table.

## Features

(a) The schedule is presented by the interviewer. The questions are asked and the answers are noted down by him.
(b) The list of questions is a more formal document; it need not be attractive.
(c) The schedule can be used in a very narrow sphere of social research.

## Objectives of Schedule

The main purposes of schedule are three fold: (i) To provide a standardized tool for observation or interview in order to attain objectivity. (ii) To act as memory tickler i.e., the schedule keeps the memory of the interviewer/observer refreshed and keeps him reminded of the different aspects that are to be particularly observed. (iii) To facilitate the work of tabulation and analysis.

## Types of Schedules

1. *Rating Schedules:* In the field of business guidance, psychological research, and social research, the rating schedules are used to assess the attitudes, opinions, preferences, inhibitions and other like elements.
2. *Documents Schedules:* The schedules of this type are used to obtain data regarding written evidence and case histories. In these schedules, those terms are included which occur frequently in documents and are to be generally found in case histories. For example, in the field of criminology, rating schedules are used to gather data to be found in crime studies, the different kinds of crime, their incidence, the nature of earlier crime and the personal data on criminals.
3. *Institutional Survey Forms:* It is used to gather data about specialized institutions or agencies. The form and the size of evaluational schedules is determined by the nature and the complexity of the problems of an institution: more complex the problem, bigger the size of the schedule.
4. *Observation Schedule:* Observer records the activities and responses of an individual or a group under specific conditions. The observation schedules may need one or more research workers.
5. *Interview Schedules:* In an interview schedule, and interviewer presents the questions of the schedule to the interviewers and records their responses on blank spaces.

## Steps in Framing a Schedule

The problem under study should first of all be split up into various aspects. The determination of these aspects needs clear understanding of the problem under study.

(a) Each aspect has again to be broken up in to a number of sub-parts. These sub-parts should be quite exhaustive to give a full picture.

(b) Care should be taken to see that the questions convey the exact sense, are easily followed by the response and they will be willing to supply information without any hesitation, bias or distortion of facts.

(c) It is necessary that the questions should be presented to the respondents in a well-ordered serial.
(d) Whatever may be the degree of precaution taken, some slips are bound to be left out and cannot be located unless the schedule has been put into operation.

## Contents of Schedule

The schedule is divided into three parts according to the nature of the contents. These are:

(a) *Introductory Part:* In this part, the name of the survey, the address of the surveyor, serial number of the case, place of interview, date and time of the interview and so on are mentioned clearly.
(b) *Main Schedule:* This is the main part of the schedule, consisting of titles, columns and questions.
(c) *Instructions:* In this part, the researcher or interviewer is given directions regarding the method of interview.

## Type of Questions

The questions of the schedule may be classified into the following:

1. *Open-end questions:* In these questions, the respondents are given freedom to express their views, as there is a wide range choice.
2. *Closed Questions:* These types of questions do not allow the respondents to give answers freely.
3. *Pictorial Questions:* In these types of questions, pictures are drawn, and the respondent indicates the answer by selecting the pictures he prefers.
4. *Dichotomous Questions:* In these questions, two alternatives are given: a positive one and a negative one.
5. *Multiple-Choice Questions:* These questions consist of many questions. The respondent has to select any one of these.
6. *Leading Questions:* In these questions, the reply is suggested in an indirect way. These types of questions create confusion. Thus as far as possible, leading questions should be avoided.
7. *Ambiguous Questions:* Questions, which indicate alternate meanings and lack clarity are called ambiguous questions.
8. *Ranking Items of Questions:* Through these questions, the preferences of the respondents are obtained.

## Questions (to be avoided) Requiring more Diligence

1. Long or Circumlocutory Questions.
2. Complex Questions.
3. Presumptuous Questions or Presuming Questions.
4. Personal Questions.

5. *Questions involving memory:* More factual questions to some extent involve the respondent in recalling information. His degree of success in doing this accurately is thus a basic determinant of the quality of his response.
6. *Embarrassing Questions:* Subjects which people do not like to discuss in public present a problem to the questionnaire designer. Respondents are often embarrassed to discuss private matters, to give low-prestige answers.
7. *Questions on Periodical Behaviour:* An interesting choice arises in studying the frequency of periodical behaviour. The main choice of questions can be illustrated with reference to cinema-going:

   (a) 'How often have you been to the cinema during the last fortnight (or any other period chosen)?'
   (b) 'How often do you go to the cinema on the average?'
   (c) 'When did you last go to the cinema?'

   The first question covers a number of different possibilities corresponding to the period chosen, and answers will depend on the type of activity and on the extent to which one is willing to rely on the respondent's memory.

8. *Questions that are Insufficiently Specific:* A common error is to ask a general questions when an answer on a specific issue is wanted.
9. *Questions regarding Social and Moral Ideals:* Even when one flouts in private life the moral and social ideals of a society, one would not like to publicly express his disapproval of these.
10. Unrelated Questions.
11. Unnecessary Questions.
12. Upsetting Questions.

## COLLECTION OF SECONDARY DATA

Secondary data means data that are already available i.e., they refer to the data, which have already been collected and analysed by someone else. When the researcher utilizes secondary data, then he has to look into various sources from where he can obtain them. In this case he is certainly not confronted with the problems that are usually associated with the collection of original data. Secondary data may either be published data or unpublished data. Usually published data are available in:

A. various publications of the central, state and local governments,
B. various publications of the foreign governments or of international bodies and their subsidiary organizations,
C. technical and trade journals,
D. books, magazines and newspapers,

E. reports prepared by research scholars, universities, economists, etc. in different fields,

F. reports and publications of various associations connected with business and industry, banks, stock exchanges, etc., and

G. public records and statistics, historical documents, and other sources of published information. The sources of unpublished data are many; they may be found in dairies, letters unpublished biographies and also may be available with scholars and research workers, trade associations, labour bureaus and other public/ private individuals and organizations.

## Typical Objectives for Secondary Data Research Designs

There are two general categories of research objectives: fact finding and model building. The simplest form of secondary data research is fact, finding. A typical secondary research objective for a study might be to uncover all available information about consumption patterns for a particular product category or to identify demographic trends that affect an industry. For example, the chapter began by describing the sports market in the United States. A common secondary data study designed to find facts might be a market tracking study. Market tracking refers to the observation and analysis of trends in industry volume and brand share over time.

Model building, as a general objective for secondary research, is more complicated than simple fact finding. Model building involves specifying relationships between two or more variables. Model building can involve the development of descriptive or predictive equations; however, model building need not be a complicated mathematical process. In fact, decision-makers using simple models, ones that everyone can readily understand, often find these models superior to complex models that are difficult to comprehend.

Managers often estimate market potential using secondary data. The researcher may estimate market potential by converting different types of data that are available from two or more sources. For example, if one source of data indicates that 10 percent of all electrical contractors intend to buy a drill and another source indicates that there are 80,000 electrical contractors then it may be estimated that 8,000 drills will be sold to electrical contractors.

Managers need information about the future. They need to know what company sales will be next year and in future time periods. Sales forecasting is the process of predicting sales totals over a specific future time period. Accurate sales forecasts, especially when products are in mature, stable markets, frequently are the result of secondary data research that identify trends and extrapolates past performance into the future. Business researchers often use internal company sales records to project sales.

The term data mining refers to the use of powerful computers, to dig through volumes of data to discover patterns about an organization's customers and products. It is a broad term that applies to many different forms of analysis. For example, neural networks are a data-mining form of artificial intelligence in which a computer is programmed to mimic the way in which human brains process information.

Market basket analysis is a form of data mining that analyze anonymous point of sale transaction logs to identify coinciding purchases or relationships between products purchased and other retail shopping information. When the identity of the customer who makes repeated purchases from the same organization is known, an analysis can be made of sequences of purchases. Sequence discover, the use of data mining to detect sequence patterns, is a popular application among direct marketers, such as catalog retailers.

## Classification of Secondary Data

*Internal and Proprietary Sources:* Data that are external to the organization refers to data created, recorded, or generated by another entity. Most organizations routinely gather, record, and store internal data for solving future problems. For example, accounting departments continually gather data. Aggregating or desegregating internal data is a frequent form of internal research. By exhausting all sources within the company, researchers can avoid duplicating another department's data collection and research efforts.

### *External Sources of Data can be Categorized as Follows*

1. *Books and Periodicals:* Books and periodicals provide a wealth of information. Libraries stock many bibliographies, guides, directories, and indexes. Professional journals and commercial business periodicals can be especially valuable sources of data.
2. *Government Sources:* Government agencies produce a prolific amount of data. Federal government data (e.g., the Census of Population) can be counted on for accuracy and quality of investigation. State, county, and local government data is often more current and structured to meet local needs than federal data.
3. *Media Sources:* Information on a broad range of subjects is available from broadcast and print media. The media like to show that their vehicles for advertising are viewed or heard by the advertising target market. Such information is generally free of charge and can be useful. However, it should be given careful evaluation as it often covers limited aspects of a topic.
4. *Commercial Sources:* Numerous firms specialize in selling information. These firms provide diverse types of data, examples of which follow:

   (a) *Market Share Data:* Market tracking refers to the observation and analysis of trends in industry volume and brand share over time.

(b) *Scanner Data:* Market tracking through optical character recognition such as the universal product code and other optical scanners provides a wealth of accurate and rapid product and brand sales information collectively known as scanner data.

(c) Demographic and census updates.

(d) *Attitude and Public Opinion Research:* Specialized syndicated services report the findings of attitude research and opinion polls.

(e) *Stock Market Sources*: Numerous firms sell information on aggregate market and individual stocks.

## Merits of Documentary Sources

*Provides an insight in to total situation:* The purpose of the use of available materials is to explore the nature of the data and the subjects to get an insight into the total situation. While looking for the data requires by the researcher he may uncover many more available data than are often assumed to exist and hence contributes significantly to the unfolding of hidden information.

*Helps in the formulation of Hypothesis:* The use of documentary sources sometimes, helps in the formulation of research hypothesis. While an investigator may have one or two hypothesis, which he might have deduced from theory the study of available materials, may suggest further hypothesis.

*Helps in testing the Hypothesis:* The available records may also help in testing the hypothesis.

*Provides Supplementary Information:* Available documents may be used to supplement or to check information gathered specifically for the purpose of a given investigation.

## Disadvantages of Secondary Sources of Data

1. *Collected for a Specific Purpose*
   Data are often collected with a specific purpose in mind, a purpose that may produce deliberate or unintentional bias. Thus, secondary data were collected originally for particular purposes may produce other problems.
2. *Old Data*
   Secondary data are by definition, old data. Thus the data may not be particularly timely for same purposes.
3. *Aggregation of Data in an appropriate Unit*
   Seldom are secondary data available at the individual observation level. This means that the data are aggregated in some form, and the unit of aggregation may be inappropriate for a particular purpose.

## SURVEY

The term 'Survey' has come from two words, 'Sur' and 'Vor', which means ' to see' a particular thing from a high place. But the term is used in different ways in different sciences. In social sciences, it indicates the investigation of social problems, the technique of collection of data through interview, questionnaire, etc.

Survey research is characterized by the selection of random samples from large and small populations to obtain empirical knowledge of a contemporary nature.

### Aims of Survey

1. To collect first hand information.
2. To collect accurate and efficient information.
3. To identify the characteristics of a particular group.
4. By conducting descriptive studied one can understand the depth of a subject matter.
5. To quantify certain factual information.
6. The qualitative survey aims to test new product concept and to make refinement.
7. To make stylistic, aesthetic, or functional changes on the basis of respondents suggestions.
8. To provide casual explanations and to new explore new ideas.

### Advantages of Survey

To provide quick, accurate and efficient means of information about the population.

It is flexible.

It is very valuable to the managers in their decision-making

*Errors in Survey Research:* Outlines the various forms of survey error that can affect the accuracy of a survey.

A. *Random Sampling Error:* Most surveys try to portray a representative cross-section of a particular target population, but even with technically proper random probability samples, statistical errors will occur because of chance variation. Without increasing sample size, these statistical problems are unavoidable.
B. *Systematic Error:* Systematic errors result from some imperfect research design or from a mistake in the execution of the research. These errors are also called non-sampling errors. A sample bias exists when the results of a sample show a persistent tendency to deviate in one direction from the true value of the population parameter. The two general categories of systematic error are *respondent error* and *administrative error.*

### 1. Respondent Error

If the respondents do not cooperate or do not give truthful answers then two types of error may occur.

(a) *Non-responsive Error:* To utilize the results of a survey, the researcher must be sure that those who did not respond to the questionnaire were representative of those who did not. If only those who responded are included in the survey then non-responsive error will occur. Non-respondents are most common in mail surveys, but may also occur in telephone and personal surveys in the form of no contacts (not-at-homes) or refusals. The number of no contacts has been increasing because of the proliferation of answering machines and growing usage of Caller ID to screen telephone calls. Self-selection may also occur in self-administered questionnaires; in this situation, only those who feel strongly about the subject matter will respond, causing an over-representation of extreme positions. Comparing demographics of the sample with the demographics of the target population is one means of inspecting for possible biases. Additional efforts should be made to obtain data from any underrepresented segments of the population. For example, call-backs can be made on the not-at-homes.

(b) *Response Bias:* Response bias occurs when respondents tend to answer in a certain direction. This bias may be caused by an intentional or inadvertent falsification or by a misrepresentation of the respondent's answer.

  (a) *Deliberate falsification:* People may misrepresent answers in order to appear intelligent, to avoid embarrassment, to conceal personal information, to "please" the interviewer, etc. It may be that the interviewees preferred to be viewed as average and they will alter their responses accordingly.

  (b) *Unconscious Misrepresentation:* Response bias canarise from question format, question ambiguity or content. Time-lapse may lead to best-guess answers.

  (c) *Types of response bias*: There are five specific categories of response bias. These categories overlap and are by no means mutually exclusive.

    (1) *Acquiescence bias:* This is a response bias caused by a respondent's tendency to concur with a particular position. For example, "yea Sayers" who accept all statements they are asked about.

    (2) *Extremity bias:* Some individuals tend to use extremes when responding to questions, which may cause extremity bias.

(3) *Interviewer bias:* If an interviewer's presence influences respondents to give untrue or modified answers, the survey will contain interviewer bias. Respondents may wish to appear wealthy or intelligent, or they may try to give the right answer or the socially acceptable answer.

(4) *Auspices bias:* The answers to a survey may be deliberately or unintentionally misrepresented because the respondent is influenced by the organization conducting the survey.

(5) *Social desirability bias:* This may occur consciously or subconsciously. Answers to questions that seek factual information or matters of public knowledge are usually quite accurate, but the interviewer's presence may increase a respondent's tendency toward an inaccurate response to a sensitive question in an attempt by the respondent to gain prestige in the interviewer's mind.

### 2. Administrative Error

The results of improper administration or execution of the research task are examples of administrative error. Such errors are inadvertently caused by confusion, neglect, omission, or some other blunder. There are four types of administrative error:

(1) *Data processing Error:* The accuracy of the data processed by computer depends on correct data entry and programming. Mistakes can be avoided if verification procedures are employed at each processing stage.

(2) *Sample selection Error:* This type of error is a systematic error that results in an unrepresentative sample because of an error in either the sample design or execution of the sampling procedure.

(3) *Interviewer Error:* Interviewers may record an answer incorrectly or selective perception may influence them to record data supportive of their own attitudes.

(4) *Interviewer Cheating:* To avoid possible cheating, it is wise to inform the interviewers that a small sample of respondents will be back to confirm that the interview actually took place.

## Classifying Survey Research Methods

Surveys can be classified in three ways:

### A. Method of Communication

Surveys can be classified according to the method of communication, telephone, mail, or personal interviews.

### B. Structured and Disguised Questions

A structured question limits the number of responses available;

whereas unstructured questions tend to be open-ended which allows the respondent considerable freedom in responding. The researcher can also disguise the questions, which is particularly advisable if the subject matter is of a threatening nature. Other questions do not require disguising as it is assumed that the respondent is willing to reveal the information. Questions can be categorized according to their degree of structure and disguise. This helps in the selection of the appropriate communication medium for conducting the survey. However, it is not always easy to categorize the surveys as the categories are not clear-cut and most surveys are a hybrid of structured and unstructured questions.

## C. Classifying Surveys on a Temporal Basis

### 1. Cross-sectional Study

This is the most common type of study in which the data is collected at a single point in time. In such a study, various segments of the population are sampled so that relationships among variables may be investigated by cross-tabulation.

### 2. Longitudinal Study

In longitudinal studies, respondents are questioned at different points in time so that changes occurring can be observed over time. Longitudinal studies which involve two or more samples at different times are called cohort studies because similar people are expected to be in each sample over time. Such studies can also be called tracking studies because they are designed to compare aggregate trends and identify changes. Having two or three different sample groups avoids response bias which might normally result from prior interview, but the researcher can never be sure that the changes in the variable being measured are not actually due to having different people in the sample.

### Panel Study

This is a longitudinal study, which includes gathering data from the same sample over time. Panels are generally expensive and, thus, are usually managed by contractors, which specialize in maintaining consumer panels. Such panels enable the investigator to keep track of repeat purchases, behaviour habits affected by changes in price, special promotions, or other aspects of business strategies.

## Important Statistical Measures that are used in the Survey/Research

(1) Measures of central tendency or statistical averages;
(2) Measures of dispersion;
(3) Measures of asymmetry (skewness);
(4) Measures of relationship; and
(5) Other measures.

Amongst the measures of central tendency, the three most important ones are the arithmetic average or mean, median and mode. Geometric mean and harmonic mean are also sometimes used. From among the measures of dispersion, variance and item square root—the standard deviation are the most often used measures. Other measures such as mean deviation, range, etc. are also used. For comparison purpose, we use mostly the coefficient of standard deviation or the coefficient of variation. In respect of the measures of skewness and kurtosis, we mostly use the first measure of skewness based on mean and mode or on mean and median.

Other measures of skew ness, based on quartiles or on the methods of moments, are also used sometimes. Kurtosis is also used to measure the peaked ness of the curve of the frequency distribution. Amongst the measures of relationship, Karl Pearson's coefficient of correlation is the frequently used measure in case of statistics of variables, whereas Yule's coefficient of association is used in case of statistics of attributes.

Multiple correlation coefficient, partial correlation coefficient, regression analysis, etc., are other important measures often used by a researcher. Index numbers, analysis of time series, coefficient of contingency, etc., are other measures that may as well be used by a researcher, depending upon the nature of the problem under study. We give below a brief outline of some important measures (out of the above listed measures) often used in the context of research studies.

### Percentages

The expression of data in terms of percentages is one of the simplest statistical devices used in the interpretation of business and economic statistics. Percentages are useful chiefly for the purpose of aiding comparison. A percent is the number of hundredth parts one number is of another. Generally percentages are recorded to one decimal place.

### Frequency Distribution

In this device the various items of a series are classified into groups and the number of items falling into each group is stated. For preparing frequency distribution, the unclassified data is to be arranged from low to high or from high to low in the form of an array. With such rearrangements, it would be very much easier to note the lowest or highest number. This array enables us to see the range of data, the concentration of data, and the fair degree of continuity. Thus the frequency of each value can be obtained on the basis of number of times it appears. This may be further condensed by indicating the number of times each value occurred. Each class interval is identified by the lowest and highest value and each frequency value indicates the total number of values contained in the corresponding interval. This is known as group frequency distribution.

1. Arrange a data sheet with three headings value, tabulation and

frequency. Under value, list in order from low to high all possible values included in the data, which are to be tabulated.

2. *Tabulation*: Begin with the first item in the original unordered list of values. Place a tally mark in the tabulation column opposite to the appropriate value figure-proceed in the same way for the remaining items in the original list. The subsequent counting is facilitated if every fifth mark in a row is made standing across the preceding four marks.
3. Count the number of tally marks opposite each interval and write the result in the frequency column.
4. *Determine the range of items:* Find the highest and the lowest items in the series. Find the difference between these numbers. This difference is called the range of distribution.
5. Divide the range by 10 or 20 round off the resultant (The minimum and maximum units recommended in an interval are 10 and 20).
6. Determine the size and the starting point of interval.
7. *Construct frequency distribution:* Begin at the top with the class interval, which contains the smallest value and continue until the interval containing the highest value is reached. The number entered in the frequency column should be the sum of the frequency from the data sheet included within each class interval.

### Measures of Central Tendency

An average represents the whole series by a single figure and thus reduces the complexity of data. In statistics, an average plays a very important role because condensation of data is essential in statistical analysis and interpretation. There are three types of averages, which are commonly used in business statistics mean or arithmetic mean, median and mode.

### Mean from Ungrouped Data

Mean is a mathematical average and it is most popular measure of central tendency. The arithmetic mean of a series of measures is equal to the sum of the measures divided by their number.

$$\text{Arithmetic mean} = X/N$$

### Median from Ungrouped Data

It may be simply defined as the middle measure in a series in which all measures have been arranged in the order of their size. The median is the value of the variable, which divides the group into two equal parts, one part comprising all values greater, and the other all values less than the median. Then the following formula should be applied:

$$\text{Md} = ((N+1)/2)^{th} \text{ item}$$

Where Md stands for median, and N stands for the number of items.

Mode from ungrouped data.

Mode may be defined as the item, which occurs most frequently in a series of values. For example, in a series of 3, 5, 6, 10, 11, 6.5, 20, 19, 6 the variable 6 has occurred more frequently three times—hence it is the mode of the series.

### *Arithmetic Mean from a Frequency Distribution*

Sometime, it is more convenient to derive mean from a frequency distribution. An additional column may be opened to record the products of F*X. The total of this F*X will be divided by the total of "f", i.e., N to get mean.

Mean = Summation of (f*X)/N

The mean of a grouped frequency distribution can be computed in a similar fashion by taking the midpoint of the interval as the value X and then adopting the similar above procedure.

### *Measures of Variability*

From the measures of central tendency one can know about the distribution of data but it is also important to know how compactly the measures are distributed about this point of central tendency or, conversely, how far they are scattered away from it. This condition in a frequency distribution is variously referred to as dispersion, spread, and ways to describe this characteristic quantitatively. Simplest way describing the variability is to state the lowest and highest measures of the range of the distribution. This distribution, called the range, is not very meaningful, since it is dependent only upon the two extreme individuals in the group. Mean deviation or average deviation is an important measure of dispersion in business statistics. Mean deviation of a series is the average of the deviations of various items from mean, median or mode. This measure is relatively easier to interpret. For example, the mean deviations in height of a group of individuals differ from the average individual by 2 inches. In calculation of the mean deviation of various items from a measure of central tendency, algebraic signs (+ or –) are totally ignored. The following are the different formulae for the calculation of mean deviation:

sigma = summation d/N

where sigma stands for mean deviation,

summation d stands for sum of deviation from mean, and

N stands for total items.

Standard deviation is the square root of the arithmetic average of the squares of deviations measured from the value of mean series. The most important difference between mean deviation and standard deviation is that algebraic signs (+ or –) are not ignored in the calculation of standard deviation, and hence it is more accurate and justified measures of dispersion. Standard deviation is calculated by the following formulae:

Standard deviation or sigma = square root (summation $d^2/N$)

where square root (summation d2) – sum of squares of deviation from mean, and

N – total number of items.

## Time Series

Economists and business experts have very often to deal with quantities (i.e. variates), which change, in value with time. Variation of such quantities with time can be systematically studied. Use of graphs considerably helps such a study. Time series is a record of the values of a variate (i.e. quantity) during a particular period, taken at successive intervals of time. When the values of the variate are plotted against time, on a graph paper, and the points so obtained are joined by straight line segments, a graphical record of the behaviour of the variate becomes available. Graph of a time series obtained is called histogram of that time series. The historigram gives a rough idea about the nature of changes in the values of the variate with time. The fluctuations showed in the histogram may be due to various causes. The causes, which operate over long period, are to be segregated from the causes, which operate over short time. This process is called analysis of time series. The variations in the values of the variate can be analysed into the following three main components:

1. The basic or long-time trend
2. Short-time or periodic changes
3. Irregular fluctuations

The short-time changes can further be analysed into:

(a) Cyclical movements, and
(b) Seasonal movements.

*Basic or long-time trend:* The time series over a long interval of time to show a steady increase or decrease which is known as basic trend or secular trend or just as the trend of the time series. The trend indicates the normal pattern of the changes in values of the variants. An estimate of prediction of the normal behaviour of the variate can only be made from the knowledge of its trend.

*Short-time changes:* But during the short durations, the same above variate may show a different behaviour. These deviations from trend are very often periodic in nature. The periodic changes occurring in a time series may be mainly of two types:

(a) Cyclical changes which result in repeated booms and slumps over regular periods of time.
(b) Seasonal variations are regular and repeatedly occur over a short duration. The duration of this movement depends upon the nature of the variate e.g., sales of ice cream has its peak in summer.

*Irregular Fluctuations:* Many time series show a sudden rise or fail at certain instants of time. Such sharp changes have no tendency to recur, e.g. wholesale prices of consumer goods may rise sharply due to war, flood, etc. These are known as irregular or random fluctuations.

### Focus Groups

Focus groups became widely used in marketing research during in the 1980s and they are increasingly used in application research today. The most common focus group in research continues to be in the consumer area. However, many corporations are using focus group results for diverse exploratory applications. The objective of the focus group is often a new product or product concept. These are often used for quantitative. As a group interview tool, focus groups have applied research potential for other areas of business, particularly where the generation and evaluation of ideas or the assessment of needs is indispensable. In exploratory research, the qualitative data that focus groups produce may be used for enriching all levels of research questions and hypothesis and comparing the effectiveness.

A focus group is a panel of people headed by a trained moderator. He meets the participants for 90 minutes to 2 hours.

Features of focus group:

(1) The group dynamic principles are applied.
(2) There will be exchange of ideas among the participants. Feelings, ideas and experiences are shared among the participants.
(3) The panel is normally made up of 6 to 10 members.
(4) The participation will be less effective when the group is too small or too big. The facilitator will introduce the topic and encourages the group to discuss among themselves.
(5) The moderator will drive the group so that all relevant information is considered by the group. The moderator will take steps to control and avoid domination by few people.
(6) The moderator will ensure uninterrupted proceedings of the discussion. Mind writer could use focus groups involving employees of the call centers and service centers to determine changes and provide analysis of change ideas.

(7) It can discuss with both satisfied and dissatisfied customers to uncover what has occurred with their experiences.

## Types of Focus Groups

### *(A) Telephone Focus Groups*

Traditional focus groups participants meet face to face. However, it is need to reach people that traditional focus group cannot attract. With modern telephone conferencing facilities telephone focus groups can be particularly effective in the following situations.

(1) When it is difficult to recruit desired participants.
(2) When target group members are rare, low incidents and placed in a wider area.
(3) When issues are so sensitive that anonymity is needed but respondents must be from a wide geographical area.
(4) When you want to conduct only a couple of focus groups but want nation wide representation.

### Advantages

1. Telephone focus groups are usually less expensive than face to face focus groups.
2. This can be productive.
3. People in traditional superior subordinate roles can be mixed as long as they are not from the same city.
4. A Telephone focus group is likely to be effective under the following conditions:
   (a) When participants need to handle a product;
   (b) When an object of discussion cannot be sent through the mail in advance;
   (c) When sessions will run long, and
   (d) When the participants are group of young children.

### *(B) Online Focus Groups*

An emerging technique for exploratory research is to use the latest communication techniques like e-mail, websites, Usenet news groups and an Internet chat room. The latest technology also made it possible to do live voice chats on line, reducing or eliminating the cost associated with telephone focus groups. Questions to a new group with an interest in the research problem can generate considerable discussion.

### Drawbacks

1. However on line discussions are not confidential;

2. Online forum discussions are likely to reflect lesser number of participants;
3. Power computers are needed; and
4. This is not enforceable in all areas of marketing.

### (C) Video Conferencing Focus Groups

It is non face to face focus groups which is conducted via video conferencing. There is adequate growth in this medium. Like telephone focus groups, video conferencing discussions are cost saving. It reduces the travel time to the moderator and the client. Within a short time, more accomplishments can be made via this system. Large corporations and universities have their own internal video conferencing facilities and most video conferencing focus groups will tend to occur within this setting.

In face to face methods the moderators use large sheets of paper to record trends. Others use personnel note pad. Facility managers use both video and audiotapes to enable a full analysis. The recorded conversations are grouped by using content analysis.

#### Advantages

1. It is less expensive and quick in action;
2. It is extremely flexible;
3. It provides the manager, researcher and client a chance to observe reactions in an open-ended group setting;
4. Participants respond in their own words and they are not compelled to express;
5. Surprise informations and new ideas are explored;
6. Agendas can be modified as the research team moves on to the next focus groups; and
7. There is more chances for greater depth of understanding.

#### Disadvantages

1. It is only a qualitative device.
2. There is limited sampling. Hence, accuracy cannot be ensured.
3. This cannot be considered as a replacement for quantitative analysis.

## Advantages of Focus Group Interviews

Specific advantages of focus group interviews have to be categorized as follows:

(a) *Synergism:* The combined effort of the group will produce a wider range of information, insights and ideas than will the accumulation of separately secured responses.

(b) *Serendipity:* An idea may drop out of the blue, and affords the group the opportunity to develop such an idea to its full significance.

(c) *Snowballing:* A bandwagon effect occurs. One individual often triggers a chain of responses from the other participants.

(d) *Stimulation:* Respondents want to express their ideas and expose their opinions as the general level of excitement over the topic increases.

(e) *Security:* The participants are more likely to be candid because they soon realize that the things said are not being identified with any one individual.

(f) *Spontaneity:* People speak only when they have definite feelings about a subject; not because a question requires an answer.

(g) *Specialization:* The group interview allows the use of a more highly trained moderator because there are certain economies of scale when a large number of people are "interviewed" simultaneously.

(h) *Scientific scrutiny:* The group interview can be taped or even videoed for observation. This affords closer scrutiny and allows the researchers to check for consistency in the interpretations.

(i) *Structure:* The moderator, being one of the groups, can control the topics the group discusses.

(j) *Speed:* A number of interviews are, in effect, being conducted at one time.

## SAMPLING

### Meaning of Sample

A sample, as the name implies, is a smaller representation of a large whole. In other words, a section of the population selected from the latter in such a way that they are representative of the universe called a sample. A single member of a population; is referred to as population element. When some of the elements are selected with the intension of finding out something about the population from which they are taken, that group of elements is referred as a sample and the process of selection is called sampling. The method of selecting for studying a portion of the universe with a view to draw conclusion about the universe is known as sampling. Sampling may be defined as "The selection of part of part of an aggregate or totality on the basis of which a judgement or inference about the aggregate or totality is made".

### Sampling and Sample Design

A sample design is the theoretical basis and the practical means by which we infer the characteristics of some population by generalizing from the characteristics of relatively few of the units comprising the population. There are certain other terms that are characteristics of all sampling discussion and with which the reader should be familiar. These terms are listed and defined below:

*Population or Universe:* Population or universe is the aggregate of all units possessing certain specified characteristics on which the sample seeks to draw inferences.

*Frame:* The frame describes the population in terms of sampling units. It may often be a geographical area, such as a list of city blocks or counties. Sometimes it may even be the subscription list for a magazine. In essence, a frame lists or maps elements of the universe.

*Census:* "Census" denotes a total enumeration of individual's elements, or units in a defined population.

*Sample:* A sample is composed of some fraction or part of the total number of elements or units in a defined population. Sampling therefore is a method of selecting some fraction of a population.

*Design:* The design describes the method by which the sample is chosen.

*Random:* A mathematical term random means that every element in the total population has an equal chance of being chosen.

*Unit:* Any population or universe should contain some specifications in terms of contents, units, extent and time.

*Variable:* A variable can always be transformed into an attribute by a broad grouping.

*Parameter*: Parameter is the value of a variable or attribute calculated from the population, which is being studied. The characteristics of population are referred to as parameters.

*Estimating:* One major aspect of data analysis interpretation is the estimation of population parameters by using descriptive statistic from a sample of a population.

*Bias:* The tendency to have an error in one direction is called bias.

*Sample error:* Sample error refers to the error characteristics of the sample design and indicates how closely the measurement obtained from the sample is to the parameter.

*Accuracy:* It is considered distinct from precision. It refers to unavoidable errors in measurement of estimation, probably not measurable or known.

### Methods of Sampling

The various methods of sampling techniques can be classified under two main categories. They are random sampling and non-random sampling. Random sampling is also referred to as probability sampling since the Law of probability can be applied in this method. It is to be noted that the term random sampling is not used to describe the data in the sample but the process employed to select the sample. Therefore, in sampling process the randomness is the property.

## Probability Sampling Methods

1. Simple random sampling (unrestricted random sampling)
2. Restricted random sampling:

   a. Stratified sampling
   b. Systematic sampling
   c. Cluster and area sampling
   d. Multiphase-stage sampling
   e. Sequential sampling

## Non-Probability Sampling Methods (Non-Random)

1. Accidental sampling
2. Quota sampling
3. Purposive sampling
4. Convenience sampling

## Simple or Unrestricted Random Sampling

Simple random sampling is the basic theme of all scientific sampling. It is the basic probability sampling design. All other methods of scientific sampling are variations of the simple random sampling. Simple random sampling refers to the sampling technique in which each and every item or each possible sample combination in the whole population (which is essentially homogenous in terms of some characteristics relevant to the enquiry) has an equal and independent chance of being included in the sample.

The random sampling is based on the concept of equi-probable outcomes. Therefore it is also known as a probable sample as it refers to a definite method of selection of individual items under such a condition that each item has equal opportunity or probability or chance of being selected. Random sampling is sometimes referred to as 'representative sampling'. This method is suitable for a small homogenous population. To ensure randomness of selection one may adopt either the Lottery method or consult Table of random numbers. Three such tables are noteworthy. They are: 1. Tippett's table of random numbers, 2. Kendall and Babington Smith Numbers, and 3. Fisher and Yate's Numbers. Tippett's numbers is the most popular.

### *Merits*

1. No possibility of personal bias affecting the results because the selection of items in the sample depends entirely on chance,
2. It presents the universe in a better way,
3. Probability theory can be used to measure the precision of sample results because sampling errors follow the principle of chance.

### *Demerits*

Expensive and time consuming especially when the population is large.

### Mixed or Stratified Random Sampling

Under this process, the entire universe or population is divided/ subdivided in to homogenous groups or types or classes called strata(s) and a sample is drawn from each stratum at random. These samples are then combined to form a single sample of the universe. A stratified sample is thus equivalent to a set of random samples of a number of such populations, each representing a single type or stratum. The sample drawn will be typical of the whole population, as it will represent all the different segments. A stratified sampling may be either proportionate or disproportionate. In a proportionate stratified sampling plan, the number of items drawn from each stratum is proportional to the size of the strata. On the other hand, if an equal number of units are drawn from each stratum regardless of how the stratum represented in the universe, then such a plan is known as disproportionate stratified sampling. This method is suitable for a large heterogeneous population. This method differs from the simple random sampling in as much as that all the members of the universe are not taken to be as equally important.

### Systematic Sampling or Quasi-random Sampling

A systematic sample is one in which every kth item (e.g. Every tenth item) is selected in a list representing a population or a stratum. The number K is called the sampling interval. The items of a population are arranged in a systematic order on the basis of its important characteristics. The first number is chosen at random from the first K items, as described below: Arrange the farm households of a village in an ascending or descending order of the size of their farms. Then the sample is drawn at regular intervals with a random start. For example, in selecting a sample of 20 farm households out of 300, the population total viz., 300 is divided by 20. The quotient is 15. Any random number between 1 to 15 is selected say 5. Then items numbered 5, 20, 35, 50, 65, 80...etc., are selected. This method is popularly used in those cases where a complete list of the population from which sample is to be drawn is available.

### Multi-stage Sampling or Cluster Sampling

As the name implies this method refers to a sampling procedure, which is carried out in several stages. The population is distributed in to a number of first stage sampling units, and a sample is taken of these first stage units by some suitable methods. Each of these (selected) first sample units is further sub-divided in to second stage units, and from these again a sample is taken by some suitable method. Further stages may be added if required. The method adopted in the first stage may be the same or different for subsequent stages. Large groupings within the population (at the first stage) are called clusters. Where the population is broken in to area that constitutes the primary sampling units, the sample is called an Area Sample-Chunk Sample. It is convenient to confine certain questions about details to a fraction of the sample, while other information is collected from the whole sample. This procedure is known as 'multi-phase sampling'.

### Sequential Sampling

The ultimate size of the sample under this technique is not fixed in advance but is determined according to mathematical decision rules on the basis of information yielded as survey progresses. When a particular lot is to be accepted or rejected on the basis of a single sample, it is known as single sampling when the decision is to be taken on the basis of two samples, it is known as double sampling and in case the decision rest on the basis of more than two samples but the number of samples is certain and decided in advance, that sampling is known as multiple sampling. But when the number of samples is more than two but how many is neither certain nor decided in advance, this type of system is often referred to as sequential sampling.

## NON-RANDOM/NON-PROBABILITY SAMPLING

This type of sampling technique gives no assurance that every element has some specifiable chance of being included. It is clear that for the non-probability samples there is no way of calculating the margin of error and the confidence level.

### Accidental Sampling

In accidental sampling, the researcher simply reaches out and takes the cases that fall to hand continuing the process till such time as the sample reaches a designated size. The researcher may take 100 persons in a railway platform or in a street who are willing to be interviewed or to provide the kind of information that he is seeking. This type of sampling besides being economical and convenient will be helpful in stimulating insights and hypothesis. Where too much accuracy is not needed or where preoccupation is with tentative clues to provide hypothesis formulation, then accidental sampling is quite useful.

### Quota Sampling

A quota sample is one in which the investigator is instructed to collect information from an assigned number, or quota of individuals in each of several groups. The groups maybe classified according to age, sex, income, or other characteristics much like the strata in stratified sampling. The individuals selected in each group are left to the investigator's choice rather that being decided by probability methods. Quota sampling usually proceeds in three stages.

(a) The population is classified in terms of properties known or assumed to be pertinent to the characteristics being studied,
(b) The proportion of the population falling in to each group is determined on the basis of the known, assumed or estimated composition of the population, and
(c) Each observer or investigator is allotted a quota of respondents. This method is very popular in market surveys and public opinion pole because it is cheaper per sample than random sampling.

### Judgement or Purposive Sampling

A judgment sample is one, which is selected according to someone's personal judgment. The investigator uses his judgment in the choice and includes only those items of the universe in the sample, which he considers are most typical of the convenience. While choosing the sample, only the average items are considered and extreme items are omitted. Selection is based according to the object of enquiry and no significant item may be ignored. This method is more suitable when only a small number of sampling units are in the universe and in solving everyday business problems and making public policy decision-making which need urgent attention.

### Convenience Sampling

The method of convenience sampling is also called the chunk. A chunk refers to that fraction of the population being investigated which is selected neither by probability nor by judgment, but by convenience. A sample obtained by readily available lists such as automobile registration, telephone directories is a convenience sample and not a random sample even if the sample is drawn at random from the lists. Convenience sample is often used for making pilot studies. Questions may be tested and preliminary information may be obtained by the chunk before the final sample design is decided upon.

### Defects and Problems of Sampling Technique

1. *Less accuracy:* In comparison to census technique the conclusions derived from sample are more liable to error. Therefore, sampling technique is less accurate than the census technique.
2. *Changeability of Units:* If the units in the field of survey are liable to change or if these are not harmonious the sampling technique will be very hazardous.
3. *Misleading Conclusions:* If due care is not taken in the selection of samples or if they are arbitrarily selected, the conclusions derived from them will become misleading if extended to all units.
4. *Need for Specialized Knowledge:* The sample technique can be

successful only if a competent and able scientist makes the selection.

5. *When Sampling is not Possible:* Under certain circumstances it is very difficult to use the sampling technique. If the time is very short and it is not possible to make selection of the sample, the technique cannot be used. Besides if one needs 100% accuracy the sampling technique cannot be used. It can also not be used if the material is of heterogeneous nature.

## Need for having an Appropriate Sample Size

(1) Sampling design and the sample size are important to establish the representative ness of the sample for generalisability.

(2) If the appropriate sampling design is not used, a large sample size will not, in itself, allow the findings to be generalized to the population.

(3) Unless the sample size is adequate for the desired level of precision and confidence, no sampling design, however sophisticated, can be useful to the researcher in meeting the objectives of the study.

(4) Sampling decisions should consider both the sampling design and the sample size. Too large a sample size, however (say, over 500) could also become a problem in as much as we would be prone to committing Type II errors. That is, we would accept the findings of our research, when in fact we should reject them.

(5) With too large a sample size, even weak relationships (say a correlation of 10 between two variables) might reach significance levels, and we would be inclined to believe that these significant relationships found in the sample are indeed true of the population, when in reality they may not be. Thus, neither too large nor too small sample sizes help research projects.

(6) Another point to consider, even with the appropriate sample size, is whether statistical significance is more relevant than practical significance. For instance, a correlation of .25 may be statistically significant, but since this explains only about 6% of the variance (.252), how meaningful is it in terms of practical utility?

## What Size Sample is Needed?

A sample must be in such a way that it should represent the universe. A sample should bear some proportional relationship from the size of the population from which it is drawn. Precision is mostly needed in this aspect. A sample of 400 may sometimes be appropriate, while a sample of more than 2000 may be required in other circumstances. In another case perhaps a sample of only 40 is needed.

## Following are the Principles Influence the Sample Size

The greater the dispersion within the population, the larger sample must be provided. The greater the number of sub-groups in the sample, the greater the sample size must be as each sub-group must meet minimum sample size requirements. If the calculated sample size exceeds 5 percent of the population he sample size may be reduced without sacrificing the precision. Since researchers can never be hundred percent certain, a sample reflects its population, they must decide, how much precision they need. Precision is measured by the interval range in which they would expect to find the parameter estimate and the degree of confidence they wish to have in the estimate.

The size of the probability sample needed can be affected by the size of the population, but only when the sample size is large compared with the population. Other considerations are the feasibility of the technique. One type of sample may be inappropriate because we have no list of population elements. Since various designs have differing, statistical and economic efficiencies, the choice of design will also affect the size of the sample.

The researcher also may be interested in making estimates concerning various subgroups of the population. So to maintain the desired level of precision, the sample must be large enough for each of the sub groups. In more complex sampling procedures, the smaller sub-groups of sampled more heavily and then the parameter estimates drawn from these sub groups are weighted. There is a judgment rule of thumb for selecting minimum sub-group sample size. It has been suggested that, each sub-group, which is to be analysed separately, should have a minimum of hundred units in each category.

Stratified sampling involves drawing separate probability samples within the sub groups to make the sample more efficient. This makes the determination of sample size more complex.

Increased complexity is also a determining factor of the sample size. The formulas are beyond the scope of research.

Another judgment factor in the determination of the sample size is the selection of the appropriate items, question, or characteristic for the sample size calculation.

However, cost of data collection becomes a major consideration and judgment must be exercised taking into account the importance of the item information.

## Estimating the Sample Size

Determining the sample size for a simple random sample is quite easy. The researcher:

(1) Estimates the standard deviation of the population.
(2) Makes a judgment about the desired magnitude of error.
(3) Determines a confidence level.

The only problem is that of estimating the standard deviation of the population. Ideally, similar studies conducted in the past will be used as a basis for judging the standard deviation. In practice, researchers without prior information conduct a pilot study for the purpose of estimating population parameters so that another, larger sample, with the appropriate sample size, may be drawn. This procedure is called sequential sampling, because the researcher takes an initial look at the pilot study results before deciding on a larger sample providing more precise information.

A rule of thumb for estimating the value of the standard deviation is to expect it to be one-sixth of the range.

For the moment, let us assume that the standard deviation has been estimated in some preliminary work. If our concern is to estimate the mean of a particular population, the formula for sample size is $n = (ZS/E)^2$ where

Z = standardization value indicating confidence level,
S = sample standard deviation or estimate of the population standard deviation, and
E = acceptable magnitude of error, plus or minus error factor (range is one-half of total confidence interval).

### A. *The Influence of Population Size on Sample Size*

In most cases, the size of the population does not have a major effect on the sample size. However, a finite correction factor may be needed to adjust the sample size if that size is more than five percent of a finite population. If the sample is large relative to the population, the above procedures may overestimate sample size, and there may be a need to adjust sample size.

### B. *Proportions*

Sample Size Determination Requires Knowledge about Confidence Intervals.

When the sample size question involves the estimation of a proportion, the researcher requires some knowledge of the logic for determining a confidence interval around a sample proportion (p). For a confidence interval to be constructed around the sample proportion (p), an estimate of the standard error of the proportion (Sp) must be calculated and a confidence coefficient specified.

The plus or minus estimate of the population proportion is:

$$\text{Confidence interval} = p \pm Zc.l.Sp$$

where Sp = $\sqrt{pq}/n$,
p = proportion of successes, and
q = (1 p), or proportion of failures.

To determine sample size for a proportion the researcher must make a judgment about the confidence level and the maximum allowance for random sampling error. Further, the size of the proportion influences sampling error; thus an estimate of the expected proportion of successes must be made based on intuition or prior information. The formula is:

$$n = \left(Z_{c.1}^{2} pq\right) / E^{2}$$

### C. *Actual Calculation of Sample Size for a Sample Proportion*

In practice there are a number of tables that have been constructed so that the determination of sample size may be determined by inspecting the tables. Thus, in a survey of 100 people in which 50 percent agree with one statement and ten percent with another, the sampling error is expected to be ten percentage points of error and six percentage points of error, respectively.

### D. *Sample Size on the Basis of Judgment*

Sample size may also be determined on the basis of managerial judgments. Using a sample size similar to the sample size used in previous studies provides the inexperienced researcher with a comparison of other researchers' judgments.

In most studies several characteristics are of concern, and the desired degree of precision may vary for these items. The researcher must exercise some judgment to determine which item will be utilized. Often the item that will produce the largest sample size will be utilized to determine the ultimate sample size. However, the cost of data collection becomes a major consideration, and judgment must be exercised regarding the importance of such information.

Another sampling consideration stems from most analysts' need to analyze the various sub-groups within the sample. There is a judgmental rule of thumb for selecting minimum sub-group sample size. It has been suggested that each sub-group to be separately analyzed should have a minimum of 100 or more units in each category of the major breakdowns. According to this procedure, the total sample size is computed by totaling the sample size necessary for these subgroups.

### E. *Determining Sample Size for Stratified and Other Probability Samples*

Stratified sampling involves drawing separate samples within the subgroups to make the sample more efficient. With a stratified sample, the sample variances are expected to differ by strata. This makes the determination of sample size more complex.

## F. *A Reminder about Statistics*

The terms and symbols defined in this chapter provide the basics of the language of statisticians and researchers. To learn the pragmatic use of statistics in business research there can be no forgetting of these concepts.

### Issue of Precision and Confidence in Determining Size

A reliable and valid sample should enable us to generalize the findings from the sample to the population under investigation. In other words, the sample statistics should be reliable estimates and reflect the population parameters as closely as possible within a narrow margin of error. No sample statistic is going to be exactly the same as the population parameter (μ) , no matter how sophisticated the probability sampling design is. The issue of confidence interval and confidence level are addressed in the following pages.

### Precision

Precision refers to how close our estimate is to the true population characteristic. Usually, we would estimate the population parameter to fall within a range, based on the sample estimate. For example, let us say that from a study of a simple random sample of 50 of the total 300 employees in a workshop, we find the average daily production rate per person is 50 pieces of a particular product ( X bar = 50). We might then (by doing certain calculations, as we shall see later) be able to say that the true average daily production of the product (μ) would be anywhere between 40 and 60 for the population of employees in the workshop. In saying this, we offer an interval estimate, within which we expect the true population mean production to be (μ = 50 ±10). The narrower this interval, the greater the precision.

Precision is a function of the range of variability in the sampling distribution of the sample mean. That is, if we take a number of different samples from a population, and take the mean of each of these, we will usually find that they are all different, are normally distributed, and have a dispersion associated with them. The smaller this dispersion or variability, the greater the probability that the sample mean will be closer to the population mean. We need not necessarily take several different samples to estimate this variability.

Note that the standard error varies inversely with the square root of the sample size. Hence, if we want to reduce the standard error given a particular standard deviation in the sample, we need to increase the sample size. Another noteworthy point is that the smaller the variation in the population, the smaller the standard error, which in turn implies that the sample size need not be large. Thus, low variability in the population requires a smaller sample size.

### Confidence

Whereas precision denotes how close we estimate the population parameter based on the sample statistic, confidence denotes how certain we are that our estimates will really hold true for the population. In the previous example of production rate, we know we are more precise when we estimate the true mean production (μ) to fall somewhere between 45 and 55 pieces, that somewhere between 40 and 60. However, we may have more confidence in the latter estimation than in the former.

In essence, confidence reflects the level of certainty with which we can state that our estimates of the population parameters, based on our sample statistics will hold true. The level of confidence can range from 0 to 100% .

## Sample Data, Precision and Confidence in Estimation

Precision and confidence are important issues in sampling because when we use sample data to draw inferences about the population, we hope to be fairly, "on target", and have some idea of the extent of possible error. Because a point estimate provides no measure or possible error, we do a interval estimation to ensure a relatively accurate estimation of the population parameter. Statistics that have the same distribution as the sampling distribution of the mean are used in this procedure, usually a $z$ or a $t$ statistic.

In sum, the sample size, n, is a function of:

1. The variability in the population,
2. Precision or accuracy needed,
3. Confidence level desired, and
4. Type of sampling plan used for example, sample random sampling *versus* stratified random sampling.

So far we have discussed sample data as a means of estimating the population parameters, but sample data can also be used to test hypotheses about population values rather than simply to estimate population values. The procedure for this testing incorporates the same information as in interval estimation, but the goals behind the two methods are somewhat different.

We wish to determine whether or not customers spend the same average amount in purchases at department store A as in department store B. First we would set the null hypothesis which would state that, there would be no difference in terms of rupees spent by customers shopping at two different stores. This would be expressed as follows:

$H_o$: μA – μB = 0

The alternative hypothesis of differences would be stated non directionally (as we have no idea whether customers buy more at store A or store B) as :

HA: $\mu_A - \mu_B \neq 0$

If we take a sample of 20 customers from each of the two stores and find that the mean amount in value purchases of customers in store A is 105 with the standard deviation of 10, and the corresponding figures for store B are 100 and 15 respectively, we see that,

XA – XB = 105 – 100 = 5.

Our null hypothesis has postulated no difference. Should we then conclude that our alternate hypothesis is to be accepted? We cannot say. To determine this, we must first find the probability of the two group means having a difference of 5 in the context of the null hypothesis of a difference of 0. This can be done by converting the difference in the sample means to a *t* statistic and seeing what the probability of finding a *t* of that value. The *t* distribution has known probabilities attached to it. Looking at the *t* distribution table, we find that, with two samples of 20 each (the degrees of freedom become $(n_1 + n_2) - 2 = 38$) for the *t* value to be significant at the .05 lever, the critical value should be around 2.021. We need to use 2 tailed test since we do not know whether the difference between store A and store B will be +ve or –ve. For even a 90% probability, it should be at least 1.684.

We already know that,

$\overline{XA} - \overline{XB} = 5$ (the difference in the means of two series), and
μA – μB = 0 (from our null hypothesis)

then, $t = (5–0)/(4.136) = 1.209$. this *t* value of 1.209 is much below the value of 2.021. thus, we can say that, the difference of 5 that we found between the two stores is not significantly different from 0. The conclusion then is that there is no significant difference between how much customers buy at department store A and department store B. we will thus accept the null hypothesis and reject the alternative.

## Sample Size on the Basis of Judgment

Sample size may also be determined on the basis of managerial judgments. Using a sample size similar to the sample size used in previous studies provides the inexperienced researcher with a comparison of other researchers' judgments.

In most studies several characteristics are of concern, and the desired degree of precision may vary for these items. The researcher must exercise some judgment to determine which item will be utilized. Often the item that will produce the largest sample size will be utilized to determine the ultimate sample size. However, the cost of data collection becomes a major consideration, and judgment must be exercised regarding the importance of such information.

Another sampling consideration stems from most analysts' need to analyze the various sub-groups within the sample. There is a judgmental rule of thumb for selecting minimum subgroup sample size. It has been suggested that each sub-group to be separately analyzed should have a minimum of 100 or more units in each category of the major breakdowns. According to this procedure, the total sample size is computed by totaling the sample size necessary for these sub-groups.

## QUESTIONS

1. What is primary data?
2. What are the sources of secondary data?
3. What are the precautions to be taken while using secondary data?
4. What is meant by interview method?
5. Define? Interview.
6. Discuss the purpose wise classification of interview?
7. What are the basic guidelines of good interview?
8. Describe the objectives of interview method of data collection.
9. What are the principles of interview?
10. What are the types of interview in research?
11. What do you understand by electronic questionnaire?
12. What are the questions that should not be asked in the questionnaire?
13. What are the characteristics of a well designed questionnaire?
14. Discuss various forms of questionnaire.
15. What are the advantages of questionnaire method of data collection in the field of research?
16. Describe briefly various methods collecting primary data?
17. What is survey method of data collection in research?
18. What are the advantages of survey method of data collection?
19. What is observation? What are the types of observation?
20. Discuss the differences between questionnaire and schedule.
21. What do you mean by check list in questionnaire?
22. What are the types of schedule?
23. Discuss the method of framing the schedule.
24. Discuss the types of computer-assisted interview programs.
25. Briefly discuss about the computer-aided survey.
26. What is E- Mail survey? What are the merits of it?
27. What is internet survey? What are the advantages of Internet survey technique?
28. What is Graphical user interface?
29. Briefly explain about layout of Internet questionnaires.
30. What is secondary data?
31. What are the precautions to be taken while using observation method?
32. What are the methods of collecting the external secondary data?
33. What do you understand by focus groups? What are the types of focus group?
34. Discuss the features of focus group.
35. What is telephone focus group? What are the advantages of this method?
36. Describe the advantages of focus groups?
37. Make a brief discussion on Video conferencing focus groups. How this technique is useful in the present days?

38. Elucidate the advantages of focus group interviews.
39. What is a sample in research?
40. Discuss the types of samples used in business research?
41. Discuss the methods of sampling.
42. What is meant by bias in sample?
43. What do you understand by sample design?
44. What is random sample?
45. What is meant by sampling error?
46. What is a variable?
47. What is meant by parameter?
48. Discuss any four methods of probability sampling with examples.
49. Enumerate any four non-probability sampling methods with examples.
50. Discuss on the defects of sampling methods.
51. What is the need for having an appropriate sample size?
52. What are the principles, which influence the size of the sample?
53. Explain the steps involved in estimating the Sample Size.
54. What is confidence interval?

# 4

# *Data Analysis and Interpretation*

## ANALYSIS OF DATA

Analysis means examine in order to learn what the research is made up of and study about the examined parts. Analysis, particularly in case of survey or experimental data, involves estimating the values of unknown parameters of the population and testing of hypotheses for drawing inferences. Analysis may, therefore, be classified as descriptive analysis and inferential analysis (also known as statistical analysis). "Descriptive analysis is largely the study of distributions of one variable. This study provides us with largely the study of distributions of one variable. This study provides us with profiles of companies, work groups, persons and other subjects on any of a multitude of characteristics such as size, composition, efficiency, preferences, etc." This sort of analysis may be in respect of one variable (described as one-dimensional analysis), or in respect of two variables (described as bivariate analysis) or in respect of more than two variables (described as multivariate analysis).

According to Prof. Wilkins and Bhandarkar, "analysis of data involves a number of closely related operations that are performed with the purpose of summarizing the collected data and organizing these in such a manner that they will yield answer to the research questions or suggest hypothesis or questions if no such questions or hypothesis had initiated the study".

Correlation analysis studies the joint variation of two or more variables for determining the amount of correlation between two or more variables. Casual analysis is concerned with the study of how one or more variables affect changes in another variable. It is thus a study of functional relationships existing between two or more variables. This analysis can be termed as regression analysis. Casual analysis is considered relatively more important in experimental researches. In modern times, with the availability of computer facilities, there has been a rapid development of multivariate analysis, which may be defined as "all statistical methods, which simultaneously analyze more than two variables on a sample of observations". Usually the following analyses are involved when we make a reference of multivariate analysis:

(a) *Multiple regression analysis:* In the simple regression analysis, we have used the coefficient of determination as a measure to determine the strength of the relationship of Y on X. It is quite natural for the researcher to generate more precise estimates, say, of wheat production, than obtained by the simple regression method. A logical step to do this is by including additional independent variables in the analysis. The regression analysis that uses more than one independent variable is termed as multiple regression analysis.

(b) *Multiple discriminate analysis:* This analysis is appropriate when the researcher has a single dependent variable that cannot be measured, but can be classified into two or more groups on the basis of some attribute. The object of this analysis is to predict an entity's possibility of belonging to a particular group based on several predictor variables.

(c) *Multivariate analysis of variance (or multi-ANOVA):* This analysis is an extension of two-way ANOVA, wherein the ratio of among group variance to within group variance is worked out on a set of variables.

(d) *Canonical analysis:* This analysis can be used in case of both measurable and non-measurable variables for the purpose of simultaneously predicting a set of dependent variables from their joint covariance with a set of independent variables. Inferential analysis is concerned with the various tests of significance for testing hypotheses in order to determine with what validity data can be said to indicate some conclusion or conclusions. It is also concerned with the estimation of population values. It is mainly on the basis of inferential analysis and the task of interpretation (i.e., the task of drawing inferences and conclusions) is performed.

## INTERPRETATION OF DATA

Analysis and interpretation are central steps of' the research process. The goal of analysis is to summaries the collected data in such a way that they provide answers to the questions that triggered the research. Interpretation is the search for the broader meaning of research findings. This search has two major aspects. First, there is the effort to establish continuity in social research through linking the results of one study with those of another. Secondly, interpretation leads to the establishment of explanatory concepts. Through interpretation, the meanings and implications of the study become clear. Analysis is not complete without interpretation: and interpretation cannot proceed without analysis. Both are, thus, inter-dependent.

According to Jahada and cook, "Scientific interpretation for relationship between the data of a study and between the study findings and other scientific knowledge".

## Essentials for Interpretation

### 1. *Accurate Data*

One of the most important pre-requisites of interpretation and analysis is the availability of accurate and reliable data. For, in the absence of such material, the investigator fails to interpret the data in a proper and required form.

### 2. *Sufficient Data*

Another important pre-requisite of accurate interpretation is the existence of sufficient and reliable data. The main reason of it is the basic truth that unless we have sufficient data, we may never achieve the objectives of proper interpretation and analysis. For, some of the rules and methods are applicable only if there is sufficient data.

### 3. *Proper Type of Classification and Tabulation*

For attaining the objective of accurate interpretation, in most of the cases, the investigators are required to base their calculations, estimations and judgements, on data represented in a properly classified and tabulated form.

### 4. *Absence of Heterogeneous Data*

For a uniform and accurate result, the data must be homogeneous. The reason is that if the data are non-homogeneous or heterogeneous, it may fall to yield the desired result.

### 5. *Possibility of Statistical Treatment*

It is a matter of common belief that every data or information is not suited to statistical treatment. In particular, if the subject concerned is related to 'quality' or if the information available is scanty, they may not be regarded as 'suitable for statistical treatment'. Naturally, proper interpretations and statistical analysis are not possible in such cases.

### 6. *Consistency of Information*

Inconsistent information and data are always subject to inaccurate results. In mathematical and statistical treatment, however, emphasis is always laid on having stable and accurate results.

### 7. Precautions in Interpretation

The following are among the more common errors of interpretation, which need to be avoided.

### 8. Failure to see the Problem in Proper Perspective

Sometimes the investigator may have an adequate grasp of the problem in its broad sense and too close a focus on its immediate aspect.

### 9. Failure to Appreciate the Relevance of Various Elements

The investigator may fail to see the relevance of the various elements of the situation due to an adequate grasp of the problem, too rigid a mind-set or even a lack of imagination. This may cause the investigator to overlook the operation of significant factors.

### 10. Failure to Recognise Limitations in the Research Evidence

These limitations may be of many types such as non-representativeness in sampling, basis in the data, inadequacies in the research design, defective data gathering instruments and inaccurate statistical analysis.

### 11. Misinterpretation due to Unstudied Factors

A given result is composed of many factors; it is not produced simply by a single factor. The factors, which condition any result, are innumerable. In some instances the interpretation is difficult or inconsistent with another results because one ha conceived of his problem in too narrow sense.

### 12. Ignoring Selective Factors

In investigations, where a selective group is made the subject of study (e.g., institutional delinquents) or where a selective factor is operating on the situations studies (year-wise failure in a four year course) one is likely to reach unwarranted conclusions if one ignores the selective factors.

## Difficulties of Interpretative Evaluations

In studies of the descriptive nature—historical or normative survey—proper interpretation of data rests on proper evaluation of facts. Explanation of one's research findings in terms of their practical implications, which often a usual part of the research undertaken is fraught with the danger of misrepresentation.

Importance and significance of statistics in social research is considerably increasing particularly in our modern times, when the figures are playing a significant part. Since, figures help in representing data and make that easy and understandable, therefore in social research their use is increasing. The figures provide detailed description and tabulate as well as analyse data without subjectivity, but only objectively. Statistics in social research help in gaining accuracy and reliability. The results can be presented in brief and precise language and complex and complicated problems can be studied in very simple way. It becomes possible to convert abstract problems in to figures and complex data can be reduced in the form of tables. In this way every social researcher is realizing the need and necessity of statistics. This perhaps is the reason that today no serious study can be carried without the help of statistician. Statistical methods are the mathematical techniques used to facilitate the interpretation of numerical data secured from groups of individuals or groups of observations from a single individual.

The statistical methods may be classified in to four sets of techniques. The first set of techniques will enable us to organize group data, to describe and interpret these data in terms of derived measures of central tendency, of variability and to portray these data in graphical form for more convenient interpretation or more ready assimilation.

The second set of techniques will be useful to describe quantitatively the limits within which he may safely generalize about large groups or populations on the basis of facts derived from relatively small groups or samples select at random from these populations.

Third set of techniques will help to describe quantitatively the degree of relationship existing between measures of different characteristics.

The fourth set of techniques will enable the student to describe quantitatively fluctuations occurring in time series, to isolate these variations and to eliminate their influence from basic data when this is deemed desirable.

Most research studies result in a large volume of raw data, which must be suitably reduced so that the same can be read easily and can be used for further analysis. Clearly any research worker cannot ignore the science of statistics, even though he may not have occasion to use statistical methods in all their details. Classification and tabulation, as stated earlier, achieve this objective to some extent, but we have to go a step further and develop certain indices or measures to summarise the collected/classified data. Only after this we can adopt the process of generalization from small groups (i.e., samples) to population. In fact, there are two major areas of statistics viz., descriptive statistics and inferential statistics. Descriptive statistics concern the development of certain indices from the raw data, whereas inferential statistics concern with the process of generalisation.

## FACTOR ANALYSIS

Factor analysis is a generic name given to a class of multivariate statistical methods whose primary purpose is data reduction and summarization. Broadly speaking, it addresses itself to the problem of analyzing the interrelationships among a large number of variables (e.g. test scores, test items, questionnaire response) and then explaining these variables in terms of their common underlying dimensions (factors). By using factor analysis, the analyst can identify the separate dimensions being measured by the survey and determine a factor loading for each variable (test item) on each factor.

Factor analysis (unlike multiple regression, discriminant analysis, or canonical correlation, in which one or more variables is explicitly considered the criterion or dependent variable and all others the predictor or independent variables) is an interdependence technique in which all variables are simultaneously considered. In a sense, each of the observed (original) variables is considered as a dependent variable that is a function of some underlying, latent, and hypothetical set of factors (dimensions). Conversely, one can look at each factor as a dependent variable that is a function of the originally observed variables.

### Purpose of Factor Analysis

The general purpose of factor analytic technique is to find a way of condensing (summarizing) the information contained in a number of original variables into a smaller set of new composite dimensions (factors) with a minimum loss of information; that is, to search for and define the fundamental constructs or dimensions assumed to underlie the original variables. More specifically, factor analysis performs four functions:

1. Identify set of dimensions that are latent (not easily observed) in a large set of variables; this is also referred to as R factor analysis.
2. Device a method of combining or condensing large numbers of people into distinctly different groups within a large population; this is also referred to as Q factor analysis.
3. Identify appropriate variables for subsequent regression, correlation or disscriminant analysis from a much larger set of variables.
4. Create an entirely new set of a smaller number of variables to partially or completely replace the original set of variables for inclusion in subsequent regression, correlation or discriminant analysis.

## CLUSTER ANALYSIS

Cluster analysis is the name of a group of multivariate statistical techniques whose primary purpose is to identify similar entities from the characteristics they posses. It identifies and classifies objects or variables so that each object is very similar to others in its cluster with respect to some predetermined selection criteria. The resulting object clusters should then exhibit high internal (within-cluster) homogeneity and high external (between-cluster) heterogeneity. Thus, if the classification is successful, the objects within clusters will be close together when plotted geometrically, and the objects in different clusters will be far apart.

Cluster analysis has been variously referred to as Q-analysis, typology, classification analysis, and numerical taxonomy. This variety of names is due in part to the usage of clustering methods in such diverse disciplines as psychology, biology, sociology, and business. The primary value of cluster analysis lies in the preclassification of data, as suggested by "natural" groupings of the data itself.

Let us illustrate cluster analysis with a hypothetical example relating to the types of vacations taken by 12 individuals. Vacation behavior is represented on two dimensions: number of vacation days and dollar expenditures on vacations during a given year.. The Through scatter diagram we can found three clear-cut clusters. The first sub-groups, consisting of individuals L, H and B suggests group of individuals who have many vacation days but do not spend much money on their vacations. The second cluster, consisting of individuals A, I, K, G and F, represents intermediate values on both variables: an average number of vacation days and an average dollar expenditure on vacations. The third group consists of a cluster of individuals who have relatively few vacation days but who spend large amounts on these outings.

In this hypothetical example individuals are grouped on the basis of their similarity or proximity to other individuals. The logic of cluster analysis is to group individuals or objects on the bases of their similarity to or distance from each other. The actual mathematical procedures for deriving clusters will not be dealt with here, as our purpose is only to introduce the technique.

A study investigating test markets provides a pragmatic example of the use of cluster analysis. Manages are frequently interested in finding test-market cities that are sufficiently similar so that no extraneous variation causes a difference between the experimental and control markets. In this study the objects to be clustered were cities. The characteristics of the cities, such as population, retail sales, number of retail outlets, and percentage of nonwhites, were used to identify the groups.

## Application of Cluster Analysis

Application of cluster analysis can be divided into three major stages:

(1) Partitioning, (2) Interpretation, and (3) Profiling. The partitioning stage is the process of determining if and how clusters may be developed. The interpretation stage is the process of understanding the characteristics of each cluster and developing a name or label that appropriately defines its nature. The profiling stage involves (1) describing the characteristics of each cluster to explain how they may differ on relevant dimensions such as demographics. Some authors have suggested the following steps to be followed.

## Steps in Cluster Analysis

Five steps are basic to the application of most cluster analysis.

(1) Selection of the sample to be clustered (Ex. Buyers, medical patients, inventory, products and employees).

(2) Definition of the variables on which to measure the objects, events, or people (example financial status, political affiliation, market segmentation, symptom classes, productivity attributes).
(3) Computation of similarities among the entities through correlation.
(4) Selection of mutually exclusive clusters or hierarchically arranged clusters.
(5) Cluster comparison and validation.

Different clustering methods can and do produce different solutions. It is important to have enough information about the data to know when the derived groups are real and not merely imposed on the data by the method.

### Methods of Cluster Analysis

The three most popular methods used in social science research are hierarchical agglomerative, iterative partitioning and factor analytic methods.

The hierarchical agglomerative method is conceptually simple to understand. The single linkage approach does not require an understanding of matrix algebra or an extensive background in multivariate statistical methods. The method is based on a simple rule of how to search for a similarity matrix and when to combine the cases.

*Iterative partitioning* methods work on the following approach:

1. Begin with an initial partition of the given data set into some specific number of clusters, and compute the centroids of these clusters. The cluster centroid is the average value of the objects contained in the cluster on all variables included in the analysis.
2. Allocate each data point to the cluster that has the nearest centroid.
3. Compute the new centroid of the clusters. The clusters are not updated until there has been a complete pass through the data.
4. Repeat steps (2) and (3) until no data point change clusters.

The *factor analysis variant* is a popular method in psychology for cluster analysis. This method, an inverse factor analysis or Q type factoring, starts by developing a correlation matrix of similarities among individuals. Usually factor analysis is carried out on a P × P correlation matrix (P is the number of factors), but when used to define clusters, it is performed on the n × n correlation matrix (n is the number of individuals). Factors are extracted from the correlation matrix, and the cases are assigned to clusters based on their factor loadings.

## DISCRIMINANT ANALYSIS

Discriminant analysis is the appropriate statistical technique when the dependent variable is categorical (nominal or nonmetric) and the independent variables are metric. In many cases, the dependent variable consists of two groups or classifications, for example, male *versus* female or high versus low. Discriminant analysis is capable of handling either two groups or multiple groups (three or more). When two-group classifications are involved, the technique is referred to as two-group discriminant analysis; the technique is referred to as multiple discriminant analysis (MDA).

Discriminant analysis involves deriving the linear combination of the two (or more) independent variables that will discriminate best between the prior defined groups. This is achieved by the statistical decision rule of maximizing the between-group variance relative to the with-in group variance; this relationship is expressed as the ratio for between-group to with-in group variance. The linear combinations for a discriminant analysis are derived from an equation that takes the following form:

$$Z = W_1X_1 + W_2X_2 + W_3X_3 + \ldots + W_nX_n$$

where Z = discriminant score
W = discriminant weights
X = independent variables

Discriminant analysis is the appropriate statistical technique for testing the hypothesis that the group means of the two or more groups are equal. To do so, discriminant analysis multiplies each independent variable by its corresponding weights and adds these products together. The result is single composite discriminant score for each individual in the analysis. By averaging the discriminant scores for all the individuals within a particular group, group mean is found out. This group mean is referred to as a centroid. When the analysis involves two groups, there are two centroids; with three groups there are three centroids, and so forth. The centroids indicate the most typical location of an individual from a particular group, and a comparison of the group, and a comparison of the group centroids shows how far apart the groups are along the dimension being tested.

Discriminant analysis is also comparable to analysis of variance (ANOVA). In discriminant analysis the single dependent variable is categorical and the independent variables are metric. The opposite is true of ANOVA. ANOVA involves metric dependent variables and a single categorical independent variable.

Example. An illustration of the method, where Dean Merrill, a brokerage firm, is hiring MBAs for its account executives program. Over the years the firm has had indifferent success with the selection process. A procedure has to be developed to improve this. It appears that discriminant analysis is a perfect technique. Data was collected from 30 MBAs who have been hired. Fifteen of these have been successful employees while the other 15 have been unsatisfactory. The personnel files provide the following information that can be used to conduct the analysis:

$X_1$ = Years of prior work experience.
$X_2$ = GPA in graduate program.
$X_3$ = Employment test scores.

An algorithm determines how well these three independent variables will correctly classify those who are judged successful from those judged unsuccessful. The classification results are shown in the figure. This indicates that 25 of the 30(30 – 3 – 2 = 25) cases have been correctly classified using these three variables.

### Assumptions of Discriminant Analysis

The assumptions for deriving the discriminant function are multivariate normality of the distributions and unknown (but equal) dispersion and covariance structures for the groups. When classification accuracies are determined, we assumed equal costs of misclassification, equal a priori group probabilities, and known dispersion and co-variation structures. However, discriminant analysis is not very sensitive to violations of these assumptions unless the violations are extreme. This is particularly true with large sample sizes.

### Objectives of Discriminant Analysis

1. Determining if statistically significant differences exist between the average score profiles of the two (or more) a priori defined groups.
2. Establishing procedures for classifying statistical units individuals or objects) into groups on the basis of their scores on several variables.
3. Determining which of the independent variables account most for the differences in the average score profiles of the two or more groups.

### Application of Discriminant Analysis

The application of discriminant analysis can be divided into three major stages:

(1) Derivation,
(2) Validation, and
(3) Interpretation.

The derivation stage consists of several separate steps. The steps are variable selection, sample division, the computational method and statistical significance.

The validation stage involves several major considerations; the reason for developing classification matrices, cutting score determination, constructing classification matrices, chance models, and classification accuracy relative to chance. If the discriminant function is statistically significant and the classification accuracy is acceptable, the analyst continues to third stage, which focuses on making substantive interpretations of the findings

## CORRELATION ANALYSIS

Correlation is a well known statistical measure frequently used is Statistical analysis of data.

Simpson and Kafjaf, "Correlation analysis deals with the association between two or more variables".

Ya Lun Chou, "Correlation analysis attempts to determine the degree of relationship between variables".

Correlation is used only for testing and verification of the relationship. Correlation literally means related or sympathetic movement between variables. The correlation coefficient is a measure of the strength of the linear relationship between two variables. The correlation coefficient takes on values between -1 and 1, with values close to—1 or 1 indicating a strong relationship between the two variables. A value close to 0 indicates a weak or non-existent relationship. A negative value shows a negative, or inverse relationship—as one variable increases, the other decreases. A positive value shows a positive, or direct relationship—as one variable increases, the other also increases. Pearson's correlation coefficient (Pearson's r) assumes that both populations are well approximated by a normal distribution, and that their joint distribution is bivariate normal.

### Types of Correlation

#### *Positive and Negative Correlation*

When both the variables change in one direction that is when both increase or decrease the relationship between the two variables is called positive or direct. But when the change is in opposite directions that is, one is increasing and the other is decreasing, the correlation is *negative or inverse.* For determining the direction of change average values are taken.

#### *Example : (Positive Correlation)*

Age of husband and age of wife.
Price of commodity and amount of supply.
Increase in rainfall up to a point and production of rice.
Increase in heat affects temperature.
Increase in cost of advertisement and sales.

Increase in height and weight.
Example : (Negative Correlation)
Demand of a commodity may go down as a result of rise in prices.
Increase in the number of television sets and number of cinema goers.
Sale of woolen garments and day temperature.

### *Linear and Curvilinear Correlation*

If the ratio of change between two variables is uniform then there exists linear correlation between them. Linear and non-linear correlation is based upon the consistency of the ratio of change between the variables. Their relationship is described by the straight line. If the variables under study are graphed, the points will form a straight line.

### *Simple, Multiple and Partial Correlation*

Simple, multiple and partial correlation is based upon the number of variables under study. When only two variables are involved, the analysis of relationship between them is called simple correlation. When more than two variables are studied, the relationship can be either multiple or partial. Simultaneous effect of two or more dependent variables are one independent variable is a study of multiple correlation. For example, if we study relationship between agricultural production, rainfall and the amount of fertilizers used, it will be a multiple correlation. In partial correlation, the relationship of two variables is studied by eliminating the effect of other variables from the both. Partial correlation is a study of relationship of more than two variables. For example, mathematical study of combined effect of both the amount of rainfall and temperature on the yield of wheat is a problem of multiple correlations. But the correlation analysis of amount of rainfall and yield of wheat in a certain constant temperature is a problem of partial correlation. The relationship between two values can be determined by the quantitative value of coefficient of correlation, which is obtained by calculations.

### *Perfect Correlation*

Perfect correlation is that where changes in two related variables are exactly proportional. If equal proportional changes are in the same direction, there is perfect positive correlation between the two variables describes as +1; and if equal proportional changes are in the reverse direction, there is perfect negative correlation, described as –1. For example, the circumference of a circle increase in the equal proportionate ratio with an increase in the equal proportionate ratio in the length of its diameter, the amount of electricity bill increase in a perfectly definite ratio with an increase in the number of unit consumed, the volume of a gas varies inversely with the pressure at constant temperature, etc.

### *No Correlation*

When there exists no interdependence between the two variables or no relationship is found between the changes in them, there is no correlation or absence of correlation; described as 0 (zero).

### *Limited Degree of Correlation*

The variables may be correlated, but an increase in one variable need not always be accompanied by a corresponding or equal increase (or decrease) in the other variable. Correlation is said to be *limited positive* when there are unequal changes in the two variables in the *same direction*; and correlation is *limited negative* when there are unequal changes in the *reverse direction*. The limited degree of combination can be high (between ±.75 to 1); moderate (± .25 to .75). Or low between (between ± 0 to .25). Thus the calculated result of correlation must vary between –1 to +1.

The variables that are included in 'r' analysis may be easily distinguished by following the custom of representing them by the letter X with subscript. The dependent variable is always denoted by $X_1$ and the others $X_2$, $X_3$. . . . Multiple correlation is of great practical significance—for rarely it is true that a variable is influenced solely or predominantly by one or other factor. For e.g. The sales of a manufacturer are influenced among other things, by his prices, his competitive position in the industry, his sales promotion campaign, industry sales competitors price and national prosperity.

In simple correlation only one of the independent variable at a time could be correlated with the manufacturer's sales and there is no direct way of determining the extent to which the observed correlation might have been caused by the interacting influence of other factors on the two variables under study.

### *Coefficient of Multiple Correlation*

The coefficient of multiple linear correlation is represented by $R_1$ and the subscript designating the variables are also involved.

If $X_1$ is denoted as dependent variable, and $X_2$ and $X_3$ are independent variables of $X_1$, the multiple correlation can be calculated as follows

$$r_{1.23} = \frac{\text{Explained Variation}}{\text{its degree of freedom}}$$

If $X_2$ is treated as dependent variable; $X_1$ and $X_3$ as independent variables,

$$r_{2.13} = \sqrt{\frac{r^2_{21} + r^2_{23} - 2r_{21}r_{23}r_{13}}{1 - r^2_{13}}}$$

If $X_3$ is treated as dependent variable; $X_1$ and $X_2$ as independent variables

$$r_{3.12} = \sqrt{\frac{r^2_{31} + r^2_{32} - 2r_{31}r_{32}r_{12}}{1 - r^2_{12}}}$$

A coefficient of multiple correlation such as $r_{1.23}$ lies between 0 and 1. The closer it is to 1, the better is the relationship between the variables. The closer it is to 0, the worse is the linear relationship. If the multiple correlation is 1, the correlation is called perfect correlation.

### *Illustration*

Calculate multiple correlation for profit earned with sales and advertisement from the following data:

Profit and Sales $r_{12} = 0.43$

Profit and Advertisement $r_{13} = 0.54$

Sales and Advertisement $r_{23} = 0.36$

$$r_{1.23} = \sqrt{\frac{r^2_{12} + r^2_{13} - 2r_{12}r_{13}r_{23}}{1 - r^2_{23}}}$$

$$r_{1.23} = \sqrt{\frac{(0.43)2 + (0.54)2 - 2(0.43)(0.54)(0.36)}{1 - (0.36)2}}$$

$$= \sqrt{\frac{0.1849 + 0.2916 - 0.1672}{1 - 0.1296}}$$

$$= \sqrt{\frac{0.3093}{0.8704}}$$

$$r_{1.23} = 0.596$$

### *Merits*

The coefficient of multiple correlation serves the following purposes.

1. It serves as a measure of the degree of association between one variable taken as the dependent variable and a group of other variables taken as the independent variable.
2. It also serves as a measure of goodness of fit of the calculated plane of regression.
3. It also helps to measure the general degree of accuracy of estimates made by reference to equation for the plane of regression.

## Karl Pearson's Coefficient of Correlation

Karl Pearson's coefficient of correlation helps to study the numerical expression and describes the extent to which the variables are related. This method of calculating coefficient of correlation (r) is based on covariance of the concerned variables. Thus Pearson's coefficient of correlation is devoted by the symbol (r). The formula for computing Pearson coefficient (r) is:

$r = \Sigma xy/N\ \sigma x \sigma y$

where

$$x = \overline{X - X},\ y = \overline{Y - Y}$$

$\Sigma xy$ = sum of the product of deviation in x and y series calculated with reference to their arithmetic means.

$\sigma x$ = standard deviation of the series X.
$\sigma y$ = standard deviation of the series Y.

A sample form of the above formula for application to practical problem is given as follows:

$\Sigma xy/\Sigma x2 * \Sigma y2$

where

$$x = \overline{X - X},\ y = \overline{Y - Y}$$

However the above formula can be used when only deviations x and y are from respective means and these are not in fractions. The various steps involved are as follows:

(i) Calculate means of the two series, i.e. X and Y.
(ii) Taking the deviation of X series from the mean of X and also the deviation of Y series from the mean of Y, indicated as x and y.
(iii) Square the deviations and obtain the sum of the respective squares of deviation, i.e $\Sigma x^2$ and $\Sigma y^2$.
(iv) Multiply the deviation of X and Y series and obtain the table, i.e $\Sigma xy$.

Substitute the values of $\Sigma xy$, $\Sigma x^2$ and $\Sigma y^2$ in the formula.

### *Limitations of Correlation*

The following are the limitations of correlation:

### *Normality*

Correlated series are affected by numerous causes thus, there may arise a possibility of normality.

### Causal Relationship

Cause and effects are responsible for Positive and Negative correlation between two independent variables. If there is no evidence of such cause and effect reason, then the existence of correlation is doubtful.

### Linear Nature

This is also a limitation that while knowing correlation it is to be assumed that there exists a linear relationship if these are plotted on a graph-paper then the picture will be like a straight line.

The existence of correlation always moves between +1 or –1, it cannot exceeds in any case more than +1.

Difficulty in Calculation of Probable Errors. Calculation of 'Y' is not easy, yet for drawing reliable result probable error be calculated which is again a difficult task.

Calculation of Standard Errors. It is always .6745 in normal distribution 50% value are covered in it thus, it is a test of significance of 'Y'.

### Correlation and Regression

Both the correlation and regression analysis helps us in studying the relationship between two variables, yet they differ in their approach, and objective.

Correlation studies are meant for studying the co-variation of the two variables. They tell us whether the variables under study move in the same direction or in reverse direction. The degree of their co-variation is also reflected in the correlation coefficient, but the correlation study does not study the nature of relationship. It does not tell us about the relative movement in the variables under study and we cannot predict the value of one variable by taking into account the value of the other variable. This is possible through regression analysis.

Correlation between two series is not necessarily a cause and effect relationship. A high degree of positive correlation between price and supply does not mean that, supply is the effect of price. There may be no cause and effect relationship between the variables under study and yet they may be correlated. Regression on the other hand presumes one variable as a cause and the other as its effect. The independent variable is supposed to be affecting the dependent variable and as such we can estimate the values of the dependent variable by projecting the relationship between them.

The coefficient of correlation varies between ±1. The regression coefficients have the same signs as the correlation coefficient. If r is positive, regression coefficients would also be positive and if r is negative, he regression coefficients would also be negative.

Further whereas correlation coefficient cannot exceed unity of the regression coefficients can have a value higher than unity but the product of the two regression coefficients can never exceed unit because r is the square root of the product of the two regression coefficients.

## Methods of studying Correlation

### 1. *Graphic Method*

The values of two variables are plotted with the same scale and axes individually against the same third variable. The points are then joined by straight lines. For example, yields office and rainfall for a number of years are plotted individually against the years for which they are measured on the horizontal axis. We will thus get two curves. If they are running parallel, we can conclude there is positive correlation and if they are running in opposite direction, they indicate negative correlation. This method cannot give us the idea about the degree of the correlation between them.

### 2. *Scatter Diagram*

Under this, simply the values are plotted and not joined by a line. If there is some width in the band of points it will indicate imperfect correlation. If the band slopes upwards, it indicates positive correlation and if it slopes downwards then it indicates negative correlation. When the points do not form a band i.e., they are scattered in all directions, it indicates that there is no correlation between the variables.

### 3. *Co-efficient of Correlation*

For the purpose of comparison and further analysis, it is necessary to get a numerical measure for the correlation between two variables. A relative measure of this type is given by Karl Pearson's coefficient of correlation; also known as the product-movement correlation coefficient.

## REGRESSION ANALYSIS

Regression analysis establishes a functional relationship, which is mathematical, showing dependence of one variable on the other. Regression literally means return to the normal, which is true on account of an average of relationship. It may cause and effect relationship. The word regression refers to an act of returning or going back. After establishing the fact about correlation, it become necessary to know the extend to which one variable varies in response to a given change in the other related variable. For example the provision of reference service is related to the number of staff members engaged on reference work. We can determine the number of reference librarians knowing the demand of reference service, this is known as regression.

According to M.M. Blair, "Regression" as the measure of the average relationship between two or more variable in the term of the original units of the data".

Wallis and Roberts, "It is often more important to find what the relation actually is, in order to estimate or predict one variable (the dependent variable) and the statistical technique appropriate in such a case is called regression analysis".

## Regression Lines

A Regression line refers to graphic method of regression analysis, if we take the case of X and Y variables, we shall have two regression lines as the regression of X on Y which indicates the most probable value of X for the given us most probable values of Y for the given values of X. These two lines through high on correlation between the two series i.e. when the value of r is equal to +1 or –1, two regression lines would coincide and overlap each other.

## Regression Equations

The line, which graphically describes the average relationship between the two variables, is called line of regression. The equation, which describes this line of regression mathematically, is known as regression equation. Examine methods of regression equation.

### *Regression Equation of Y on X*

The regression equation of Y on X is expressed as follows:

$$Yc = a + bX$$

In the above equation a and b constants. These constants are called the parameters of the line. The parameter 'a' determines the level of the fitted line where as parameter 'b' determines the slope of the line. The symbol Yc stand for the value of Y computed from the relationship for a given X.

Regression equation of X on Y

The regression equation of X on Y is expressed as follows:

$$Xc = a + by$$

The equation Xc = a + by hold good only when there are two observations. But we always have more than two observations in a series. The values of two parameters, as such should be computed by solving the following two normal equations simultaneously. Thus regression line of X on Y can be obtained when:

$$\Sigma X = Na + b\Sigma y$$
$$\Sigma XY = a\Sigma Y + b\Sigma y^2$$

where $\Sigma Y$, $\Sigma X$, $\Sigma Y^2$, $\Sigma XY$ are the respective totals and are computed from the observed values of X and Y, to which the estimated trends is to be fitted. The regression line of Y on X can be obtained when:

$$\Sigma Y = Na + b\Sigma x$$
$$\Sigma XY = a\Sigma X + b\Sigma x^2$$

From the above two regression equation we can compute the most probable values of X for the given values of Y, the most probable values of Y for the given values of X.

### Simple Regression

Simple regression analysis deals with one dependent variable and one independent variable. This is used to find out an unknown variable from the known variable. Estimation or Prediction is possible through the regression analysis.

### Multiple Regression

In multiple regression analysis which is a logical extension of two variable regression analysis instead of a single independent variable. Two or more independent variables are used to estimate the value of a dependent variable. Multiple regression analysis is a statistical technique that can be used to analyze the relationship between a single dependent (Criterion) variable and several independent (Predictor) variables. The multiple correlation and regression analysis serves highly useful purpose in practice.

### Objectives

(a) To derive an equation which provides estimates of the dependent variable from values of the two or more variables.

(b) To obtain a measure of the error involved in using this regression equation as a basis for estimation.

(c) To obtain a measure of the proportion of variance in the dependent variable accounted for or "explained by" the independent variables.

Multiple regression involving two independent variables will be shown as follows.

$$Y_c = a + b_1 X_1 + b_2 X_2$$

If there are three variables $X_1$, $X_2$ and $X_3$ the multiple regression equation of $X_1$ on $X_2$ and $X_3$ shall have the following form:

$$X_1 = a_{1.23} + b_{12.3} X_2 + b_{13.2} X_3$$

$X_1$ is the dependent variable and $X_2$ and $X_3$ are independent variables. The constant $a_{1.23}$ is the intercept made by the regression plane; it is zero when the regression line passes through the origin. The regression coefficients denoted by $b_{12.3}$ and $b_{13.2}$ represent the rate of change of the dependent variable per unit change in each of the independent variables when the other independent variables are held constant.

### Purpose of Multiple Regression

It is a general statistical technique that can be used to examine the relationship between a single dependent variable and a set of independent variables. The following are the purposes:

1. It helps to determine the appropriateness of using the regression procedure with the problem. The results obtained from the analysis may be interpreted in such a way as to suggest whether the application was appropriate.
2. To examine the statistical significance of the attempted a prediction.
3. To examine the strength of the association between the single dependent variable and the one or more independent variables. When co linearity among the independent variables is minimal (or has been removed by factor analysis), it helps to identify the extent to which each of the independent variables is related to the dependent variable.
4. To predict the values of one variable from the values of others.

### Usages of Multiple Regression in Prediction

In multiple regression we predict two variable, to assess the accuracy of the prediction examining the sum of the squared errors of prediction is done. It will serve to acquaint the essential meaning of regression analysis. Then we have to examine our predictive ability from a statistical viewpoint (as an estimator of population characteristics). To determine the appropriateness of predictive model, analysis of residuals (the difference between the observed values and the values our model predicts) is used in terms of:

- The linearity of the phenomenon measured.
- The constant variance of the errors terms.
- The independence of the error terms.
- The normality of the error term distribution.
- The addition of other variables.

## TEST OF SIGNIFICANCE OF REGRESSION ANALYSIS

Test of significance of multiple correlation coefficient by testing for the overall significance of the regression process by analysis of variance or F-ratio. We assume that there is no relationship between the dependent variable and the independent variables, taken collectively. In other words, our null hypothesis would be that the regression is not significant, so that:

$H_0$ : The regression is not significant
$H_1$ : The regression is significant

The null hypothesis is tested on the basis of the F-test and a decision is made whether to accept the null hypothesis or reject the null hypothesis.

$$F = \frac{\text{Explained Variance}}{\text{Unexplained Variance}}$$

(Note that this is explained variance and unexplained variance, and not explained variation and unexplained variation.) Where,

$$\text{Explained variance} = \frac{\text{Explained variation}}{\text{its degree of freedom}}$$

$$\text{And,} \quad \text{Unexplained variance} = \frac{\text{Unexplained variation}}{\text{its degree of freedom}}$$

(Explained variance is also known as variance due to regression and the unexplained variance is also known as the residual variance)

Now the degrees of freedom for the explained variation are (k–1), where k is the number of constants in the regression equation. Also (k) is equal to the number of total variables, so that (k–1) would be the number of independent variables. These degrees of freedom are also known as the *degrees of freedom in the numerator of the F-ratio.*

Similarly, the degrees of freedom for the unexplained variation are (n–k), where n as the *degrees of freedom in the denominator of the F-ratio.*

$$\text{Hence,} \quad F = \frac{\sum(\bar{Y}_c - Y)^2/(k-1)}{\sum(Y - Y_c)^2/(n-k)}$$

In the problem of the yearly food expenditures, that we have followed so far, let us find the value of the F-ratio. We have:

$$\text{Explained variation} = \sum\left(\frac{112.45/2}{1.05/3} - Y\right)^2 = 112.45$$

K = 3, so that (k–1) = 2

Unexplained variation = S $(Y–Yc)^2$ = 1.05

Now,

$$F = 56.225/0.35$$
$$= 160.64$$

Now, if we want to test the null hypothesis at á = 0.05 then we look at the critical value of F from the table at á = 0.05, with df for the numerator as = 2, and df for denominator being = 3.

Since our computed value of F is higher than the critical value of F at 0.05 level of significance, we cannot accept the null hypothesis. Hence, based upon this test, we can conclude that the regression is significant and the dependent variable and the independent variables are correlated. This correlation is significant because, the coefficient of correlation ($R^2_{y.12}$) was = 0.995. Thus the significance of coefficient can be tested by F-test

## CANONICAL ANALYSIS

Canonical correlation is considered to be the general model on which many other multivariate techniques are based. Canonical correlation places the fewest restrictions on the types of data on which it operates. Since the other techniques impose more rigid restrictions, it is generally believed that the information obtained from such techniques is of higher quality and may be presented in a more interpretable manner. For this reason many researcher view canonical correlation as a last-ditch effort to be used. When all other higher level techniques have been exhausted.

### Objectives

Canonical correlation analysis is the most generalized member of the family of multivariate statistical techniques (which include multiple correlation, regression and discriminant), and is directly related to principal components-type factor analytic models. The goal of canonical correlation is to determine the primary independent dimensions that relate one set of variables to another. The objectives are as follows;

1. Determining whether two sets of variables (measurements made on the same objects) are independent of one another or, conversely, determining the magnitude of the relationships that may exists between the two sets.
2. Deriving a set of weights for each set of criterion and predictor variables such that the linear combinations themselves are maximally correlated.
3. Deriving additional linear functions that maximize the remaining correlation, subject to being independent of the preceding set (or sets) of linear compounds.
4. Explaining the nature of whatever relationships exist between the sets of criterion and predictor variables, generally by measuring the relative contribution of each variable to the canonical functions (relationships) that are extracted.

### Application of Canonical Correlation

Canonical correlation is first focuses on the canonical functions and then on the output information.

### Deriving the Canonical Functions

The basic input data for canonical correlation analysis are two sets of variables. One set is defined as independent variable and the other set is defined as dependent variable. The underlying logic of canonical correlation involves the derivation of a linear combination of variables from each of the two sets of variables so that the correlation between the two linear combinations is maximized.

The application of canonical correlation does not stop with the derivation of a single relationship between the sets of variables. Instead, a number of pairs of linear combinations – referred to as canonical variates – may be derived. The maximum number of canonical variates (functions) that can be extracted from the sets of variables equals the number of variables in the smallest data set, independent or dependent. For example, when the research problem involves five independent (predictor) variables and three dependent (criterion) variables, the maximum number of canonical functions that can be extracted is three.

### Output Information from Canonical Analysis

The four most important types of output information derived through canonical correlation analysis are : (1) canonical variates, (2) the canonical correlations between the variates, (3) the statistical significance of the canonical correlations, and (4) the redundancy measure of shared variance for the canonical functions.

Each canonical function consists of a pair of variates, one for each of the subsets of variables entered into the analysis. In the other words, each canonical function has two variates, one representing the independent variables and the other the dependent variables. The canonical variates are interpreted on the basis of a set of correlation coefficients, usually referred to as canonical loadings or structure correlations. Two other types of information provided by a canonical analysis are the canonical correlations and their respective levels of statistical significance. The strength of the relationship between the pairs of variates is reflected by the canonical correlation. When squared, the canonical correlation represents the amount of variance in one canonical variate that is accounted for by the other canonical variate. This also may be referred as the amount of shared variance between the two canonical variates. Squared canonical correlations are referred to as canonical roots or. The last type of information of concern to us at this point is the redundancy measure of shared variance. The redundancy measure can be computed to provide additional information concerning the variance shared by the two sets of variables.

### Interpretation of Canonical Functions

Most canonical problems necessitate the use of computer; the analyst frequently must use whichever method is available in the standard statistical packages. The use of cross-loadings is the preferred approach and can be applied using the SAS statistical package. If the SAS package is not available, the analyst is forced either to compute the cross-loadings by hand or to select another method of interpretation, since none of the other popular statistical software packages provide this information. The widely used SPSS package provides canonical loadings, while the BMD package provides canonical weights.

### Limitations of Canonical Analysis

1. The canonical analysis reflects the variance shared by the linear composites of the sets of variables, not the variance extracted from the variables.
2. Canonical weights derived in computing canonical functions are subject to a great deal of instability.
3. Canonical weights are derived to maximize the correlation between linear composites, not the variance extracted.
4. It is difficult to identify meaningful relationships between the subsets of independent and dependent variables because precise statistics have not yet been developed to interpret canonical analysis.

## STAGES OF DATA ANALYSIS

The process of analysis begins after the data have been collected. The Exhibit entitled Overview of the Stages in the Data Analysis shows the interrelated steps involved in data reduction and analysis.

The goal of most research is to provide information. Information refers to a body of facts that are in a format suitable for decision making, whereas data are simply recorded measures of certain phenomena. The raw data collected in the field must be translated into information that will answer the business manager's questions. The conversion of raw data into information requires that the data be edited and coded so that they may be transferred to computer or other data storage media.

## EDITING

There are many errors, such as fieldworkers' erroneous recording of responses that must be dealt with before the data can be coded. Editing procedures are conducted to make the data ready for coding and transfer to data storage. Editing is the process of checking and adjusting the data for omissions, legibility, and consistency.

Coding is the assignment of categories or classifying symbols to previously edited data. Careful editing makes the coding job easier. When an editor discovers a problem, he or she adjusts the data to make it more complete, consistent, or readable.

*Field Editing:* Field supervisors are often responsible for conducting preliminary field editing on the same day as the interview. If a field edit is conducted at the end of the day, supervisors who edit completed questionnaires will frequently be able to question interviewers, who may be able to remember the interviews and correct the problem. The daily field edit also allows for possible recontacting of the respondents to fill in omissions.

*In-house editing:* Early reviewing of the data is not always possible. In such situations, in-house editing rigorously investigates the results of data collection. The research supplier or the research department normally has a centralized office staff to perform the editing and coding function.

*Editing for Consistency:* The in-house editor's task is to ensure that inconsistent or contradictory responses are adjusted to ensure that the answers will not be a problem for coders and keyboard operators. For example, the editor's task may be to eliminate an obviously incorrect sampling unit. The in-house editor must determine if the answers given by a respondent are consistent with other, related questions—the editor must use good judgment in correcting such inconsistencies.

*Editing for Completeness:* In some cases the respondent may have answered only one portion of a two-part question. Item non-response is the technical term for unanswered questions on an otherwise complete questionnaire. Specific decision rules for handling this problem should be meticulously outlined in the editor's instructions. If an editor finds a missing answer where there can be no missing values, he or she may insert an answer (plug value) according to such a predetermined rule. Another decision rule might be to randomly select an answer.

The editor must decide whether an entire questionnaire is "usable." When a questionnaire has too many answers missing, it may not be suitable for the planned data analysis.

Editing questions answered out of order: Another task faced by an editor may be to rearrange the answers given to an open-ended questionnaire. For example, the respondent may have provided the answer to a subsequent question in his or her comments to an earlier open-ended question. As a result, the interviewer may have avoided asking the subsequent question. To make the responses uniform with other questionnaires, the editor may move certain answers to the section related to the skipped question.

*Facilitating the Coding Process:* While all the previously described editing activities will help the coders, several editing procedures are specifically designed to simplify the coding process. Any such procedures should not be arbitrary, but should be based on a systematic procedure of fixed rules.

1. *Editing and tabulating "don't know" answers*: In many situations the respondent will answer, "don't know." On the surface, this response seems to suggest "no opinion." However, there may be reasons other than the legitimate "don't know" answer. The reluctant "don't know" is given when an individual simply does not want to answer a question. If the individual does not understand the question, he or she may give a confused "don't know" answer. The editor may try to identify the meaning of the "don't know" answer from other data provided on the questionnaire. How the editor deals with such an answer should be based on a systematic procedure.

2. *Mechanics of editing*: Edited data are frequently written in with a colored pencil. The original data are usually left in to permit a subsequent edit.
3. *Pretesting edit*: Editing the questionnaires during the pretest stage can prove to be very valuable. For example, certain changes in the questionnaire, such as increasing the space for an open-ended answer because respondents' answers in the pretest were longer than anticipated, will be appreciated during the actual analysis.
4. *Pitfalls of editing*: Subjectivity can easily enter into the editing process. To do a proper editing job the editor must be intelligent, experienced, and objective. A systematic procedure for assessing the questionnaires should be developed.

## CODING

The process of identifying and classifying each answer with a numerical score or other character symbol is called coding. Codes are generally considered to be numbered symbols; however, they are more broadly defined as rules for interpreting, classifying, and recording the data. Researchers organize coded data into fields, records, and files. A field is a collection of characters that represents a single type of data. A record is a collection of related fields, and a file is a collection of related records. Each research study is recorded in a file.

A. *The data Matrix:* A data matrix is a rectangular arrangement of data into rows and columns. For example, a data matrix from a secondary study investigating each state's population (in millions), average age, and automobile registration (per 1,000 people). Each row in the matrix represents one state. Each column represents a particular field. In our example, the columns represent variables that reflect data about each state. The intersection of a row and column indicates a place to enter a number or other code assigned to one state on a particular variable. Today the use of an on-line computer terminal for direct data entry is the most common input device for data storage.

B. *Code Construction:* When the question has a fixed-alternative (closed-ended) format, the number of categories requiring codes is determined during the questionnaire design stage. The codes "8" and "9" are conventionally given to the respective "don't know" and "no answer" responses.

There are two basic rules for code construction. First, the coding categories should be exhaustive; that is, coding categories should be provided for all subjects, objects, or responses. Second, the coding categories should be mutually exclusive and independent. There should be no overlap between the categories so that a subject or response can be placed in only one category. This frequently requires that an "other" code category be included to ensure that the categories are all inclusive and mutually exclusive.

When a questionnaire is highly structured, the categories may be precoded before the data are collected. In many cases, such as when researchers are using open-ended response questions, a framework for classifying responses to questions cannot be established before data collection. This situation requires *post coding*, or simply coding.

## Coding Open-Ended Response Questions

The usual reason for using open-ended questions is that the researcher has no clear hypotheses regarding the answers, which will be numerous and varied. Code construction in these situations necessarily must reflect the judgment of the researcher.

A major objective in the code building process is to accurately transfer the meaning from written responses to numeric codes. Experienced researchers recognize that the key idea in this process is that code building is based on thoughts, not just words. The end result of code building should be a list, in an abbreviated and orderly form.

Differentiating categories of answers for the coding of open-ended questions is more difficult than that for fixed-alternative questions and is somewhat of an art. Researchers generally perform test tabulation. The test tabulation is a small sample of the total number of replies to a particular question. Its purpose is preliminary identification of the stability and distribution of the answers that will determine how to set-up a coding scheme.

The second stage after tabulating the basic responses is to determine how many answer categories will be acceptable. This will be influenced by the purpose of the study and limitations of the computer program or storage medium.

A. *Codes should not be too elaborate:* The coding scheme should not be too elaborate. The coder's task is to summarize the data. A preliminary scheme having too many categories can always be collapsed or reduced at a later time in the analysis. If initial coding is too abstract and only a few categories are established, revising the codes will be difficult. Experienced coder's group answers under generalized headings that are pertinent to the research question. The coding of open-ended questions is a very complex issue.

B. *Code book:* Up to this point, it has been implied that each code's position in the data matrix has already been determined. However, this plan generally occurs after the coding scheme has been designed for every question. The code book identifies each variable in the study and its location on the computer card(s), or other input medium. With the code book the researcher can identify any variable's description, code name, and field. Researchers commonly identify individual respondents by giving each an identification number or questionnaire number.

C. *Production coding:* The actual process of transferring the data from the questionnaire or data collection form after the data have been collected is called production coding. Codes may be written directly on the instrument or on a special coding sheet, which is on 80-column ruled paper that is a facsimile of the data matrix. The coding should be done in a central location so that a supervisor may solve interpretation problems. The value of training coders should not be overlooked.

*Editing and coding combined:* Frequently certain editing functions will be performed by the person coding the questionnaire.

### Example for Coding

Comment on the coding scheme for the following: In which of these groups did your total family income, from all sources, fall last year—before taxes, that is? Just tell me the code number.

| *Response* | *Code* |
|---|---|
| Under Rs. 4,000 | 01 |
| Rs. 4,000 to Rs. 9,999 | 02 |
| Rs. 10,000 to Rs. 14,999 | 03 |
| Rs. 15,000 to Rs. 19,999 | 04 |
| Rs. 20,000 to Rs. 29,999 | 05 |
| Rs. 30,000 to Rs. 39,999 | 06 |
| Rs. 40,000 to Rs. 59,999 | 07 |
| Rs. 60,000 to Rs. 79,999 | 08 |
| Rs. 80,000 to Rs. 99,999 | 09 |
| Rs. 100,000 or over | 10 |
| Refused to answer | 11 |
| Don't know | 98 |
| No answer | 99 |

This coding seems adequate. Each response has a clear code and the "don't know" (98) and "no answer" (99) are assigned traditional codes.

Suppose the following information had been gathered about the occupations of several respondents. How would you classify the following respondents' answers in the occupational coding scheme in the chapter: plumber, butcher, retail sales, X-ray technician, and veterinarian.

Plumber (craftsmen, foremen, and kindred workers).

Butcher (operative).

*Retail sales:* This is a tough one. Most students will pick sales workers rather than clerical and kindred workers. However, counter clerks, identified as clerical, is the classification for retail sales. This should give the instructor a springboard for discussing the difficulty of coding occupation, especially when there is such a wide variety of sales jobs.

X-ray technician (professional, technical, and kindred workers); All health technologists (dental hygienists, therapy assistants) fit this category. Health administrators are classified as managers; Veterinarian (professional, technical, and kindred workers).

## TABULATION

### Meaning

Tabulation is the process of summarizing raw data and displaying it in compact form for further analysis. Analysis of data is made possible through tables. Preparing tables is a very important step. Tabulation may be by hand, mechanical, or electronic. The choice is made largely on the basis of the size and type of study, alternative costs, time pressures, and the availability of computers and computer programs. If the number of questionnaire is small, and their length short, hand tabulation is enough.

### Parts of a Table

Generally a research table has the following parts:

a. Table number,
b. Title of the table,
c. Caption,
d. Stub (row heading),
e. Body,
f. Head note, and
g. Footnote.

### Table Number

Each table should be numbered. There are different practices with regard to the place where this number is to be given. The number may be given either in the center at the top above the title or in the side of the table at the top or at the bottom of the table on the left-hand side. However, if space permits the table number should be given in the center. Where there are many columns, it is also desirable to number each column so that easy reference to it is possible.

### Title of the Table

Every table must have a suitable title. The title is a description of the contents of the table. A complete title has to answer the questions what, where and when in that sequence. In other words,

What precisely are the data in the table (i.e., what categories of statistical data are shown)?

Where the data occurred (i.e., the precise geographical, political or physical area covered)?

When the data occurred (i.e., the specific time or period covered by the statistical material on the table)?

### Caption

Caption refers to the column headings. It explains what the column represents. It may consist of one or more column headings. Under a column heading there may be sub-heads. The caption should be clearly-defined and placed at the middle of the column.

### Stub

As distinguished from caption, stubs are the designation of the rows or row headings. They are at the extreme left ad perform the same function for the horizontal rows or numbers in the table as the column headings do for the vertical columns or numbers. The stubs are usually wider than column headings but should be kept as narrow as possible without sacrificing precision and clarity of statements.

### Body

The body of the table contains the numerical information. This is the most vital part of the table. Data presented in the body arranged according to descriptions are classifications of the captions and stubs.

### Head Note

It is a brief explanatory statement applying to all or a major part of the material in the table, and is placed below the title entered and enclosed in brackets. It is used to explain certain points relating to the whole table that have been included neither in the title nor in the captions or stubs.

### Footnotes

Anything in a table, which, the reader may find difficult to understand from the title, captions and the stubs should be explained in footnotes. If footnotes are needed, they are placed directly below the body of the table. Footnotes are used for four main purposes:

a. To point out any exceptions as to the basis of arriving at the data.
b. Any special circumstances affecting the data, for example, strike, lockout, fire, etc.
c. To clarify anything in the table.
d. To give the source in case of secondary data.

## TYPES OF TABLES

Tables are of different types. They are listed on the next page.

### (a) Simple Table

This is made on the basis of just one quality or characteristics. Hence it is called one-way table. Examples of such tabulation are the classification of states on the basis of population, distribution of students on the basis of subjects of their study, etc.

**Number of Employees According to Age Group**

| *Age in years* | *Number of Employees* |
|---|---|
| Below 25 | 50 |
| 25 - 35 | 67 |
| 35 - 45 | 43 |
| 45 - 55 | 15 |
| 55 and above | 5 |
| Total | 180 |

### (b) Complex Table

This is formed on the basis of more than one quality or characteristic- e.g. distribution of students on the basis of sex and marks obtained, etc. If complex table is based on two qualities, it is called two-way table and if it is based on three qualities, it is called three-way table. If it is based on more than three qualities, it is called manifold table.

**Number of Employees According to Age and Sex**

| *Age in Years* | *Males* | *Females* | *Total* |
|---|---|---|---|
| Below 25 | 32 | 18 | 50 |
| 25 - 30 | 40 | 27 | 67 |
| 35 - 45 | 25 | 18 | 43 |
| 45 - 55 | 10 | 5 | 15 |
| 55 and above | 5 | — | 5 |
| Total | | | 180 |

### (c) General-purpose Tables

General-purpose tables, also known as the reference tables or repository tables, provide information for general use or reference. They usually contain detailed information and are not constructed for specific discussion. In other words, these tables serve as a repository of information and are arranged for easy reference. Tables published by governmental agencies are mostly of this kind, such as the tables contained in the Statistical Abstract of the Indian Union, detailed tables tell facts which are not for particular discussion. When a researcher uses such tables, they are usually placed in the appendix of the report for easy reference.

### (d) Special-purpose Tables

Special-purpose tables, also known as summary or analytical tables, provide information for particular discussion. They show relationship between different groups of figures. When attached to a report they are found in the body of the text. These tables are also called derivative tables since they are often derived from general tables. Thus the large detailed tables in the census records of the Government of India are general-purpose tables. When such data are used, they are ordinarily taken from the general-purpose tables and presented as special-purpose tables, which emphasize the relation the user wishes to stress.

## Methods of Tabulation

### *Manual Tabulation*

If the survey has used a small sample and a limited number of cross tabulations, it is probably more efficient to tabulate manually than by machine.

### *Mechanical Tabulation*

In large studies with many cross tabulations of a two dimensional, three-dimensional, and four-dimensional nature, questionnaires must be prepared for machine tabulation.

### *Electronic Data Processing*

In many involved tabulations where a number of multiple correlations must be determined, it is sometimes more efficient to put survey data on a computer. However, this does not save money or time if the tabulations involve a "one-shot" study. On the other hand, studies of a continuing nature, such as retail audits, are particularly amenable to electronic data processing.

## CHARTS

One of the most convincing and appealing ways in which data may be presented is through charts. Evidence of this can be found in the financial pages of newspapers, journals, advertisements, etc. Pictorial presentation helps in quick understanding of the data. A picture is said to be worth 10,000 words, i.e., through pictorial presentation data can be presented in an interesting form. Charts have greater memorising effect as the impressions created by them last much longer than those created by the figures. A chart can take the shape of either diagram or graph. For the sake of clarity we will discuss them under two separate heads:

- Diagrams, and
- Graphs.

## Diagrams

For representing data, diagrams are more commonly used than graphs. General Rules for constructing Diagrams:

## General Rules to be Observed while Constructing Diagrams

### *Title*

Every diagram must be given a suitable title. The title should convey in as few words ad possible the main idea that the diagram is intended to portray.

### *Proportion Between Width and Height*

A proper proportion between the height and the width of the diagram should be maintained. If either the height or the width were too short or too long in proportion, the diagram would give an ugly look.

### *Selection of Appropriate Scale*

The scale showing the values should be in even numbers or in multiples of 5 or 10, example, 25, 50, 75 or 20, 40, 60. Odd values like 1, 3, 5, 7 should be avoided. No rigid rules can be laid down about the selection of appropriate scale.

### *Footnotes*

In order to clarify certain points about the diagram, footnotes may be given at the bottom of the diagram.

### *Index*

,An index illustrating different types of lines or different shades, colors, should be given so that the reader can easily make out the meaning of the diagram.

### *Neatness and Cleanliness*

Diagrams should be absolutely neat and clean.

### *Simplicity*

Diagrams should be as simple as possible so that the reader can understand their meaning clearly. For the sake of simplicity, it is important that too much material should not be loaded in a single diagram.

## TYPES OF DIAGRAMS

Different types of Diagrams are divided under the following heads:

1. One-dimensional diagrams, e.g., bar diagrams.
2. Two-dimensional diagrams, e.g., rectangles, squares and circles.
3. Pictograms and cartograms.

Each of these types is discussed below in detail.

## 1. One-Dimensional or Bar Diagrams

Bar diagrams is the most common type of diagrams used in practice. A bar is a thick line whose width is shown merely for attention. They are called one-dimensional because it is only the length of the bar that matters and not the width. When the number of observations is large, lines may be drawn instead of bars to economies space. Special merits of bar diagrams are the following:

1. They are readily understood.
2. They possess the outstanding advantage that they are the simplest and the easiest to make.
3. When a large number of observations are to be compared they are the only form that can be used effectively.

### Types of Bar Diagrams

Bar diagrams are of the following types:

a. Simple bar diagrams
b. Sub-divided bar diagrams
c. Multiple bar diagrams
d. Percentage bar diagrams
e. Deviation bars
f. Broken bars

#### *Simple Bar Diagrams*

A simple bar diagram is used to represent only one variable. For example the figures of scales, production, population etc., for various years may be shown by means of a simple bar diagrams. Since the bars are of the same width and only the length varies, it becomes very easy for the reader to study the relationship.

#### *Sub-Divided Bar Diagrams*

These diagrams are used to represent various parts of the total. For example, the number of employees in various departments of a company may be represented by a sub-divided bar diagrams. While constructing such a diagram, the various components in ach bar should be kept in the same order.

#### *Multiple Bar Diagrams*

In multiple bar diagrams two or more sets of inter-related data are represented. The technique of drawing such a diagram is the same as that of simple bar diagram. The only difference is that since more than one phenomenon is represented, different shades, colours, dots, or crossings are used to distinguish between the bars.

### *Deviation Bars*

Deviation bars are popularly used for representing net quantities—excess of deficit, i.e., net profit, net loss, net exports or imports, etc. Such bars can have both positive and negative values. Positive values are shown above the base line and negative values below it.

## 2. Two-Dimensional Diagrams

As distinguished from one-dimensional diagrams in which only the length of the bars is taken in to account, in two-dimensional diagrams the length as well as the width of the bars is considered. Thus the area of the bar represents the given data. Two-dimensional diagrams are also known as surface diagrams or area diagrams. The important types of such diagrams are:

(A) Rectangles,
(B) Squares, and
(C) Circles.

### *Rectangles*

This form is quite popular. Since the area of a rectangle is equal to the product of its length and width, while constructing such a diagram both the length and width are considered. When two sets of figures are to be represented by rectangles, either of the two methods may be adopted. We may represent the figures as they are given or may convert them to percentages and then subdivide the length in to various components. The latter method is more popular than the former as it enables comparison to be made on a percentage basis.

### *Squares*

The rectangular method of diagrammatic presentation is difficult to use where the values of items vary widely. The method of drawing a square diagram is very simple. One has to take the square root of the values of various items that are to be shown in the diagram and then select a suitable scale to draw the squares.

### *Circles*

Another way of preparing a two dimensional diagram is in the form of circles. In such diagrams both the total and the component parts or sectors can be shown. The area of a circle is proportional to the square of its radius. Circles can be used in all those cases in which squares are used.

### *PIE Diagram*

This type of diagram enables us to show the partitioning of a total in to component parts. A very common use of the pie chart is to represent the division of a sum of money in to its components. For example, the entire circle, or pie, may represent the budget of a family for a month and the sections may represent portions of the budget allotted to rent, food, clothing and so on. Similarly, through a pie diagram we can show how a rupee spent by a firm is distributed over various heads such as wages, raw materials, administration expenses, etc.

## 3. Pictograms and Cartograms

### Pictograms

Pictograms, also known as picture grams, are very popularly used in presenting statistical data. They are not abstract presentations such as lines or bars, but really depict the kind of data we are dealing with. Pictures are attractive and easy to comprehend and as such this method is particularly useful in presenting statistics to the layman. The picture symbol should be self-explanatory in nature, i.e., it should represent clearly the phenomena.

### Cartograms

Cartograms or statistical maps are used to give quantitative information on geographical basis. They are thus used to represent special distribution. The quantities on the map can be shown in many ways, such as, through shades of colours, by dots, by placing pictograms in each geographical unit and by placing the appropriate numerical figure in each geographical unit.

## GRAPHS

A large variety of graphs are in practical use. However, we shall discuss only some important ones, which are more popularly used in practice. Broadly the various graphs can be divided under the following two heads:

1. Graphs of time series or line graphs.
2. Graphs of frequency distribution.

### Graphs of Time Series or Line Graphs

When we observe the values of a variable at different points of time the series so formed is known as the time series. The technique of graphic presentation is extremely helpful in analyzing changes at different points of time. On the X-axis we generally take the time and on the Y-axis the value of the variable and join the various points by straight lines. The graph so formed is known as line graph. Such graphs are most widely used in practice. They are simplest to understand, easiest to make and most same graph and a comparison can be made.

### Graphs of Frequency Distributions

A frequency distribution can be presented graphically in any of the following ways:

1. Histogram.
2. Frequency Polygon.
3. Smoothed frequency curve.
4. Cumulative frequency curves or 'Ogives'.

### *Histogram*

Out of several methods of presenting a frequency distribution graphically, histogram or the column diagram, as it is sometimes called, is the most popular and widely used in practice. The statistical meaning of histogram is that it is graph that represents the class frequencies in a frequency distribution by vertical adjacent rectangles. A histogram is a graphical method for presenting data, where the observations are located on a horizontal axis (usually grouped in to intervals) and the frequency of those observations is depicted along the vertical axis.

### *Frequency Polygon*

A frequency polygon is a graph of frequency distribution. It has more than four sides. It is particularly effective in comparing two or more frequency distributions. There are two ways in which a frequency polygon may be considered:

We may draw a histogram of the given data and then join by straight lines the midpoints of the upper horizontal side of each rectangle with the adjacent ones. The figure so formed is called the frequency polygon.

Another method of constructing frequency polygon is to take the midpoints of the various class intervals and then plot the frequency corresponding to each point and to join all these points by straight lines. The figure obtained would exactly be the same as obtained by method No. 1. The only difference is that here we do not have to construct a histogram.

### *Smoothed Frequency Curve*

A smoothed frequency curve can be drawn through the various points of the polygon. The curve is drawn freehand in such a manner that the area included under the curve is approximately the same as that of the polygon. The object of drawing a smoothed frequency curve is to eliminate as far as possible all accidental variations that might be present in the data. While smoothing a frequency polygon the fact that it really derived from the histogram should always be kept in mind. This would imply that the top of the curve would overtop the highest point of the polygon particularly when the magnitude of class interval is large. The curve should look as regular as possible and all sudden turns should be avoided.

### *Cumulative Frequency Curves or 'Ogives'*

Sometimes one needs to know the answers to questions like 'how many workers of a factory earn more than Rs. 1,500 per month' or 'how many workers earn less than Rs. 1,200 per month'. To answer these questions it is a necessary to add the frequencies. When frequencies are added, they are called cumulative frequencies. These frequencies are then listed in a table called a cumulative frequency table. The graph of such a distribution is called a cumulative frequency curve or an Ogive (pronounced Ojive).

There are two methods of constructing Ogive, namely:

The 'less than' method, and
The 'more than' method.

*'Less than' method:* In the 'less than' method we start with the upper limits of the classes and go on adding the frequencies. When these frequencies are plotted we get a declining curve.

*'More than' method:* In the 'more than' method we start with the lower limits of the classes and from the total frequencies we subtract the frequency of each class. When these frequencies are plotted we get a declining curve.

## COMPUTERIZED DATA PROCESSING

*Input medium:* Most studies having large sample sizes use a computer for data processing. Technological changes now offer researchers several alternative means of putting data into the computer. A research study using computer-assisted telephone interviewing or a self-administered Internet questionnaire with direct data entry can automatically store and tabulate responses as they are collected. Direct data capture substantially reduces clerical errors that occur during the editing and coding process. A research system using on-line direct data entry equipment can reduce a three-to-four week research study to a few days. Also, for highly structured questionnaires, optical scanning systems may be used to directly read material from marked sensed questionnaires onto magnetic tape.

*Data entry (keyboarding):* The process of transforming data from a research project, such as answers to a survey questionnaire, to computers is referred to as data conversion. As computers have become more sophisticated, data entry is either instantaneous, or converted to magnetic media for storage. When data are not directly entered into the computer the moment they are collected, data processing for the computer begins with keyboarding. This keyboard equipment transfers coded data from the questionnaires or coding sheets onto a magnetic tape or floppy disk. However, keyboard operators may make errors. To ensure 100 percent accuracy, the job is verified by a second keyboard operator who checks the accuracy of the data entered. Keyboard operators prefer to have the data on coding sheets so that they do not have to page through the questionnaire to punch the data. However, this usually increases the time and effort required for coding. The particular resources of the project will dictate which source is used as input to the keyboard operators

## MEASURES OF CENTRAL TENDENCY

The value or the figure which represents the whole series is neither the lowest value in the series nor the highest it lies somewhere between these two extremes, that is in the centre of the series or the distribution, where most of the items of the series tend to cluster. Because of this tendency towards the centre of the distribution the value are called the measures of Central Tendency.

Simpson and Kafka defined it as "A measure of central tendency is a typical value around which other figures congregate".

Waugh has expressed "An average stand for the whole group of which it forms a part yet represents the whole".

### Types of Averages

The following are the various types of common averages used in statistical analysis.

1. Arithmetic mean
2. Median
3. Mode
4. Geometric mean
5. Harmonic mean

### Arithmetic mean

Arithmetic mean is a mathematical average and it is the most popular measures of central tendency. The arithmetic mean is frequently referred to simply as the "mean".

Mean of a series is the simplest and the most widely used of all the measures of averages. It is obtained by dividing sum of the values of all observations in a series (Sx) by the number of items (N) constituting the series.

Thus, mean of a set of numbers $X_1, X_2, \ldots X_n$.

$$\therefore \text{Mean} = \frac{\text{Sum of the items}}{\text{number of items}} = \frac{\Sigma X}{N}$$

where

X = Mean
X = Sum of items in a series
N = Number of observations

### Calculate the Arithmetic Mean

Calculate the Arithmetic mean of the daily Book issues of the College Libraries in a certain district:

Total number of book issues = 1423
Total number of libraries = 10

$$\therefore \text{Mean} = \frac{\text{Sum of the items}}{\text{number of items}} = \frac{\Sigma X}{N} = 1423/10 = 142.3$$

## Merits of Mean

(i) It is rigidly defined.
(ii) It is easy to understand the arithmetic average even if some of the details of the data are lacking.
(iii) It is not based on the position in the series.
(iv) It gives weight to all items in direct proportion to their size.

## Demerits of Mean

(i) It cannot be located through a frequency graph nor obtained by inspection.
(ii) It may lead to fallacious conclusion if the details of the data are not given.
(iii) It can ignore any single item only at the risk of losing its accuracy.
(iv) It cannot be employed in the study of qualitative phenomenon.
(v) It is very mush affected by extreme values.

## Median

Median is a central value of the distribution, or the value, which divides the distribution in two equal parts, each part containing equal number of items. Thus it is the central value of the variable, when the values are arranged in order of magnitude. The various definitions of median are given below.

Connor has defined, as "The median is that value of the variable which divides the group into two equal parts, one part comprising of all values greater, and the other all values less than median".

Kenney and Keeping have defined it as "the central value of the distribution, a value such that greater and smaller values occur with equal frequency".

Secrist has expressed, as "Median of a series is the value of the items as actual estimated when a series is arranged in order of magnitude which divides the distribution into two parts".

According to Bowley, "if a number of the group are ranked in order to the measurement under consideration, then the measurement of the number most nearly one half is the median".

Let the annual circulation of books in seven College libraries be 10001, 10500, 11000, 11800, 12300, 13567, 15987. The middle value of this series of number is 12300. This is the Median of this distribution, that is the median for circulation of Books in the seven college libraries.

In the calculation of median, there are two stages:

(i) The search for the middle items which is located by the size of {N + ½} or $N^{th}$ item.
(ii) The value of this middle item is the median value.

### Calculation of Median—Discrete series

Step:

(i) Arrange the data in ascending or descending order.
(ii) Calculate the cumulative frequencies.
(iii) Apply the formula.

Median = Size of $(N + 1)/2^{th}$ item.

### Calculation of median—Continuous series

For calculation of median in a continuous frequency distribution the following formula will be employed. Algebraically,

Median = L + (N/2 – c.f/f) i
L = lower limit of median
f = frequency of median class
c.f = cumulative frequency
i = class interval of the median class

### Mode

Mode is the third type of average. It is denoted by the capital letter Z. it is defined as that value of the item in a series, which occur frequently, i.e. greatest number of times. Mode is defined by;

Croxton and Cowden: "the mode of a distribution is the value at the point armed with the item tend to be most heavily concentrated. It may be regarded as the most typical of a series of value".

Zizek has defined mode in the following words: "The value which occurs most frequently in a series (or group) of items and around which the other items are distributed most densely".

An important thing to note about mode is that it shows the center of concentration of the frequency in and around a given value. Its importance is very great in library science studies where a librarian is interested in knowing about the size, which has the highest concentration of items. It is also helpful in making a choice of approximate sizes, which must be ordered for.

The mode is the most frequently occurring value in the data set. For example, in the data set {1, 2, 3, 4, 4}, the mode is equal to 4. A data set can have more than a single mode, in which case it is multimodal. In the data set {1, 1, 2, 3, 3} there are two modes: 1 and 3.

The exact value of mode can be obtained by the following formula:

$$Z = L_1 + (\Delta_1 / \Delta_1 + \Delta_2)\ i$$

where

$Z$ = mode
$L_1$ = lower limit of the modal class
$i$ = the size of the class interval of the modal class

$\Delta_1$ = the difference between the frequencies in the modal class and the premodal class,
$\Delta_2$ = the difference between the frequencies in the modal class and the post modal class

$\Delta_1 = f_1 - f_o$
$\Delta_2 = f_1 - f_2$

$f_1$ = frequency of the modal class
$f_o$ = frequency of the class preceding the modal class
$f_2$ = frequency of the class succeeding the modal class

## Merits of Mode

(i) Mode is readily comprehensible and easily calculated.
(ii) It is the best representative of data.
(iii) It is not at all affected by extreme value.
(iv) The value of mode can also be determined graphically.
(v) It is usually an actual value of an important part of the series.

## Demerits of Mode

(i) It is not based on all observations.
(ii) It is not capable of further mathematical manipulation.
(iii) Mode is affected to a great extent by sampling fluctuations.
(iv) Choice of grouping has great influence on the value of mode.

It is therefore, said the mode is the most unstable average and its true value is difficult to determine. Moreover, the value of the mode is affected significantly by the size of the class intervals used in grouping data into a frequency distribution. A change in the size of the class intervals will change the value of the mode.

## Geometric Mean

The geometric mean, in *mathematics*, is a type of *mean* or *average*, which indicates the central tendency or typical value of a set of numbers. It is similar to the *arithmetic mean*, which is what most people think of with the word "average," except that instead of adding the set of numbers and then dividing the sum by the count of numbers in the set, *n*, the numbers are multiplied and then the *nth root* of the resulting *product* is taken.

For instance, the geometric mean of two numbers, say 2 and 8, is just the square root (i.e., the second root) of their product, 16, which is 4. As another example, the geometric mean of 1, ½, and ¼ is the cube root (i.e., the third root) of their product (0.125), which is ½.

The geometric mean can be understood in terms of *geometry*. The geometric mean of two numbers, *a* and *b*, is simply the side length of the *square* whose area is equal to that of a *rectangle* with side lengths *a* and *b*. That is, what is *n* such that $n^2 = a \times b$? Similarly, the geometric mean of three numbers, *a*, *b*, and *c*, is the side length of a cube whose volume is the same as that of a *rectangular prism* with side lengths equal to the three given numbers.

The geometric mean only applies to positive numbers.[1] It is also often used for a set of numbers whose values are meant to be multiplied together or are exponential in nature, such as data on the growth of the *human population* or interest rates of a financial investment. The geometric mean is also one of the three classic *Pythagorean means*, together with the aforementioned arithmetic mean and the *harmonic mean*.

The geometric mean of a data set $[a_1, a_2, ..., a_n]$ is given by

$$\left(\prod_{i=1}^{n} a_i\right)^{1/n} = \sqrt[n]{a_1 - a_2 .....a_n}$$

The geometric mean of a data set *is less than or equal to* the data set's *arithmetic mean* (the two means are equal if and only if all members of the data set are equal). This allows the definition of the *arithmetic-geometric mean*, a mixture of the two which always lies in between.

The geometric mean is also the arithmetic-harmonic mean in the sense that if two sequences $(a_n)$ and $(h_n)$ are defined:

$$a_{n+1} = \frac{a_n + h_n}{2}, a_o = x$$

and

$$h_{n+1} = \frac{2}{\frac{1}{a_n} + \frac{1}{h_n}}, h_o = y$$

then $a_n$ and $h_n$ will converge to the geometric mean of $x$ and $y$.

## Harmonic Mean

In mathematics, the harmonic mean (formerly sometimes called the subcontrary mean) is one of several kinds of average. Typically, it is appropriate for situations when the average of rates is desired.

The harmonic mean $H$ of the positive real numbers $x_1, x_2, \ldots, x_n$ is defined to be:

$$H = \frac{n}{\frac{1}{x_1} + \frac{1}{x_2} + \ldots + \frac{1}{x_n}} = \frac{n}{\sum_{i=1}^{n} 1/x_i}, \; x_i > 0 \text{ for all } i.$$

Equivalently, the harmonic mean is the *reciprocal* of the *arithmetic mean* of the reciprocals.

A geometric construction of the three *Pythagorean means* (of two numbers only). Harmonic mean denoted by $H$ in purple colour.

The harmonic mean is one of the three *Pythagorean means*. For all data sets *containing at least one pair of nonequal values*, the harmonic mean is always the least of the three, while the *arithmetic mean* is always the greatest of the three and the *geometric mean* is always in between. (If all values in a nonempty dataset are equal, the three means are always equal to one another; e.g. the harmonic, geometric, and arithmetic means of {2, 2, 2} are all 2.)

It is the special case $M_1$ of the *power mean*.

Since the harmonic mean of a list of numbers tends strongly toward the least elements of the list, it tends (compared to the arithmetic mean) to mitigate the impact of large outliers and aggravate the impact of small ones.

The arithmetic mean is often incorrectly used in places calling for the harmonic mean.[1] In the speed example below for instance the arithmetic mean 50 is incorrect, and too big.

## Harmonic Mean of Two Numbers

For the special case of just two numbers $x_1$ and $x_2$, the harmonic mean can be written

$$H = \frac{2x_1 x_2}{x_1 + x_2}$$

In this special case, the harmonic mean is related to the *arithmetic mean* $A = (x_1 + x_2)/2$ and the *geometric mean* $G = \sqrt{x_1 x_2}$ by

$$H = \frac{G^2}{A}$$

So $G = \sqrt{AH}$, which means the geometric mean, for two numbers, is the geometric mean of the arithmetic mean and the harmonic mean.

Calculte harmonic mean from the following data :

| *Marks* | *Frequency* |
|---|---|
| 0-10 | 7 |
| 10-20 | 10 |
| 20-30 | 5 |
| 30-40 | 3 |
| 40-50-2 | |

## Solution

| *Marks* | *F* | *Mid Point m* | *1/m* | *Fx1/m* |
|---|---|---|---|---|
| 0-10 | 7 | 5 | 0.20000 | 1.00000 |
| 10-20 | 10 | 15 | 0.0666 | 0.66667 |
| 20-30 | 5 | 25 | 0.04000 | 0.2800 |
| 30-40 | 3 | 35 | 0.2857 | 0.08571 |
| 40-50 | 2 | 45 | 0.02222 | 0.04444 |
| | N=27 | Σ(f × 1/m) = 2.07682 | | |

**Harmonic Mean** $= \frac{N}{\Sigma(f \times 1/m)} = 27\ /2.07682 = 13$

## THE CHI-SQUARE TESTS

The chi –square(chi, the Greek letter pronounced "kye") test is one of the most commonly used tests of significance. The test is used in assessing the goodness of fit of the theoretical distribution to the observed frequency distribution and for the test of independence of attributes, when the frequencies are presented in a two-way classification. The chi- square (x2) distribution is a continuous probability distribution and is skewed to the right.

Data used in a chi-square analysis has to satisfy the following conditions:

- Randomly drawn from the population,
- Reported in raw counts of frequency,
- Measured variables must be independent,
- Observed frequencies cannot be too small, and
- Values of independent and dependent variables must be mutually exclusive.

There are two types of chi-square test:

- *The Chi-square test for goodness of fit* which compares the expected and observed values to determine how well an experimenter's predictions fit the data.
- *The Chi-square test for independence,* which compares two sets of categories to determine whether the two groups are distributed differently among the categories. (McGibbon, 2006)

## The Goodness-of-Fit Test

One of the more interesting goodness-of-fit applications of the chi-square test is to examine issues of fairness and cheating in games of chance, such as cards, dice, and roulette. Since such games usually involve wagering, there is significant incentive for people to try to rig the games and allegations of missing cards, "loaded" dice, and "sticky" roulette wheels are all too common.

So how can the goodness-of-fit test be used to examine cheating in gambling? It is easier to describe the process through an example. Take the example of dice. Most dice used in wagering have six sides, with each side having a value of one, two, three, four, five, or six. If the die being used is fair, then the chance of any particular number coming up is the same: 1 in 6. However, if the die is loaded, then certain numbers will have a greater likelihood of appearing, while others will have a lower likelihood.

One night at the Tunisian Nights Casino, renowned gambler Jeremy Turner (a.k.a. The Missouri Master) is having a fantastic night at the craps table. In two hours of playing, he's racked up $30,000 in winnings and is showing no sign of stopping. Crowds are gathering around him to watch his streak—and The Missouri Master is telling anyone within earshot that his good luck is due to the fact that he's using the casino's lucky pair of "bruiser dice", so named because one is black and the other blue.

Unbeknownst to Turner, however, a casino statistician has been quietly watching his rolls and marking down the values of each roll, noting the values of the black and blue dice separately. After 60 rolls, the statistician has become convinced that the blue die is loaded.

### Value on Blue Die, Observed Frequency and Expected Frequency

| *Value on Blue Die* | *Observed Frequency* | *Expected Frequency* |
|---|---|---|
| 1 | 16 | 10 |
| 2 | 5 | 10 |
| 3 | 9 | 10 |
| 4 | 7 | 10 |
| 5 | 6 | 10 |
| 6 | 17 | 10 |
| Total | 60 | 60 |

At first glance, this table would appear to be strong evidence that the blue die was, indeed, loaded. There are more 1's and 6's than expected, and fewer than the other numbers. However, it's possible that such differences occurred by chance. The chi-square statistic can be used to estimate the likelihood that the values observed on the blue die occurred by chance.

The key idea of the chi-square test is a comparison of observed and expected values. How many of something were expected and how many were observed in some process? In this case, we would expect 10 of each number to have appeared and we observed those values in the left column.

With these sets of figures, we calculate the chi-square statistic as follows:

$$x^2 = \sum \frac{(\text{observed} \times \text{frequency} - \text{expected} \times \text{frequency})^2}{(\text{expected} \times \text{frequency})}$$

Using this formula with the values in the table above gives us a value of 13.6.

Lastly, to determine the significance level we need to know the "degrees of freedom." In the case of the chi-square goodness-of-fit test, the number of degrees of freedom is equal to the number of terms used in calculating chi-square minus one. There were six terms in the chi-square for this problem—therefore, the number of degrees of freedom is five.

We then compare the value calculated in the formula above to a standard set of tables. The value returned from the table is 1.8%. We interpret this as meaning that if the die was fair (or not loaded), then the chance of getting a $\div^2$ statistic as large or larger than the one calculated above is only 1.8%. In other words, there's only a very slim chance that these rolls came from a fair die. The Missouri Master is in serious trouble.

## Recap

To recap the steps used in calculating a goodness-of-fit test with chi-square:

1. Establish hypotheses.
2. Calculate chi-square statistic. Doing so requires knowing:
   - The number of observations.
   - Expected values.
   - Observed values.
3. Assess significance level. Doing so requires knowing the number of degrees of freedom.
4. Finally, decide whether to accept or reject the null hypothesis.

## Testing Independence

The other primary use of the chi-square test is to examine whether two variables are independent or not. What does it mean to be independent, in this sense? It means that the two factors are not related. Typically in social science research, we're interested in finding factors that are related-education and income, occupation and prestige, age and voting behaviour. In this case, the chi-square can be used to assess whether two variables are independent or not.

More generally, we say that variable Y is "not correlated with" or "independent of" the variable X if more of one is not associated with more of another. If two categorical variables are correlated their values tend to move together, either in the same direction or in the opposite.

**Example**

Return to the example discussed at the introduction to chi-square, in which we want to know whether boys or girls get into trouble more often in school. Below is the table documenting the percentage of boys and girls who got into trouble in school:

| | *Got in Trouble* | *No Trouble* | *Total* |
|---|---|---|---|
| Boys | 46(40.97) | 71 (76.02) | 117 |
| Girls | 37(42.03) | 83 (77.97 | 120 |
| Total | 83 | 154 | 237 |

To examine statistically whether boys got in trouble in school more often, we need to frame the question in terms of hypotheses.

**1. Establish Hypotheses**

As in the goodness-of-fit chi-square test, the first step of the chi-square test for independence is to establish hypotheses. The null hypothesis is that the two variables are independent—or, in this particular case that the likelihood of getting in trouble is the same for boys and girls. The alternative hypothesis to be tested is that the likelihood of getting in trouble is not the same for boys and girls.

***Cautionary Note***

It is important to keep in mind that the chi-square test only tests whether two variables are independent. It cannot address questions of which is greater or less. Using the chi-square test, we cannot evaluate directly the hypothesis that boys get in trouble more than girls; rather, the test (strictly speaking) can only test whether the two variables are independent or not.

**2. Calculate the Expected Value for each Cell of the Table**

As with the goodness-of-fit example described earlier, the key idea of the chi-square test for independence is a comparison of observed and expected values. How many of something were expected and how many were observed in some process? In the case of tabular data, however, we usually do not know what the distribution should look like (as we did with rolls of dice). Rather, in this use of the chi-square test, expected values are calculated based on the row and column totals from the table.

The expected value for each cell of the table can be calculated using the following formula:

$$\frac{\text{Row Total} \times \text{Column Total}}{\text{Total } \eta \text{ for Table}}$$

For example, in the table comparing the percentage of boys and girls in trouble, the expected count for the number of boys who got in trouble is:

$$= \frac{(\text{Total number of boys} \times \text{Total number of students who got in trouble})}{(\text{Total } \eta \text{ for Table})}$$

The first step, then, in calculating the chi-square statistic in a test for independence is generating the expected value for each cell of the table. Presented in the table below are the expected values (in parentheses and italics) for each cell:

| | *Got in Trouble* | *No Trouble* | *Total* |
|---|---|---|---|
| Boys | 46 (40.97) | 71 (76.02) | 117 |
| Girls | 37 (42.03) | 83(77.97) | 120 |
| Total | 83 | 154 | 237 |

### 3. Calculate Chi-square Statistic

With these sets of figures, we calculate the chi-square statistic as follows:

$$\text{Chi-square} = \text{Sum of } \frac{(\text{Observed} \times \text{frequency} - \text{expected} \times \text{frequency})^2}{(\text{Expected} \times \text{frequency})}$$

In the example above, we get a chi-square statistic equal to:

| *Sl. No.* | *Observed Frequency (O)* | *Expected Frequency (E)* | *O–E* | *(O–E)2* | *(o–E)2/E* |
|---|---|---|---|---|---|
| 1. | 46 | 40.97 | 5.03 | 25.30 | 0.62 |
| 2. | 71 | 76..03 | -5.03 | 25.30 | 0.33 |
| 3. | 37 | 42.03 | -5.03 | 25.30 | 0.60 |
| 4. | 83 | 77.97 | 5.03 | 25.30 | 0.32 |
| | | | | | $\Sigma(O-E)^2/E=1.87$ |

$$\chi^2 = \frac{(46-40.97)^2}{40.97} + \frac{(37-42.03)^2}{42.03} + \frac{(71-76.03)^2}{76.03} + \frac{(83-77.97)^2}{77.97}$$

$$\chi^2 = 1.87$$

## 4. Assess Significance Level

Lastly, to determine the significance level we need to know the "degrees of freedom." In the case of the chi-square test of independence, the number of degrees of freedom is equal to the number of columns in the table minus one multiplied by the number of rows in the table minus one.

In this table, there were two rows and two columns. Therefore, the number of degrees of freedom is: One

Tabulated value at 5% level = 3.841

Hence the calculated value is less than the tabulated value at the 5% level of significance. Thus, we cannot reject the null hypothesis and conclude that boys are not significantly more likely to get in trouble in school than girls.

### *Recap*

To recap the steps used in calculating a goodness-of-fit test with chi-square:

1. Establish hypotheses.
2. Calculate expected values for each cell of the table.
3. Calculate chi-square statistic. Doing so requires knowing:
   (a) The number of observations.
   (b) Observed values.
4. Assess significance level. Doing so requires knowing the number of degrees of freedom.
5. Finally, decide whether to accept or reject the null hypothesis.

## Chi-square Test Calculation in Library and Information Science Research

### *Illustration 1*

From the users of seven large libraries random samples of male and female users as given below were taken. Can it be said that there is a significant variation among the Male and Female users of different Libraries in the tendency to using the Library?

| *Libraries* | *A* | *B* | *C* | *D* | *E* | *F* | *G* | *Total* |
|---|---|---|---|---|---|---|---|---|
| Male | 170 | 285 | 165 | 106 | 153 | 125 | 145 | 1149 |
| Female | 37 | 120 | 33 | 35 | 51 | 34 | 35 | 345 |
| Total | 207 | 405 | 198 | 141 | 204 | 159 | 180 | 1494 |

### *Solution*

Ho: There is no significant difference in the tendency of male and female users of different large Libraries:

$$\chi^2 = \sum \frac{(O-E)^2}{E}$$

O = Observed Frequency
E = Expected Frequency

$$\text{Expected frequency} = \frac{\text{Row Total} \times \text{Column Total}}{\text{Grand Total}}$$

### *Expected Values*

1. 170 1149 × 207/1494 = 159.19
2. 285 1149 × 405/1494 = 311.47
3. 165 1149 × 198/1494 = 152.277
4. 106 1149 × 141/1494 = 108.43
5. 153 1149 × 204/1494 = 156.89
6. 125 1149 × 159/1494 = 122.28
7. 145 1149 × 180/1494 = 138.43
8. 37 345 × 207/1494 = 47.80
9. 120 345 × 405/1494 = 93.52
10. 33 345 × 198/1494 = 45.72
11. 35 345 × 141/1494 = 32.56
12. 51 345 × 204/1494 = 47.10
13. 34 345 × 159/1494 = 36.71
14. 35 345 × 180/1494 = 41.56

| *Sl. No.* | *O* | *E* | *O–E* | *(O–E)2* | *(O–E)2/E* |
|---|---|---|---|---|---|
| 1. | 170 | 159.19 | 10.81 | 116.85 | 0.73 |
| 2. | 285 | 311.47 | -26.47 | 700.66 | 2.24 |
| 3. | 165 | 152.27 | 12.73 | 162.05 | 1.06 |
| 4. | 106 | 108.43 | -2.43 | 5.90 | 0.054 |
| 5. | 153 | 156.89 | -3.89 | 15.13 | 0.096 |
| 6. | 125 | 122.28 | 2.72 | 7.39 | 0.060 |
| 7. | 145 | 138.43 | 6.57 | 43.16 | 0.31 |
| 8. | 37 | 47.80 | -10.8 | 116.64 | 2.40 |
| 9. | 120 | 93.52 | 26.48 | 701.19 | 7.49 |
| 10. | 33 | 45.72 | -12.72 | 161.79 | 3.53 |
| 11. | 35 | 32.56 | 2.44 | 5.95 | 0.18 |
| 12. | 51 | 47.10 | 3.9 | 15.21 | 0.32 |
| 13. | 34 | 36.71 | -2.71 | 7.34 | 0.19 |
| 14. | 35 | 41.56 | -6.56 | -43.03 | 1.035 |
| | | | | | $\Sigma(O–E)^2/E=19.416$ |

$X^2 = \Sigma(O–E)^2/E = 19.416$
df = (r–1) (c–1) = (2–1) (7–1) = 1 × 6=6
For d.f = 6; $X^{2\ 0.05}$ = 12.592

The calculated value of $X^2$ is greater than the table value. Hence the hypothesis is rejected and it is concluded that there is difference in the tendency of users of male and female for use of Libraries.

### *Illustration 2*

A very useful statistical test commonly used by researchers to test the hypothesis is the chi-square test. This test may be applicable in dealing with statistics in Library and Information Science field such as book stock, clientele served, number of staff, expenditure, circulation etc. In a library the number of overnight issues of textbooks recorded as follow.

| *Years* | *Overnight issues observed* |
|---|---|
| 2000 | 1500 |
| 2001 | 1700 |
| Total | 3200 |

As a first step let us Null Hypothesis: "There is no real difference between the number of overnight issues in the two years".

In that case we should expect the total number of issues for the two years to be equally divided between them.

| *Years* | *Expected overnight issues* |
|---|---|
| 2000 | 1600 |
| 2001 | 1600 |

The formula for the Chi square test

$$\text{Chi-square test } X^2 = \frac{(O-E)^2}{E}$$

| *Years* | *Observed frequency (O)* | *Expected frequency (E)* | *(O–E)* | *(O–E)2* | *(O–E)2 / E* |
|---|---|---|---|---|---|
| 2000 | 1500 | 1600 | 100 | 10000 | 6.25 |
| 2001 | 1700 | 1600 | 100 | 10000 | 6.25 |

$X^2 = 6.25 + 6.25 = 12.50$

The chi-square for the data given in the above table is 12.50. The next step is to compare this calculated value of $X^2$ with the sampling distribution of $X^2$.

It is two tailed since find out the number of overnight issues in the year 2001 is significantly greater or significantly less than in 2000.

The number of degrees of freedom is one less than the number of categories of observation. In this case the number of observation is two. Therefore the number of degree of freedom is one.

From the statistical table for $X^2$ distribution against one degree of freedom and under two tailed test the 0.01 significance level is 6.635. The calculated value of $X^2$, that is, 12.50, is greater than table value 6.635. Therefore, it is highly significant. Therefore we reject the Null hypothesis and conclude that the number of overnight issues for the year 2001 is significantly greater than year 2000.

## STATISTICAL PACKAGES

### 1. SPSS Package

In 1968, Norman H. Nie, C. Hadlai (Tex) Hull and Dale H. Bent, three young men from professional backgrounds, developed a software system. It was based on the idea of using statistics. It aims to turn raw data into information, which is essential to decision-making. These three professionals were pioneers in their field, visionaries who recognized early that data and how you analyze it is the driving force behind sound decision-making.

This revolutionary statistical software system was called SPSS, which stood for the Statistical Package for the Social Sciences. Nie, Hull and Bent developed SPSS out of the need to quickly analyze volumes of social science data gathered through various methods of research. The initial work on SPSS was done at Stanford University The main intension at that time was to make it available only for local consumption and not international distribution.

## Innovators of SPSS

Nie, a social scientist and Stanford doctoral candidate represented the target audience and set the requirements;

Bent, a Stanford University doctoral candidate in operations research, had the analysis expertise and designed the SPSS system file structure;

Hull, who had graduated from Stanford with a master of business administration degree, programmed the software system.

As is typical of creations born of necessity, SPSS quickly caught on at universities throughout America and was soon in demand. It is an effective and efficient method of analyzing data. It is a viable product. In addition to the usage to the academicians it is useful in pricing, shipping and other issues of commerce and industry. They made sure that tapes of source code were sent to a small, but enthusiastic, user community, and continually maintained and enhanced SPSS.

The early success of SPSS was directly related to the quality and availability of the documentation that accompanied the software. McGraw-Hill published the first SPSS user's manual in 1970. Once the manual was available in college bookstores, demand for the program took-off. Nie, Bent, and Hull received a royalty from sales of the manual but nothing from distribution of the program. In Nie's words, "It was like Gillette selling razors at cost and getting its profits from the blades."

With the sales of SPSS growing rapidly, the IRS determined in 1971 that SPSS was a small software company, which threatened the non-profit status of the University of Chicago within which SPSS had been housed. In 1975, the two founders, Nie and Hull, became the new company's executives. In spite of having no venture capital or financial backing, these two entrepreneurs secured for SPSS universal control of the academic marketplace due to the fact that SPSS was, and is, a portable code that enabled academic institutions to port it to most of the large mainframe computer systems, which included Control Data 6000 series, Burroughs large systems, Univac 1108, GE (subsequently Honeywell) large systems, Digital Equipment Corporation (DEC) large systems. SPSS also quickly became useful to the government and commercial markets. NASA began using SPSS for mean time between part failure on the space shuttle in the mid-1970s, and the National Forest Service used the software for incidences of injuries and bear encounters throughout the national parks system. Consumer products companies like Procter & Gamble and Anheuser-Busch also realized the value of SPSS in analyzing marketing research data.

In the mid-1980s they introduced the first mainframe statistical package to appear on a personal computer. The organization was first again in 1992 with the release of statistical products for the Microsoft Windows personal computer operating system. SPSS Inc.'s reputation for thought leadership and innovators continued to grow with the onset of the Internet and the dawn of the Information Economy.

Under Noonan's leadership SPSS Inc. continued to flourish by keeping in touch with its customers' needs and staying abreast of technological advances. The Company strengthened its leadership in the analytical marketplace through acquisitions that expanded the depth and breadth of its analytical offerings. Acquisitions included the addition of technologies such as data mining, a business intelligence suite for the IBM® e-Server, Web analytics, sophisticated analytical components, a Web interface for online analytical processing (OLAP) technology and text mining. These technologies were introduced by SPSS Inc. to better capitalize on the expanding need in decision-making.

Over its thirty-seven year history, SPSS Inc. has evolved into an international corporation that delivers analytical tools and solutions to organizations around the globe. While customers and their industries vary, they share a common need to gather insight from the analysis of data. Through SPSS one can understand what is happening today and anticipate the future in order to manage it effectively.

## Uses of SPSS

(1) It is very useful to the academicians in the field of research.
(2) By this we can understand what is happening in the world around.
(3) It turns raw data into information, which is essential to decision-making.
(4) It is widely used by the industries and commerce all over the world.
(5) Data mining, Web analytics, a Web interfaces for online analytical processing (OLAP) technology and text mining were introduced by SPSS which is used by multinational software companies.
(6) SPSS is recognized tool in the predictive analytics market space.

## Stages of Growth in the Institutional History of SPSS

*1968-75:* "SPSS becomes a product", when the technology was first developed and grew on its own as an academic enterprise.

*1975-84:* "SPSS becomes a corporation". The Company is separately incorporated when its revenues threatened the non-profit status of its original hosting institution. During this start-up phase, the business was organized and a number of development initiatives were undertaken.

*1984-92:* "The age of the PC", with the Company growing from $ 18 m to $ 38 m on the strength of the market-leading statistical analysis system for

PC DOS. SPSS was the first to market with a statistical software product on PC DOS.

*1992-96:* "The age of Windows", with the Company shipping the first Windows version of a statistical software package in 1992. The business was focused on statistical products.

*1997-2002:* "The transition to the enterprise". This period has been the age of growth by acquisition and the rise of analytic applications as a complement to the core statistical products business. The Company grew from $ 110 m in 1997 to a $ 209 m in 2002 through the acquisitions of Quantime (market research application software), ISL (data mining software), Showcase (business intelligence software for the middle market), NetGenesis (analytical application for Web data), LexiQuest (text mining software), and netExs (a Web interface for OLAP technology).

*2003:* Predictive analytics is successfully established as a market segment. SPSS played a thought-leadership role in the emergence during 2003 of predictive analytics as an important, distinct segment within the broader business intelligence software sector. Predictive analytics complements and enhançes other information technologies. Organizations that employ predictive analytics not only know what has happened, they also know what is likely to happen next. Most importantly, they know what to do about it by using this knowledge to increase revenue, reduce costs, and improve outcomes. SPSS saw a growing awareness of these benefits among the commercial, public sector, and academic organizations its serves. To enhance it focus on predictive analytics, SPSS acquired Dutch-based Data Distilleries, a provider of predictive analytic applications in November of 2003.

*2004:* Predictive analytic applications come of age. In 2004, SPSS a ccelerated the introduction of predictive analytics applications, leveraging skills and integrating technologies from recent acquisitions, including Data Distilleries. A new version of PredictiveMarketing was introduced, as well as a new application, PredictiveCallCenter. Additional development work set the stage for additional applications to be introduced in 2005.

*Today:* SPSS is recognized as a leader in the predictive analytics market space. Predictive analytics, which combines advanced analytics and decision optimization, will continue to be a focus for the organization as it seeks to increase marketplace understanding of the business benefits that predictive analytics provides.

## 2. IDAMS (Internationally-developed Data Analysis and Management Software)

*IDAMS* is a software package for processing and analysing numerical *data* developed, maintained and disseminated by UNESCO. It provides a great number of data manipulation and validation facilities and a wide range of classical and advanced statistics techniques. Interactive components allow for construction of multi-dimensional tables, graphical exploration of data and time series analysis.

*IDAMS* was originally derived from the software package OSIRIS III.2 developed in the early 1970s by the Institute for Social Research of the University of Michigan, USA. It has been modified and updated by the UNESCO Secretariat with the co-operation of experts from Belgium, Colombia, Hungary, Russia, Ukraine, United Kingdom and USA. Release 4 is available for PCs and Release 3.02 for IBM mainframes. Version 1.2a of WinIDAMS for 32-bit Windows was released in 2006.

*WinIDAMS* as well as its documentation are available in English, French and Spanish. The software itself is free but national distributors are allowed to charge for their expenses.

*WinIDAMS* is a software package for the validation, manipulation and statistical analysis of data, developed by the UNESCO Secretariat in co-operation with experts from various countries. It is distributed free-of-charge upon request.

### It Offers

- Modern graphical user interface and on-line Reference Manual,
- Possibility to customize the environment for an application,
- Facilities for editing/creating data files and data description files,
- Interactive data import/export,
- Editor for creating/updating files with instructions for program execution,
- Viewer for displaying and quick navigation through results,
- Advanced text editing facilities,
- Facilities for sorting and merging files, data editing, checking of codes and consistencies, correcting, listing, subsetting, aggregating, merging and transforming data, including construction of new variables,
- Wide range of data analysis techniques such as: table building, regression analysis, one-way analysis of variance, discriminant analysis, cluster analysis, principal components factor analysis and analysis of correspondences, partial order scoring, rank ordering of alternatives, segmentation and iterative typology,
- Interactive components for construction of multi-dimensional tables and their graphical presentation, for graphical exploration of data and for times series analysis.

## QUESTIONS

1. What is correlation matrix?
2. What are the purposes of factor analysis?
3. What is common factor analysis?
4. Draw a factor analysis decision diagram
5. What do you mean by a factor?
6. What is called cluster?
7. Explain Wards method of cluster analysis.
8. What is meant by Algorithm?
9. What are the objectives of discriminant analysis?
10. What are the uses of discriminant analysis?
11. What are the major stages in the application of Discriminant analysis?
12. Explain discriminant function.
13. What is meant by tolerance?
14. What is meant by centroid?
15. What is simple correlation?
16. What do you understand by multiple correlations?
17. Write a short note on cluster analysis?
18. What are the types of correlation?
19. Discuss the limitations of correlation?
20. What do you mean by perfect correlation?
21. Write few examples of positive and negative correlation.
22. What is meant by simple regression? What are the objectives of regression?
23. Discuss about the purpose of multiple regressions.
24. Briefly discuss about the test of significance of regression analysis.

# 5

# Research Report

## MEANING OF RESEARCH REPORT

Research reporting is the oral or written presentation of the evidence and the findings in such detail and form as to be readily understood and accessed by the reader and as to enable him to verify the validity of the conclusions. Such communications should be of the problem, the method, the facts and the conclusions in themselves as well as in their inter-relationships. It also helps the researcher himself to evaluate the success of his research effort and, in this process, to clarify and check his own thoughts.

### Essentials of a Scientific Report

The preparation of the report is final stage of the research and its purpose is to convey to interested persons the whole result of the study in sufficient detail and so arranged to enable each reader to comprehend the data and to determine for himself the validity of the conclusions.

### *Basic Quality of Good Scientific Sriting is Accuracy and Clarity*

The first step is to decide just what information one wants to convey and to understand how the various bits of it are related to one another.

One should begin with preparing a detailed outline of his report. Once the outline has been prepared, it is a good idea to carefully go through it. Check whether anything important has been omitted and whether ideas that have been grouped together logically belong together. It may be helpful to have someone else read it and comment upon it.

Although, the best guarantee of a good report is a well-organised study, there are common aids to clarify which deserve mention i.e., mechanical aids to clear presentation.

## STRUCTURE OF RESEARCH REPORT

Generally, a research report, whether it is called a dissertation or thesis, consists of three parts.

1. The preliminary i.e., preface pages
2. The text of the Report/Main body of the report
3. The reference material

### 1. Preliminary Section

The preliminaries consist of the following components:

a. The title page
b. Certificate
c. Declaration
d. Preface including acknowledgements
e. Table of contents
f. List of tables
g. List of figures (and illustrations)
h. List of abbreviations

### 2. Text or Context

The text of a dissertation/thesis consist of the following sections:

a. Introduction (Introductory chapters)
b. Review of the related literature
c. Main body of the report (usually divided in to chapters and sections)
d. Conclusion (summary, Recommendations/suggestion)

### 3. Reference Material

The reference material is generally divided as follows:

a. Bibliography
b. Appendices
c. Glossary of terms (if any)
d. Index (if any)

### Title page

The first page of the report is the title page. The title page should carry a concise and adequately descriptive title of the research study. Although title page format differ from one institution to another they usually include:

a. The name of the topic,
b. The relationship of the report to a course or the academic degree for which the degree is conferred,
c. The name of the author,
d. The name of the institution where the report is to be submitted, and
e. The date of presentation of the report.

The entire title should be typed in all capital letters. The statement with respect to the university course and the academic degree for which the report is submitted should be typed in lower case with capitalized initial letters. The name of writer/researcher should be typed in capital letters. The researcher's academic or professional degree and designation(s) need not be included here. The name of the institution where the report is to be submitted and the date/month of presentation of the report are typed.

### Acknowledgement and Preface

A 'preface' is not a synonym to either 'Acknowledgement' or 'foreword'. A preface may include reasons why; in the first place, the researcher selected the topic. If the researcher has opted to discuss the significance and nature of his research in a subsequent chapter, usually in 'Introductory Chapter', then he may not write a 'preface'. But he may use the page for only 'Acknowledgements.'

Acknowledgements are written to thank those who have helped the researcher for a variety of reasons, including guidance during the period of study. The comments, given in acknowledgements, and given only for substantial assistance and cooperation of a non-routine character which warrants public recognition.

### Table of Contents

The purpose of table of contents is to provide an outline of the content of the report. It may contain only a list of titles of chapters and their appropriate Roman numerals, followed by page number on which each chapter titles, subheads or section headings or words or phrases indicating the subject matter of the chapters. The table of contents should also include the acknowledgements/preface, list of tables figures, etc., the first page is not referred in the table of contents because it is always the title page. Similarly, the table of contents page is also not referred in the table of contents. While typing a dissertation/thesis, the table of contents is typed last. The heading "table of contents" should be in the center at the top of the page and in capital letters.

### List of Tables and Figures

If tables and figures are included in this report, separate pages for then should follow the table of contents. Both tables and figures sometimes are given together in the same page itself. Figures and illustrations are synonymous terms and refer to maps, drawings, graphs, charts, diagrams and photographs.

### The Text (Content) Chapters

The division of the text in to chapters/sections/sub-divisions should reflect the organizations of the parts with one another and with the whole i.e., the division should be logical to make the contents meaningful. The text usually consists of:

a. Introduction,
b. Review of the related literature,
c. Main body of the report devoted for analysis, interpretation and presentation of data, and
d. Summary and conclusion.

### (a) Introduction Section

Introduce the subject by highlighting its special features in about two to four paragraphs/pages. The introduction should create interest to the reader in the subject matter of research. It must not be dull, confused, aimless and lacking in precision.

1. *Statement of the Problem* : A clear statement of the nature and importance of the problem with specific questions to be answered or hypothesis to be tested; a consideration of significance of the problem and its historical background is also appropriate.
2. *The objective/purposes of the research study.*
3. *Review of Literature:* That is, summarising the current status of research works already done. A review of the pertinent past work and contradictions, pitfalls and other failings of the earliest work, mainly to substantiate the need for another research study.
4. *Significance of and Justification for the Present Study.*
5. *The scope of the study* pointing out the exact coverage reported upon, and position the research within its larger context
6. *Conceptual Framework:* That is, various concepts or domains proposed to be used in a research require to be stated. Definitions or special meanings of all-important terms so as to enable the reader to understand the concepts underlying the un development of the investigation.
7. *Methodology Adopted:* The methodology describing the research describing design used, the data collection methods employed, sampling design, how the fieldwork was carried out, the variables and controls employed, the reliability of instruments selected or

constructed and the statistical tools and procedure used in the analysis.

8. *Chapterisation:* Preview of the scheme of chapters in the main body of the thesis and their interrelationship.

### (b) Review of the Related Literature

The goal of the introduction and literature review is to demonstrate "the logical continuity between previous and present work". This does not mean anybody needs to provide an exhaustive historical review. Analyze the relationships among the related studies instead of presenting a series of seemingly unrelated abstracts or annotations. The introduction should motivate the study. The reader should understand why the problem was researched and why the study represents a contribution to existing knowledge. Unless the study is an evaluation of a program, it is generally inappropriate to attempt to motivate the study based on its social importance.

### (c) Main Body of the Report

This is the heart of the research report and probably the largest section of the report. It should be an organised presentation of results and each major division of the problem should be presented in a separate chapter. This may take a few chapters, an optimum number being five, to present all the arguments, documentation, ideas, concepts, interpretations and findings. The chapter should include a discussion of the issue or part of the problem investigated and the evidence used in its solution. If this becomes lengthy, a summary of the evidence may be made at the end of the chapter. The data themselves should be described fully, they should be analysed in detail, and all the evidence resulting from the analysis should be presented.

### (d) Summary and Conclusion

This is the last part of the text (or the context) of the report. It consists of the summary, conclusions/generalizations, suggestions and recommendations. Findings are statements of factual information based upon the data analysis. Conclusions are the answers to the questions raised, or the statements of acceptance or rejection of the hypothesis proposed. The conclusions do not need to repeat the evidence, on which they are based, but extreme case should be exercised to present them with whatever limitations or qualifications are necessary.

## REPORT FORMAT

Although every research report is custom-made for the project it represents, some conventions of *report format* are universal. They represent a consensus about what parts are necessary to a good research report and how they should be ordered.

## Tailoring the Format to the Project

The format may need adjustment for two reasons: (1) to obtain the proper level of formality and (2) to alter the complexity of the report. The format given here is for the most formal type of report. How does the researcher decide on the appropriate level of formality? The general rule is to include all the parts needed for effective communication in the particular circumstances and no more. This factor relates to how far up in management the report is expected to go and on how routine the matter is.

## Parts of the Report

1. *The title page:* The title page should include the title of the report, for whom the report was prepared, who prepared it, and the date of release or presentation. The title should give a brief but complete indication of the purpose of the research project.
2. *Letter of transmittal:* This element is included in relatively formal to very formal reports. Its purpose is to release or deliver the report to the recipient. It also serves to establish some rapport between the reader and the writer.
3. *Letter of authorization:* This is a letter to the researcher approving the project, detailing who has responsibility for the project, and what resources are available to support it. The researcher would not write this personally.
4. *Table of contents:* The table of contents is essential to any report more than a few pages long. It should list the divisions and sub-divisions of the report with page references. If the report includes many figures or tables, a list of these should also be included, immediately following the table of contents.
5. *Summary:* The summary is a vital part of the report. Studies have indicated that nearly all managers read a report's summary while only a minority read the rest of the report. The summary should be written only after the rest of the report has been completed. Its length should be about one page, so the writer must carefully sort out what is important enough to include in it. The summary contains four elements. First, the objectives of the report are stated, including the most important background information and the specific purposes of the project. Second, the major results regarding each purpose are presented. Third come the conclusions. Finally come the recommendations, or suggestions for action, based on the conclusions. In many cases, managers prefer not to have recommendations included in the report or summary.
6. *The body:* The body constitutes the bulk of the report. It begins with an introduction, which explains why the project was done and what it aimed to discover. Enough background should be included to explain why the project was worth doing, but

essential historical factors should be omitted. The last part of the introduction explains what this particular project tried to discover. The second division of the body explains the research methodology. This involves an explanation of the research design, data collection methods, sampling procedures, and other technical procedures dealing with collection of data such as fieldwork and analysis. The presentation of results should occupy the bulk of the report. No report is perfect so its limitations should be indicated. However, the discussion of limitations should avoid overemphasizing the weaknesses. The last division of the body presents the conclusions and recommendations. The conclusions and recommendations should be presented here in more detail than in the summary, with whatever justification is needed.

7. *The appendix:* Any material that is too technical or too detailed to go in the body of the paper should appear in the appendix.

## EFFECTIVE USE OF GRAPHIC AIDS

Used properly, graphic aids can clarify complex points or emphasize a message, but used improperly or sloppily they can be distracting or misleading. The key to effective use of graphic aids is to make them an integral part of the text; the key points should be pointed out and related to the discussion in progress. Several types of graphic aids may be useful in research reports.

A. *Tables:* Tables are most useful for presenting numerical information, especially when several pieces of information have been gathered about each item discussed. Each table should include a table number, which allows simple reference from the text, a title, a boxhead and stubhead, footnotes, and a source note.

B. *Charts:* Charts translate numerical information into visual form so that relationships can be easily grasped. The accuracy of the numbers is reduced to gain this advantage. Each chart should include a figure number, allowing easy reference from the text, a title, an explanation of the chart, and a source and footnotes. Charts are subject to distortion, whether unintentional or deliberate. A particularly severe kind of distortion comes from treating unequal intervals as if they were equal. Another common distortion is to begin the vertical scale at some value larger than zero; graphs should always start at zero on the vertical axis.

1. *Pie charts:* One of the most useful type of charts is the pie chart. A pie chart shows the composition of some total quantity at a particular time. Each angle or "slice" is proportional to its percentage of the whole and should be labeled with its description and percentage. The writer should not try to include too many slices—about six slices is a usual maximum.
2. *Line graphs:* Line graphs are useful to show the relationship of one

variable to another. The dependent variable is generally shown on the vertical axis and the independent variable on the horizontal axis. A simple line graph shows the relationship of one dependent variable to the independent variable, whereas a multiple line graph shows the relationship of more than one dependent variable to the independent variable. The lines for each dependent variable should be distinguishable and clearly labeled. A second variation is the stratum chart, which shows the composition of a total quantity and its changes as the independent variable changes.

3. *Bar charts:* Bar charts show changes in the dependent variable at discrete intervals of the independent variable. In each of these cases, each variable needs to be clearly identified. Too much detail obscures the essential advantage of charts, which is to make relationships easy to grasp

### The Oral Presentation

The conclusions and recommendations of most research reports will be presented orally as well as in writing. The oral presentation is a verbal summary of the major findings and conclusions, and the recommendations given to clients or line managers to provide them with the opportunity to clarify any ambiguous issues by asking questions.

The key to effective presentation is preparation. The researcher should select the three or four most important findings for emphasis and rely on the written report for full summary. The researcher needs to be ready to defend the results.

Another key to effective oral presentation is adaptation to the audience. Also, the presenter should plan to rely on brief notes, along with memory, and as much rehearsal as the occasion calls for. Graphic aids and other visual aids can be useful in an oral presentation as in a written one. Whatever medium is chosen, the visual aids should be designed to convey a simple, attention-getting message that supports a point on which the audience should focus its thinking.

### Reports on the Internet

Many clients want many employees to have access to research findings. One easy way to share data is to have executive summaries and reports available on a company Intranet. Information technology exists so that a company can use the Internet to design questionnaires, administer surveys, analyze data, and share the results in a presentation-ready format. Real-time data capture allows for beginning-to-end reporting. A number of companies offer fully Web-based research management systems.

## COMPUTER PROGRAMS FOR ANALYSIS

The proliferation of computer technology within businesses and universities has greatly facilitated tabulation and statistical analysis. Many collections or packages of computer programs have been designed to tabulate and analyze numerous types of data. Most of these packages consist of a sizeable array of programs for descriptive analysis and univariate, bivariate, and multivariate statistical analysis. Exhibits in the text show examples of printout of statistical packages. A SAS, statistical analysis system computer printout of descriptive statistics for two variables is shown: EMP (number of employees working in an MSA or Metropolitan Statistical Area) and SALES (sales volume in dollars in an MSA) in 10 MSAs. The number of data elements (N), mean, standard deviation, and other descriptive statistics are calculated. Other Exhibits show output from the SPSS software program.

Microsoft Excel, Lotus 1-2-3, and Quatro Pro are spreadsheet packages that emphasize database management and allow for entering and editing data with minimal effort. They also incorporate some programs for descriptive analysis, graphic analysis, and limited statistical analysis. In Excel statistical calculations can be performed using the Data Analysis and Paste Function menus.

### Computer Graphics/Computer Mapping

Graphic aids prepared by computers are rapidly replacing graphic aids drawn by artists. They are extremely useful for descriptive analysis. The versatility of the new software programs for computer-generated graphics allows researchers to explore many alternative ways of visually communicating the findings. An innovation that has tremendous potential is computer mapping. Computer maps portray demographic, sales, or other data on two- or three-dimensional maps generated by a computer.

## TYPES OF REPORT

### Oral Report

Unlike the written report, the oral one is a two way process. Since a give and take discussion between the researcher and the audience is easier, it offers greater scope for explaining the findings and discussing the implications. By drawing the researcher and the listener closer, it enables the former to know the report has been received and if necessary, to elaborate his work and convenience to the audience.

### Written Report

Written reports themselves are different types and their planning, drafting and documentation vary with the types, purposes and readers.

*The popular Report:* The report for the intelligent layman is intended very largely to disseminate the broad facts, findings and recommendations, if any. The report must be lucid, simple and yet dignified, scrupulously avoiding distortion, jargon and technical camouflage. To inform the layman accurately and yet adequately, the research may produce Summary report, along with a full technical report.

*The report for the Administrator:* It is the general survey report designed for the administrator or the business executive, and perhaps for a few professional colleagues too. This would be of medium size, with some technical details and supporting data followed by a summary and the principal recommendations.

*The Technical Report:* It is a report by a researcher for another researcher. The technical report may take different forms like,

1. *A detailed Report*: A techno-economic survey comprising experts in geology, transport, agriculture, fisheries, forests and so forth, each expert would make his report to the overall director of the survey, who is often an economist and who would utilize the specialists reports in preparing his own economic report,
2. A monograph,
3. An article for a professional journal, and
4. The full-technical report.

## STEPS IN DRAFTING REPORTS

Three steps are involved in drafting a report irrespective of the nature of audience. In each case the first, second and final drafts-writing may have to be done quite a few times.

### First Draft

The first draft concentrates on substance, i.e., fullness of facts. All facts of value are to be brought together. In addition to fullness, accuracy of the facts incorporated in to the text becomes necessary. Another requirement is that there should be balance, proportion and development in facts. For writing the first draft the researcher should have control over his notes and should think continuously over the problem.

The objectives to be aimed at the first draft or rough draft stage are four:

1. Comprehensiveness or fullness of facts,
2. Precision or accuracy of facts,
3. Coherence or logic of facts, and
4. Movement or transition of facts and ideas.

### Second Draft

After a lapse of some time from the completion of first draft, the revision is to be made for writing the second draft. While drafting the second one, the researcher should concentrate largely on form and language. The researcher should give the first draft, at this stage, a shape so that it can be readable, clear and lucid. Considerable trimming or editing will have to be done to make the writing precise, concise and brief. Finally, at the second draft stage, critical evaluation will have to be made of all that has been written-facts, findings, conclusions and recommendations.

At the end of the second draft stage and even all through the writing of the draft, the researcher may do well to ask himself and answer a few questions:

Does the title cover the scope of the subject?
Is the initial hypothesis tested adequately?
Are the divisions of the report and topics logical?
Does the beginning begin and the conclusions conclude?
Is there smooth development from the introduction to the recommendations?
Is the report as thorough as the writer can make it?
Are the conclusion effective and the strongest portion of the report?
Are the opening sentence, paragraphs, section etc., attractive?
Is the style smooth and phraseology formal and cultivated?
Has the audience been kept in mind?
Does the writing have too much of indecision and reserve by using too many "somewhat", "perhaps", "rather", etc.?
Has every work been weighed and used for its exact meaning and to perform a specific function?
Has the emphasis in writing been overdone by using too many "very", "invariably", "tremendous", "extraordinary", etc.?
Has too much of jargon and vague words, such as integrate, finalise area, frame of reference etc., been used?
Finally, is the researcher, as his own critic, satisfied with the report?

## The Third Draft

The final stage in drafting is the preparation of final report. It concentrates mainly on the finish and final touches, i.e., on documentation and polish to make the report weighty, authoritative, convincing and attractive. Documentation indicated the references to the sources, other previous and current work and view, additional data and discussion and suggested further reading on the specific problem as handled by the researcher. In other words, it indicated the thoroughness of the investigation and on the other a guide to further work.

### *Writing the Report*

The writer should arrange the following materials in an order and keep them on the table ready for use.

1. The detailed outline for chapters.
2. Note cards arranged in the order of chapters.
3. Source cards arranged in the alphabetical order.

4. Statistical tables, charts and results of analysis , each in a separate sheet.
5. Paper sheets.

## Revisions

1. The first draft should be read carefully again and again and edited thoroughly and revised. Any writing improves upon revision. In revising the first draft, the attention should be given to form language, readability, clarity and lucidity. With an open and critical mind the researcher must correct, carve, cut, add and polish. The following points may be kept in mind:

1. Keep in mind the requirements of a research report.
2. Fill in the blanks with appropriate ideas, words or phrases.
3. Recognize ideas wherever necessary.
4. Eliminate gaps in continuity and unclear statements.
5. Replace inappropriate words by exact and apt words.
6. Omit needless words and expressions such as "as a matter of fact", "owing to the fact that ....", etc.
7. Simplify sentences and improve their effectiveness.
8. Cut-off repetitions by giving cross references.
9. Improve the readability and clarity of the writing.
10. Correct the spelling and grammatical errors.
11. Make a critical evaluation of the draft to ensure effectiveness.

## Methodological Aspects

1. Does the research have a plan?
2. Does the report fulfil the objectives of the study?
3. Have the problem and hypothesis been stated in scientific terms?
4. Is the chapter scheme relevant to the objectives of the study?
5. Are the hypothesis tested appropriately and adequately?
6. Are the findings and inferences clear and substantiated by data?
7. Are the conclusions effective logical and based on the findings?
8. Are the recommendations flow from the findings and conclusions?
9. Are the recommendations specific, practical and convincing?
10. Does the summary really summarise the point to further research?

## Organisation and Form

1. Are the target audience been kept in mind?
2. Is the division of report into chapters logical and appropriate?
3. Does it ensure smooth flow of information from introduction to recommendation?
4. Are the quotations appropriate and accurate?

5. Is the technical information up-to-date?.
6. Have you given the techniques for the development of scales and indexes?
7. Are the tables and charts accurate and self-explanatory?
8. Are the foot notes complete and correct?

## Language and Style

1. Does the language conform to prevailing standard of usage?
2. Are the opening sentences of chapters, sections and paragraphs are attractive?
3. Is the presentation accurate, clear, concise, logical and complete?
4. Is the style smooth and continuous?
5. Is the expression strong, vigorous and dignified and free from grammatical and spelling errors?
6. Has every word been used for its exact meaning and function?
7. Are the findings and arguments concise?
8. Are there no jargons and vague words?
9. Are you sure that you are satisfied with the report?
10. Rectify the flaws, imperfections and weaknesses discovered in the course of critical evaluation?
11. Get your project report read by your friends, guide as the case may be and request them to offer constructive criticism.
12. Give weight age to constructive criticism.
13. Revise the draft in the light of valid criticism and suggestions made by the readers.

## The Purpose of the Written Report

Reports could aim at different purposes and hence the form of the written report would vary according to the situation. If the purpose is simply to offer details on some specific areas of interest requested by a manager, the report can very narrowly focused and provide the desired information to the manager in a brief format. If on the other hand, the report is intended to 'sell an idea' to management, then it has to be more detailed and convincing as to how the proposed idea is an improvement and should be adopted. Here, the emphasis would be directed on presenting all the relevant information backed by the necessary data, to persuade the reader to 'buy into the idea'.

A different form of report will be prescribed in some cases, where a manager asks for several alternative solutions or recommendations to rectify a problem in a given situation. Here, the researcher provides the requested information and the manager chooses from among the alternatives and makes the final decision. In this case, a more detailed report surveying past studies, the methodology used for the present study, different perspectives generated from interviews and current data analyses, and alternative solutions based on the conclusions drawn there from will have to be provided. How each alternative helps to improve the problem situation would also have to be discussed. The advantage and disadvantages of each of the proposed solutions, together with a cost-benefit analysis I terms of dollars and/or other resources, will also have to be presented to help the manager make the decision.

Yet another type of report might require the researcher to identify the problem and provide the final solution as well. That is, the researcher might be called in to study a situation, determine the nature of the problem, and offer a report of the findings and recommendations. Such a report has to be very comprehensive, following the format of a full-fledged study. A fifth kind of research report is the very scholarly publication presenting the findings of a basic study that one usually finds published in academic journals.

### A Simple Descriptive Report

For instance, let us say a human resources manager wants to know how many employees have been recruited during the past 18 months in the organisation, their gender composition, educational level, and the average proportion of days that these individuals had absented themselves since recruitment. A simple report giving the desired information would suffice.

In this report, a statement of the purpose of the study will be given. The methods or procedures adopted to collect the data would then be given. Finally, a narration of the actual results, reinforced by visual tabular and graphical forms of representation of the data, will be provided. Frequency distributions, cross-tabulations, and other data will be presented in a tabular form, and pictorial illustrations will include bar charts (for gender), pie charts (to indicate the proportions of individuals at various educational levels), and so on. This section will summarize the data and may look like the following.

### Details of a Report to "sell" an Idea

For example, the Information Systems (IS) manager might want to suggest to the top executives that an executive information system (EIS) would greatly enhance the effectiveness of top executives by virtue of the speed and timeliness of the electronic information delivery system. With up-to-the minute information available at the fingertips of executives—something that the current paper reporting system lacks—informed decisions could be made with much confidence. The research report for this purpose will have a different thrust and focus in greater detail on the following:

1. Explanation in clear and simple terms.
2. How it would save time (e.g. by giving immediate access to the specific information the executive needs).
3. How it would have an advantage over and be better than the current system.

4. How it would boost savings in resources in the long-run.
5. Illustration of examples from past company history (within the past 2 months, if possible) of how an EIS system would have helped the executives to make more informed decisions in those instances, and how it could have saved the system money/ resources.
6. A final forceful and convincing recommendation to adopt EIS as a way of organizational decision-making.

### The Written Report and its Audience

The organisation of a report, its length and focus on details, data presentation, and illustrations will in part, be a function of the audience for whom it is intended. The letter of transmittal of the report would clearly indicate to whom the report is being sent. An Executive Summary placed at the beginning would offer busy executives just the right amount of vital details—in less than three pages. This will help the busy managers to quickly grasp the essentials of the study and its findings, and turn to the pages that offer more detailed information on aspects that are of special interest to them.

Some managers are distracted by data presented in the form of tables and feel more comfortable with graphs and charts, while others want to see "facts and figures". Both tables and figures are visual forms of representation and need to be presented in reports. If a report were to be handled by different executives, with different orientations, it should be packaged such that they know where to find the information that meets their preferred mode of information processing. For example, in addition to mentioning about market share in the text, it can be illustrated through a pie chart, and the raw data also presented in a tabular form.

The length, organisation, and presentation modes of the report will, among other things, depend at least in part on the target audience. Some businesses might also prescribe their own format for report writing. In all cases, a good report is a function of the knowledge of whom it is intended for ad its exact purpose. As we have seen, some reports may have to be long and detailed, and others brief and specific.

## ABBREVIATIONS USED IN REPORT WRITTING

In bibliography and footnotes, English and Latin abbreviations are used to avoid repetition. The most common abbreviations are as follows.

| | | | |
|---|---|---|---|
| Anon | Anonymous | Infra | Below |
| Ante | Before | Loc. cit | In the same place and same page |
| Art., arts | Article | | |
| Bk., bks | Book, books | Ms. mss | Manuscript |

| | | | |
|---|---|---|---|
| Cf. | Compare | n.d. | No. date given |
| Ch. | Chapter | n.p | No. place given |
| col., cols | Column, columns | no., nos | Number, numbers |
| div | Division | nb | Taken notice |
| ed., eds | Editor, editors | op. cit. | In the work cited |
| edn. | Edition | post | After |
| Et al. | And others | rev | Revised |
| e.g. | For example | sec | Sections |
| et seq | And the following | supra | Above |
| et passin | And here and there | viz | Namely |
| ex. | Example | vol., vols | Volume, Volumes |
| fig., figs | Figure, figures | Vs | Versus, against |
| Idem | reference | fn. | Footnote |
| i.e. | Same person | Illus | That is illustrated |
| Ibid. | In the same | | |

## QUESTIONS

1. What is meant by report?
2. What are the qualities of a good research report?
3. What are the objectives of preparing a research report?
4. What are the purposes of written report?
5. What is meant by audience?
6. What is meant by footnotes?
7. What is meant by tabulation?
8. What are the types of tables?
9. Describe the parts of a table.
10. How the computers are used in the analysis of data in research?
11. What are the uses of computer in the preparation of a research report?
12. Describe the structure of a business research report.
13. What are the steps followed in the preparation of first draft?
14. What are the uses of preparing the second report?
15. Discuss various types of report.
16. What is a technical report?
17. What is popular report?
18. What is business research report?
19. Compare and contrast the findings and conclusions of the research study.
20. Can a single multi-purpose report aiming at all categories of target audience be written? Why or why not?
21. What is bibliography? What is its purpose?
22. Describe how a research report should be presented?
23. Distinguish between bibliography and footnotes.
24. What are the various categories of target audience for research report?

# Research in Library and Information Science

Library is one of the Service production systems facilitating generation and regeneration of information or knowledge. A library is an essential component of academic environment. A first step in research is to go to the library to read books and other source materials pertaining to his/her own field of interest to formulate a research problem.

P.V. Young writes, "As a preliminary to field research, or in connection with it, a sustained and high-quality search for data in the library is a most pressing need in the social sciences".

There are, implications about the increasing research activities for libraries. The research workers visit libraries for their information needs. It is the duty of the librarian to give them the required information as quickly and exhaustively as possible. Therefore, it is necessary for librarians to know in detail, their information requirement and hence to know what exactly research is, how it is conducted, what techniques and tools the researchers use and how they arrive at generalizations and generate new knowledge. Herein lies the need for a student of library and information science to know the process of research. Such a knowledgeable person will be better equipped to serve the scientists, academic community and other research workers.

## SCIENTIFIC RESEARCH IN LIBRARIANSHIP

Scientific research in Librarianship is a careful process by which librarians can acquire more accurate knowledge and understanding of libraries and librarianship. Knowledge about the numerous facets of Library and Information Science can be obtained by asking questions, thinking of possible answers, and testing the possibilities by means of careful inquiry. Specifically, a researcher in Library and Information Science should have a clear grasp of the user's behaviour, nature and demand of the clientele, size and nature of the library, types of collection it possess and above all, the type and extent of information service that can be rendered to the benefit of the users. With the continuous advancement taking place in information technology, the researcher in Information Science runs the risk of being out dated if he/she is not dynamic enough to keep track of these fast developments. A more careful and concerned researcher on the other hand may bring in enormous benefits to a developing country like India.

Formulation of Hypothesis forms the second stage of the research process. This process has to count upon the objectives of the study framed. Objectives of the study and the set of hypotheses are mutually dependent. A high sounding clarity and precision in the set of hypotheses shall put the investigator on the right track and lead him/her to the successful completion of the mission.

## USER STUDIES

The concept of 'User study' is sort of research activity on the part of librarian. The methodology involves psychological and sociological factors in finding the readers choice and varieties of interest. This requires a deep study about the user. 'User' is the term used in place of library reader, to mean a person or group of person who make use of the library facilities either within the library or outside of the library premises. More than anything as a measure, the services of libraries depend on the user need, and as a means of determining these needs, the organizes study of user has gained prominence.

The term user studies has been defined variously by different information scientists. According to Wysoki user studies or use studies could be concerned with studying information-processing activities of the users. Empirical studies of the use of, the demand for information are usually called user studies.

### Objectives of User Studies

According to Sangameswaran and Gopinath, the objectives of user studies are:

(a) Identify the potential users and categories of them,
(b) Identify the Information requirements category-wise by the class of information needed, the level and type of communication media, etc.,
(c) Identify the existing resources and services so that

comprehensiveness of information can be achieved without unnecessary duplication of efforts and finance,

(d) Evaluate the various existing services in respect of their utility to users to effect suitable modifications and introduce new services wherever necessary, and

(e) Achieve overall improvements in information systems from feedback obtained as above.

Kawatra attributes the following reasons for conducting various users studies:

(a) Identifying the actual systems and weaknesses of library resources and services;

(b) Identifying the levels and kinds of user needs;

(c) Identifying faculty and students' priorities for library resources and services;

(d) Identifying the limitations or problems which seem to discourage the use of the library;

(e) Identifying the level of involvement or participation of faculty and students in the library programme; and

(f) Improving the organization and planning for library services at both the local and national levels.

For finding out the information seeking attitudes of users he suggests the following questions to be asked:

(a) What do users require from the library in terms of type, quality, and range of services to satisfy their need?

(b) What does user do about his/her needs?

(c) How does user select available sources?

(d) How does the user carry out a search for information?

## User Studies : A Statistical Survey

A number of works of a reviewing, methodological or theoretical nature on user studies has appeared. The most inclusive bibliography is 'Bibliography of user Surveys 1950-70' compiled by Atkins in 1971. Her collection of 687 Studies for all types of libraries except for special libraries is based upon a review of 1,200 studies during the two decades, 1950-70.

The paper 'Discovering the user and his information needs' by D.N. Wood lists user studies conducted during 1966-70. The compilation 'User studies: A Review for librarians and Information Scientists' by Bates cite 181 studies up to 1968.

In 1970 the New York Library Association issued a publication 'Use, Misuse and Non-use of academic libraries', including and annotated bibliography of user requirements. This is a selected list (20 Pages) of papers dealing with use, the making of surveys, and the problems of library use instruction.

## User Study Methods

Various methods for the study of information use behaviour largely include survey methods used in social sciences, such as questionnaire, interview, participant observation and also experiments in field settings. Most frequently used method is that of questionnaire. Paisley (1965) speaks of questionnaire as a compromise technique expedient to use shortcomings as low response, respondents' understanding and interpretation of the questions and inability to clarify incomplete responses.

Guha categories the methods used for the information needs assessment under the following heads:

1. General or conventional methods
2. Questionnaire
3. Interview
4. Diary
5. Observation by self
6. Operations research study

## Techniques of User Studies

The important techniques that are commonly helpful in developing the resource collection are discussed below:

### *General Method*

1. Questionnaire
2. Interview
3. Observation
4. Operation research study
5. Diary

## Indirect Methods in the Context of Information Use

Analysis of Library records.

Citation analysis.

## Special and Unconventional Methods

1. Computer feedback.
2. Unconventional methods.

Three important aspects are involved in the selection of methods:

1. Selection of sample of user population.

2. Determination of procedures for collection of data from or about the sample.
3. Determination of procedures for analysis of collected data to derive or summarise results.

It is always useful to consult a statistician and take his help in the selection of appropriate methods to be followed in the envisaged user study. This would greatly enhance the usefulness of the results derived from the user study.

As to the question of selection of a sample of user population, there are a number of methods available which would facilitate this task. The most common in this regard being:

1. *Convenience Sampling:* Which means picking the first 2550 etc. users that come along as subject of study;
2. *Random Sampling:* Which involves picking users for the study from a population at random;
3. *Stratified Sampling:* Which involves sub-dividing the population into sub-groups and then picking users for study at random; and
4. *Representative Sampling:* Which involves determining beforehand individuals, pairs of individuals, or small groups with some characteristics in common as subject of study.

## User Behaviour

User studies are being conducted on the behaviour of the user in seeking information, instead of the needs of the user. These studies are more useful to study the user, his psychology, the working condition, the impact of his position in the society, etc.

## Information Seeking Behaviour

According to Wilson information seeking behaviour results from the recognition of some need, perceived by the user. That behaviour may take several forms: the user may make demands upon formal systems, such as libraries on-line services, information centers; or upon systems which may perform information functions in addition to a primary, non-information function such as estate agents' offices or car sales agencies that give current information of their field viz., prices and models, etc.

Girja Kumar has emphasized that the information seeking behaviour is mainly concerned with who needs what kind of information and for what reasons; how information is found, evaluated and used, and how there needs can be identified and satisfied. According to him the following process takes place in the information seeking behaviour.

1. Identifying objective
2. Define need
3. Accessing information system

4. Establishing sources of information
5. Information acquisition
6. Use of Information
7. Satisfaction/Dissatisfaction

The Information seeking behaviour essentially refers to the strategies and actions undertaken to locate discrete knowledge elements. It is concerned with the integrative utilization of the three basic resources: People, Information and System. It can be said that the behaviour, which yields the highest information satisfaction, is the best.

## Survey Research in Library and Information Science

Survey methods are widely used in many disciplines including Library and Information Science. Busha and Harter state that "Librarians have long conducted surveys". Usually in Library and Information Science, community surveys are conducted to gather information about Libraries and their clientele.

"Community Surveys are conducted to gather recorded or unrecorded data about social, political and economic factors of the Libraries community". It is used in decision-making, in planning, developing and conducting library services.

Library Surveys on the other hand are concerned with systematic in-depth examination of libraries, library systems, library networks, etc.

## Development in Library Surveys

The survey research in Librarianship is of recent origin. Formerly libraries were very small in size and number, and their study was considered rather insignificant. They were then managed easily, without recourse to any scientific method to study their functioning. Libraries now have grown in number, size and in complexities. These factors have added to the growth in the number of staff, collections and users.

Library Surveys as a result of above factors of change began to emerge during the 1930's. Because of increasing and urgent needs of users, there is a shift in emphasis in Library Surveys, from profiles of Libraries to users of Libraries. Literature Survey and analysis on Library Surveys show that user studies did not appear as a heading in "Library Literature" till 1960's.

## Use of Library Surveys

Library Surveys are used to bring complex situations under control. The uses of Library Survey are:

- To provide information to the librarian and authorities as well;
- To satisfy curiosity of the information seeker;
- To plan and evaluate library services; and
- At the least the library survey method would help to do is answer or anticipate grievances of users.

## User Survey

User component will have a bearing on almost all aspects of library and information system. Research enquiries about users facilitate the understanding of their characteristic features, needs, preferences, practices, opinions, attitudes, behaviour, evaluation and the like. User studies or surveys are quite familiar to library and information science professionals.

User studies, use studies, information-need studies, user satisfaction and dissatisfaction studies, information transfer studies, communication behaviour studies, Information use Pattern studies, Choice of materials and preference studies, are all closely related.

User studies are fundamental for designing any information system and services. User studies should be undertaken periodically in order to evaluate and update measures for the betterment of collection and services in a library.

By observing users and eliciting information from them through user studies, the librarian discovers the characteristics of users, their information needs and their library behaviour, attitudes, opinions, priorities, preferences and ultimately evaluation of user related facets.

User category studies include Non-users, habitual users, potential users, under served users and deprived users.

## Research Design

User surveys and use studies normally come under the purview of Descriptive design with questionnaire mode of data collection.

Right from the choice of topic to report writing, user surveys also follow the general facets prescribed for any social science research.

## Presentation of Data

The data collected through Survey must be transformed into data files (for computer analysis) or compiled into tables. This operation is considered as presentation of analysed data.

## Steps in Presentation

Analysis involves many steps such as :

- Categorization
- Coding
- Tabulation
- Statistical Analysis and Inference.

But practically presentation is done before analysis. In brief the basic steps of presentation are :

## Coding

It consists of assigning symbols, usually numeric, to each answer through coding, raw data are transformed into symbols that may be tabulated.

### Tabulation

It is an orderly arrangement of data in columns and rows. It is a part of the technical process in statistical analysis of data. The essential element in tabulation is the summarization of results in the form of statistical tables. This is of great help in the analysis and interpretation of data. While preparing tabulation, the purpose of the Study has always to be kept in mind.

### Statistical Analysis and Inference

The range of statistical techniques used in the survey analysis is too large and varied. According to Busha and Harter, the statistical methodology consists of :

#### (a) *Descriptive Statistics*

It consists of methods and procedures for summarizing, simplifying, reducing and presenting of raw data to communicate the essence of data to another. The purpose of such method is essentially reporting.

#### (b) *Inferential Statistics*

These are somewhat more ambitious. Inferential methods and techniques are used to make predictions to list hypothesis and to infer characteristics of a population from the characteristics of the sample. In general, techniques of inferential statistics proceed well beyond mere description of a set of data in some sense. They also attempt to shed some light and meaning to the data. Statistical tests that could be employed in inferential analysis includes : chi-square test, t-test, f-text, etc.

## READING HABIT OF STUDENTS—LIBRARY USE STUDY

### Questionnaire

1. Name of the student
2. Sex — M / F
3. Course — UG / PG / Faculty
4. Residence — Rural / Urban / Hostel
5. Education of the Parents — Uneducated / +2 / UG / PG / PG+
6. Income of the Parents — <2500 / 2501 to 5000 / 5001 to 8000 / >8001
7. Whether there are other educated brothers/sisters in the family
   Yes / No
8. Frequency of visit to the college library
   a. Almost daily
   b. Once in a week
   c. Once in a month
   d. Rarely
   e. Never
9. Why do you use the college library?
   a. Pleasant and enjoyable atmosphere
   b. To locate books for recreational reading
   c. To locate books for school assignments
   d. Quiet study areas
   e. To look at magazines
   f. To use reference materials
   g. Helpful library staff
10. If you cannot find the materials that you are looking for in the college library, what do you do?
    a. I browse along the shelves
    b. I ask a friend for help
    c. I give up and leave
    d. I ask staff for assistance
    e. I visit another library
    f. I use the Internet
    g. Others
11. Who encourages you to use the school library?
    a. Mother, Father, or Guardian
    b. Brother or Sister
    c. Friend
    d. Teacher
    e. Librarian
    f. Others
12. Time spent in the college library
    a. Less than an hour
    b. One hour

c. Two-Tthree hour
d. More than three hours

13. What type of reading materials you usually consult
    a. Text books
    b. Reference books
    c. Journals
    d. Magazines
    e. Story books
14. Is the library hours adequate?
    a. Yes
    b. No
15. Is the library reading space adequate?
    a. Yes
    b. No
16. Opinion about the library staff
    a. Friendly
    b. Not friendly
17. Adequacy of the library collection
    a. Adequate
    b. Not adequate
18. Is the total number of books lent enough?
    a. Yes
    b. No
19. Adequacy of loan period
    a. Adequate
    b. Not adequate
20. For reading books you will consult
    a. Librarian
    b. Catalogue
    c. Go directly to racks
    d. Get the help of friends

## Questionnaire for Information Seeking Behaviour of Users of Academic Library/College/University

### QUESTIONNAIRE

1. Name of the User
2. Gender
   (a) Male ☐ (b) Female ☐
3. Status :
   (a) Faculty Members ☐ (b) Administrative Staff ☐
   (c) Student ☐
4. Residence
   (a) Rural ☐ (b) Urban ☐
5. Educational Qualification
   (a) UG ☐ (b) PG ☐
   (c) M.Phil. ☐ (d) Ph.D. ☐
6. How often do you visit the Library?
   (a) Every day ☐
   (b) Once in a week ☐
   (c) Once in a fortnight ☐
   (d) Once in a month ☐
   (e) Occasionally ☐
7. Purpose of Seeking Information
   (a) Developing knowledge ☐
   (b) Academic Improvement ☐
   (c) Employment Information ☐
   (d) Writing Journal articles ☐
   (e) Paper presentation for seminar conference ☐
   (f) Entertainment Information ☐
8. What Type of Resources You Consult for Seeking Information ?
   (a) Text Books ☐
   (b) News papers ☐
   (c) Journals/Periodicals ☐
   (d) Digital Resources ☐
   (e) Internet ☐
   (f) Thesis and Dissertations ☐
9. If Internet What is the Predominant Search Engine for Searching the Information?
   (a) Google ☐
   (b) Yahoo ☐
   (c) Khoj ☐
   (d) MSN ☐
   (e) Altavista ☐
   (f) Others ☐
10. Which Books you Prefer more for Seeking Information?

(a) Books in general nature ☐
(b) Text books ☐
(c) Reference books ☐
(d) E-books ☐
(e) Others ☐

11. Level of satisfaction of information obtained from Library
(a) Very satified ☐
(b) Satisfied ☐
(c) Less Satisfactory ☐
(d) Dissatisfied ☐

12. Which newspaper you prefer more for seeking information?
(a) Regional Language News papers ☐
(b) English News papers ☐

13. Do you consult the Digital resources?
(a) Yes ☐
(b) No. ☐

14. If yes: specify the type of resources you consult for seeking information
(a) E. Journals ☐
(b) Data base of thesis and dissertation ☐
(c) Subjects gate ways ☐
(d) Portals ☐
(e) Web blogs ☐

15. Mention the level of satisfaction attained over seeking the Information from the books
(a) Very satisfied ☐
(b) Satisfied ☐
(c) Less Satisfactory ☐
(d) Dissatisfied ☐

16. Mention the level of satisfaction attained over seeking the Information from journals/magazines/periodicals
(a) Very Satisfied ☐
(b) Satisfied ☐
(c) Less Satisfactory ☐
(d) Dissatisfied ☐

17. Mention the level of satisfaction attained over seeking the Information from Digital resources:
(a) Very Satisfied ☐
(b) Satisfied ☐
(c) Less Satisfactory ☐
(d) Dissatisfied ☐

18. Opinion about the Services of the Library
(a) Very good ☐
(b) Good ☐
(c) No comments ☐
(d) Satisfactory ☐
(e) Poor ☐

## INTERNET USERS SURVEY QUESTIONNAIRE

1. Name :
2. Gender :
   (a) Male (b) Female
3. Course :
   (a) U.G (b) P.G.
   (c) M.Phil. (d) Ph.D.
4. Dwelling
   (a) Rural (b) Urban (c) Sub-Urban
5. Do you use Internet?
   (a) Yes (b) No
6. If yes, where do you access the Internet?
   (a) Home
   (b) College
   (c) Computer center
   (d) Internet cafe
7. How long have you been using Internet?
   (a) 1-2 years
   (b) 3-4 years
   (c) 5-6 years
   (d) 7-8 years
8. Time spend in Internet per day
   (a) One hour
   (b) 1½ hour
   (c) 2 hour
   (d) 2½ hour
   (e) 3 hour
   (f) More than four hour
9. What is the purpose of using Internet?
   (a) Developing knowledge
   (b) Academic Improvement
   (c) Employment Information
   (d) Writing Journal articles
   (e) Entertainment Information
10. What is the Search engine do you use in Internet?
    (a) google
    (b) yahoo
    (c) MSN
    (d) ltavista
    (e) Hotbot
    (f) Khoj
    (g) Kapok
    (h) Others
11. What devices do you prefer to store the Information from Internet?
    (a) CD-ROM
    (b) Floppy
    (c) Pen drive

(d) Hard Disc
(e) Others

12. Do you use E-mail for Communication?
(a) Yes
(b) No

13. If yes, what is the Name of the E-mail provider?
(a) Yahoo (b) Hotmail
(c) Gmail (d) Rediffmail
(e) VSNL

14. What are the problems that you are facing while using Internet?
(a) Slow access speed
(b) Difficulty in finding relevant Information
(c) Overload of information on the Internet
(d) Takes too long to view/download pages
(e) Privacy problem
(f) Any other

15. How do you browse the required Information from the Internet?
(a) From the Web address directly
(b) Use search engines
(c) Use subscription database
(d) Any other

16. Methods of learning Internet Skills
(a) Guidance from friends
(b) From college
(c) Self-instruction
(d) External course

17. Satisfaction of Internet Facilities
(a) Very satisfied
(b) Satisfied
(c) Dissatisfied
(d) Not satisfied

18. Do you use Library?
(a) Yes (b) No

19. Opinion about the Services of the Library
(a) Very good
(b) Good
(c) No comments
(d) Satisfactory
(e) Poor

20. Mention the level of satisfaction attained over seeking the Information from Libraries
(a) Very good
(b) Good
(c) No comments
(d) Satisfactory
(e) Poor

## BIBLIOMETRICS

Bibliometrics is a set of methods used to study or measure texts and information. *Citation analysis* and *content analysis* are commonly used bibliometric methods. While bibliometric methods are most often used in the field of *library and information science*, bibliometrics have wide applications in other areas. In fact, many research fields use bibliometric methods to explore the impact of their field, the impact of a set of researchers, or the impact of a particular paper.

Historically bibliometric methods have been used to trace relationships amongst academic journal citations. Citation analysis, which involves examining an item's referring documents, is used in searching for materials and analyzing their merit. *Citation indices*, such as *Institute for Scientific Information*'s *Web of Science*, allow users to search forward in time from a known article to more recent publications which cite the known item.

The terms *bibliometrics* and *scientometrics* have been introduced almost simultaneously by Alan Pritchard and by Nalimov and Mulchenko in 1969. While Pritchard explained the term bibliometrics as "the application of mathematical and statistical methods to books and other media of communication" (*Pritchard, 1969*), Nalimov and Mulchenko defined scientometrics as "the application of those quantitative methods which are dealing with the analysis of science viewed as an information process" (*Nalimov and Mulchenko, 1969*). According to these interpretations, scientometrics is restricted to the measurement of science communication, whereas bibliometrics is designed to deal with more general information processes.

According to Faithorne, Bibliometrics today is the quantitative treatment of the properties of recorded discourse and behaviour appertaining to it.

Bibliometrics utilizes quantitative analysis and statistics to describe patterns of publication within a given field or body of literature. Researchers may use bibliometric methods of evaluation to determine the influence of a single writer, for example, or to describe the relationship between two or more writers or works. One common way of conducting bibliometric research is to use the *Social Science Citation Index*, the *Science Citation Index* or the *Arts and Humanities Citation Index* to trace citations.

### Librametry

S.R. Ranganathan coined the term 'Librametry'. The term Librametry is a wider term, which includes in it the concept of Bibliometrics. He said there is a need to develop this subject on the lines of Bibliometry, Econometry, Psychometry, etc.

### Scope

Bibliometric studies may broadly be classified into two, namely, Descriptive studies and Behavioural studies.

### Descriptive Studies

It include those that describe the characteristic features of documents or Literatute. The following characteristics have been identified and studied.

1. Study of bodies producing documents. These include individual authors and research institutions.
2. Documents that carry information
3. Geographical origins
4. Quantity of information
5. Time and frequency of studies
6. Form of transmission such as books, journals etc.

### Behavioural Studies

Behavioural studies are those which that examine the relationship between various elements are following:

1. Authorship
2. Title statement
3. Bibliographic history ; Publication dates
4. Bibliographic; previous titles (serials)
5. Content
6. Form
7. Subscription prices
8. Subject
9. Related documents
10. Translation
11. Citation
12. Level of market orientation

### Use of Bibliometrics

It can be used with advantage to achieve
Productivity counts of Literature
Identification of peers, social change
Impact Literature
Types and amount of publications

### Bibliometrics and Scientometrics in Library and Information Science Research

Nowadays the major thrust areas of research in Library and Information Science is the application of Biblionmetrics and Scientometrics to various disciplines. These Studies include:

1. To examine the growth Literature output in a subject during a period of time.

2. To identify the quantum and structure literature on a specific subject during a particular period.
3. To identify the source and country-wise distribution of research literature output on a particular subject
4. To study the trend in authorship pattern
5. To analyse the trend in the language of publication on research literature on a particular subject
6. To analyse the degree of single *versus* multiple authored publications

## Laws of Bibliometrics

One of the main areas in bibliometric research concerns the application of bibliometric laws. The three most commonly used laws in bibliometrics are: Lotka's law of scientific productivity, Bradford's law of scatter, and Zipf's law of word occurrence.

## Lotka's Law

In 1926, Alfred J. Lotka proposed his 'Inverse Square Law' correlating contributors of scientific papers to their number of contributions.

Lotka's Law describes the frequency of publication by authors in a given field. It states that ". . . the number (of authors) making $n$ contributions is about $1/n^2$ of those making one; and the proportion of all contributors, that make a single contribution, is about 60 percent" (Lotka 1926, cited in Potter, 1988). This means that out of all the authors in a given field, 60 percent will have just one publication, and 15 percent will have two publications ($1/2^2$ times .60). 7 percent of authors will have three publications ($1/3^2$ times .60), and so on. According to Lotka's Law of scientific productivity, only six percent of the authors in a field will produce more than 10 articles. Lotka's Law, when applied to large bodies of literature over a fairly long period of time, can be accurate in general, but not statistically exact. It is often used to estimate the frequency with which authors will appear in an online catalog (Potter, 1988).

The general formula says:

$$X^nY = C$$

or

$$Y = C/X^n$$

where $X$ is the number of publications, $Y$ the relative frequency of authors with $X$ publications, and $n$ and $C$ are constants depending on the specific field ( ).

This law is believed to have applications in other fields for example in the military for fighter pilot kills.

For 100 authors, who on average each write one article each over a specific period, we have also:

| *Number of articles written* | *Number of authors writing that number of articles* |
|---|---|
| 10 | $100/10^2 = 1$ |
| 9 | $100/9^2$ H" 1 (1.23) |
| 8 | $100/8^2$ H" 2 (1.56) |
| 7 | $100/7^2$ H" 2 (2.04) |
| 6 | $100/6^2$ H" 3 (2.77) |
| 5 | $100/5^2 = 4$ |
| 4 | $100/4^2$ H" 6 (6.25) |
| 3 | $100/3^2$ H" 11 (11.111...) |
| 2 | $100/2^2 = 25$ |
| 1 | 100 |

of those making one contribution, i.e. a power law, where $a$ is often nearly 2. It is an empirical observation rather than a necessary result. This form of the law is as originally published and is sometimes referred to as the "discrete Lotka power function".

## Bradford's Law

Bradford in 1934 described a scattering pattern in the area of applied geophysics and lubrication.

Bradford's Law serves as a general guideline to librarians in determining the number of core journals in any given field. It states that journals in a single field can be divided into three parts, each containing the same number of articles: (1) a core of journals on the subject, relatively few in number, that produces approximately one-third of all the articles, (2) a second zone, containing the same number of articles as the first, but a greater number of journals, and (3) a third zone, containing the same number of articles as the second, but a still greater number of journals. The mathematical relationship of the number of journals in the core to the first zone is a constant $n$ and to the second zone the relationship is $n^2$. Bradford expressed this relationship as $1{:}n{:}n^2$. Bradford formulated his law after studying a bibliography of geophysics, covering 326 journals in the field. He discovered that 9 journals contained 429 articles, 59 contained 499 articles, and 258 contained 404 articles. So it took 9 journals to contribute one-third of the articles, 5 times 9, or 45, to produce the next third, and 5 times 9, or 225, to produce the last third. As may be seen, Bradford's Law is not statistically accurate, strictly speaking. But it is still commonly used as a general rule of thumb (Potter 1988).

## Zipf's Law

Zipf's Law is often used to predict the frequency of words within a text. The Law states that in a relatively lengthy text, if you "list the words occurring within that text in order of decreasing frequency, the rank of a word on that list multiplied by its frequency will equal a constant. The equation for this relationship is: $r \times f = k$, where $r$ is the rank of the word, $f$ is the frequency, and $k$ is the constant (Potter, 1988). Zipf illustrated his law with an analysis of James Joyce's *Ulysses*. "He showed that the tenth most frequent word occurred 2,653 times, the hundredth most frequent word occurred 265 times, the two hundredth word occurred 133 times, and so on. Zipf found, then that the rank of the word multiplied by the frequency of the word equals a constant that is approximately 26,500" (Potter, 1988). Zipf's Law, again, is not statistically perfect, but it is very useful for indexers.

## Theoretical issues

Zipf's law is most easily observed by scatterplotting the data, with the axes being log (rank order) and log (frequency). For example, "the" as described above would appear at $x = \log(1)$, $y = \log(69971)$. The data conform to Zipf's law to the extent that the plotted points appear to fall along a single line segment.

## Formally, let

- $N$ be the number of elements;
- $k$ be their rank; and
- $s$ be the value of the exponent characterizing the distribution.

Zipf's law then predicts that out of a population of $N$ elements, the frequency of elements of rank $k$, $f(k; s, N)$, is:

$$f(k; s, N) = f\frac{1/k^s}{\sum_{n=1}^{N}(1/n^s)}$$

In the example of the frequency of words in the English language, $N$ is the number of words in the English language and, if we use the classic version of Zipf's law, the exponent $s$ is 1. $f(k; s, N)$ will then be the fraction of the time the $k$th most common word occurs.

It is easily seen that the distribution is normalized, i.e., the predicted frequencies sum to 1:

$$\sum_{k=1}^{N} f(k;s,N) = 1$$

The law may also be written:

$$f(k; s, N = \frac{1}{k^s H_{N,s}}$$

where $H_{N,}$ is the $N$th generalized *harmonic number*.

The simplest case of Zipf's law is a "$1/f$ function". Given a set of Zipfian distributed frequencies, sorted from most common to least common, the second most common frequency will occur ½ as often as the first. The third most common frequency will occur 1/3 as often as the first. The $n^{th}$ most common frequency will occur $1/n$ as often as the first. However, this cannot hold exactly, because items must occur an integer number of times: there cannot be 2.5 occurrences of a word. Nevertheless, over fairly wide ranges, and to a fairly good approximation, many natural phenomena obey Zipf's law.

Mathematically, it is impossible for the classic version of Zipf's law to hold exactly if there are infinitely many words in a language, since the sum of all relative frequencies in the denominator above is equal to the harmonic series and therefore.

$$\sum_{n=1}^{\infty} \frac{1}{n} = \infty$$

In English, the frequencies of the approximately 1000 most-frequently-used words are approximately proportional to $1/n^s$ where $s$ is just slightly more than one.

As long as the exponent $s$ exceeds 1, it is possible for such a law to hold with infinitely many words, since if $s>1$ then

$$\zeta(s) = \sum_{n=1}^{\infty} \frac{1}{n^s} = < \infty$$

where $\zeta(s)$ is Riemann's zeta function.

Just why data conform to Zipfian distributions is a matter of some controversy. That Zipfian distributions arise in randomly-generated texts with no linguistic structure suggests that in linguistic contexts, the law may be a statistical artifact

## Citation Analysis

Another major area of bibliometric research uses various methods of citation analysis in order to establish relationships between authors or their work. Here is a definition of citation analysis, and definitions of co-citation coupling and bibliographic coupling, which are specific kinds of citation analysis. Weinstock isolates fifteen specific reasons for using citations:

1. Paying homage to pioneers
2. Giving credit for related work
3. Identifying methodology, equipment, etc.
4. Providing background reading
5. Correcting one's own work
6. Correcting the work of others
7. Criticizing previous work
8. Substantiating claims
9. Alerting research
10. Providing leads to poorly disseminated, poorly indexed or uncited work
11. Authentication data and classes of fact—physical constants, etc.

12. Identifying the original publications in which an idea or constant was discussed
13. Identifying original publications describing an eponymic concept of term as Hodgkin's disease, Pareto's law, Friedel-Crafts reaction
14. Disclaiming work or ideas of others
15. Disputing priority claims of others

When one author cites another author, a relationship is established. Citation analysis uses citations in scholarly works to establish links. Many different links can be ascertained, such as links between authors, between scholarly works, between journals, between fields, or even between countries. Citations both from and to a certain document may be studied. One very common use of citation analysis is to determine the impact of a single author on a given field by counting the number of times the author has been cited by others. One possible drawback of this approach is that authors may be citing the single author in a negative context (saying that the author doesn't know what's/he's talking about, for instance) (Osareh, 1996).

### Co-citation Coupling

Co-citation coupling is a method used to establish a subject similarity between two documents. If papers A and B are both cited by paper C, they may be said to be related to one another, even though they don't directly cite each other. If papers A and B are both cited by many other papers, they have a stronger relationship.

### Bibliographic Coupling

Bibliographic coupling operates on a similar principle, but in a way it is the mirror image of co-citation coupling. Bibliographic coupling links two papers that cite the same articles, so that if papers A and B both cite paper C, they may be said to be related, even though they don't directly cite each other.

## CONTENT ANALYSIS

Content analysis is a research technique used for analysing and describing objectively the content of communication. Bernard Berelson defined content analysis as "a research technique for the objective, systematic, and quantitative description of manifest content of communication".

The word 'Content', according to the Oxford English Dictionary means, that which is contained in anything. Again, the word 'Content' in the context of a book or a periodical refers to the table of contents or just contents appearing at the beginning. It gives the list of chapter headings in a book or captions or list of articles appearing in a periodical caption.

According to Bernard Berelson "Content Analysis is a research technique for the objective, systematic and quantitative description of the manifest content of communication"

According to Holsti, "Content Analysis is a technique for making inferences by objectively and systematically identifying specified characteristics of message".

Harold Lasswell formulated the core questions of content analysis: "Who says what, to whom, why, to what extent and with what effect?." Ole Holsti (1969) offers a broad definition of content analysis as "any technique for making inferences by objectively and systematically identifying specified characteristics of messages."

Kimberly A. Neuendorf (2002) offers a six-part definition of content analysis:

> "Content analysis is an indepth analysis using quantitative or qualitative techniques of messages using a scientific method (including attention to objectivity-intersubjectivity, *a priori* design, reliability, validity, generalizability, replicability, and hypothesis testing) and is not limited as to the types of variables that may be measured or the context in which the messages are created or presented."

## Content Analysis as a Research Tool

Content analysis is a research tool used to determine the presence of certain words or concepts within texts or sets of texts. Researchers quantify and analyze the presence, meanings and relationships of such words and concepts, then make inferences about the messages within the texts, the writer(s), the audience, and even the culture and time of which these are a part. Texts can be defined broadly as books, book chapters, essays, interviews, discussions, newspaper headlines and articles, historical documents, speeches, conversations, advertising, theater, informal conversation, or really any occurrence of communicative language. Texts in a single study may also represent a variety of different types of occurrences, such as Palmquist's 1990 study of two composition classes, in which he analyzed student and teacher interviews, writing journals, classroom discussions and lectures, and out-of-class interaction sheets. To conduct a content analysis on any such text, the text is coded, or broken down, into manageable categories on a variety of levels—word, word sense, phrase, sentence, or theme—and then examined using one of content analysis' basic methods: conceptual analysis or relational analysis.

## Types of Content Analysis

There are two general categories of content analysis: *conceptual analysis and relational analysis*. Conceptual analysis can be thought of as establishing the existence and frequency of concepts—most often represented by words of phrases—in a text. For instance, say you have a hunch that your favourite poet often writes about hunger. With conceptual analysis you can determine how many times words such as "hunger", "hungry", "famished", or "starving" appear in a volume of poems. In contrast, relational analysis goes one step further by examining the relationships among concepts in a text. Returning to the "hunger" example, with relational analysis, you could identify what other words or phrases "hunger" or "famished" appear next to and then determine what different meanings emerge as a result of these groupings.

## Conceptual Analysis

Traditionally, content analysis has most often been thought of in terms of conceptual analysis. In conceptual analysis, a concept is chosen for examination, and the analysis involves quantifying and tallying its presence. Also known as thematic analysis [although this term is somewhat problematic, given its varied definitions in current literature. The focus here is on looking at the occurrence of selected terms within a text or texts, although the terms may be implicit as well as explicit. While explicit terms obviously are easy to identify, coding for implicit terms and deciding their level of implication is complicated by the need to base judgments on a somewhat subjective system. To attempt to limit the subjectivity, then (as well as to limit problems of reliability and validity), coding such implicit terms usually involves the use of either a specialized dictionary or contextual translation rules. And sometimes, both tools are used—a trend reflected in recent versions of the Harvard and Lasswell dictionaries.

## Methods of Conceptual Analysis

Conceptual analysis begins with identifying research questions and choosing a sample or samples. Once chosen, the text must be coded into manageable content categories. The process of coding is basically one of selective reduction. By reducing the text to categories consisting of a word, set of words or phrases, the researcher can focus on, and code for, specific words or patterns that are indicative of the research question.

An example of a conceptual analysis would be to examine several Clinton speeches on health care, made during the 1992 presidential campaign, and code them for the existence of certain words. In looking at these speeches, the research question might involve examining the number of positive words used to describe Clinton's proposed plan, and the number of negative words used to describe the current status of health care in America. The researcher would be interested only in quantifying these words, not in examining how they are related, which is a function of relational analysis. In conceptual analysis, the researcher simply wants to examine presence with respect to his/her research question, i.e. is there a stronger presence of positive or negative words used with respect to proposed or current health care plans, respectively.

Once the research question has been established, the researcher must make his/her coding choices with respect to the eight category coding steps indicated by Carley (1992).

## Relational Analysis

Relational analysis, like conceptual analysis, begins with the act of identifying concepts present in a given text or set of texts. However, relational analysis seeks to go beyond presence by exploring the relationships between the concepts identified. Relational analysis has also been termed semantic analysis (Palmquist, Carley, & Dale, 1997). In other words, the focus of relational analysis is to look for semantic, or meaningful, relationships. Individual concepts, in and of themselves, are viewed as having no inherent meaning. Rather, meaning is a product of the relationships among concepts in a text. Carley (1992) asserts that concepts are "ideational kernels;" these kernels can be thought of as symbols, which acquire meaning through their connections to other symbols.

## Theoretical Influences on Relational Analysis

The kind of analysis that researchers employ will vary significantly according to their theoretical approach. Key theoretical approaches that inform content analysis include linguistics and cognitive science. *Linguistic approaches* to content analysis focus analysis of texts on the level of a linguistic unit, typically single clause units. One example of this type of research is Gottschalk (1975), who developed an automated procedure, which analyzes each clause in a text and assigns it a numerical score based on several emotional/psychological scales. Another technique is to code a text grammatically into clauses and parts of speech to establish a matrix representation (Carley, 1990).

Approaches that derive from *cognitive science* include the creation of decision maps and mental models. Decision maps attempt to represent the relationship(s) between ideas, beliefs, attitudes, and information available to an author when making a decision within a text. These relationships can be represented as logical, inferential, causal, sequential, and mathematical relationships. Typically, two of these links are compared in a single study, and are analyzed as networks. For example, Heise (1987) used logical and sequential links to examine symbolic interaction. This methodology is thought of as a more generalized cognitive mapping technique, rather than the more specific mental models approach.

*Mental models* are groups or networks of interrelated concepts that are thought to reflect conscious or sub-conscious perceptions of reality. According to cognitive scientists, internal mental structures are created as people draw inferences and gather information about the world. Mental models are a more specific approach to mapping because beyond extraction and comparison because they can be numerically and graphically analyzed. Such models rely heavily on the use of computers to help analyze and construct mapping representations. Typically, studies based on this approach follow five general steps:

1. Identifying concepts.
2. Defining relationship types.
3. Coding the text on the basis of 1 and 2.
4. Coding the statements.
5. Graphically displaying and numerically analyzing the resulting maps.

To create the model, a researcher converts a text into a map of concepts and relations; the map is then analyzed on the level of concepts and statements, where a statement consists of two concepts and their relationship.

## Steps in Conceptual Analysis

### 1. *Decide the Level of Analysis*

First, the researcher must decide upon the level of analysis. With the health care speeches, to continue the example, the researcher must decide whether to code for a single word, such as "inexpensive," or for sets of words or phrases, such as "coverage for everyone."

### 2. *Decide How Many Concepts to Code for*

The researcher must now decide how many different concepts to code for. This involves developing a pre-defined or interactive set of concepts and categories. The researcher must decide whether or not to code for every single positive or negative word that appears, or only certain ones that the researcher determines are most relevant to health care. Then, with this pre-defined number set, the researcher has to determine how much flexibility he/she allows him/herself when coding. The question of whether the researcher codes only from this pre-defined set, or allows him/herself to add relevant categories not included in the set as he/she finds them in the text, must be answered. Determining a certain number and set of concepts allows a researcher to examine a text for very specific things, keeping him/her on task. But introducing a level of coding flexibility allows new, important material to be incorporated into the coding process that could have significant bearings on one's results.

### 3. *Decide Whether to Code for Existence or Frequency of a Concept*

After a certain number and set of concepts are chosen for coding , the researcher must answer a key question: is he/she going to code for existence or frequency? This is important, because it changes the coding process. When coding for existence, "inexpensive" would only be counted once, no matter how many times it appeared. This would be a very basic coding process and would give the researcher a very limited perspective of the text. However, the number of times "inexpensive" appears in a text might be more indicative of importance. Knowing that "inexpensive" appeared 50 times, for example, compared to 15 appearances of "coverage for everyone," might lead a researcher to interpret that Clinton is trying to sell his health care plan based more on economic benefits, not comprehensive coverage. Knowing that "inexpensive" appeared, but not that it appeared 50 times, would not allow the researcher to make this interpretation, regardless of whether it is valid or not.

## 4. Decide on How to Distinguish Among Concepts

The researcher must next decide on the level of generalization, i.e. whether concepts are to be coded exactly as they appear, or if they can be recorded as the same even when they appear in different forms. For example, "expensive" might also appear as "expensiveness." The research needs to determine if the two words mean radically different things to him/her, or if they are similar enough that they can be coded as being the same thing, i.e. "expensive words." In line with this, is the need to determine the level of implication one is going to allow. This entails more than subtle differences in tense or spelling, as with "expensive" and "expensiveness." Determining the level of implication would allow the researcher to code not only for the word "expensive," but also for words that imply "expensive." This could perhaps include technical words, jargon, or political euphemism, such as "economically challenging," that the researcher decides does not merit a separate category, but is better represented under the category "expensive," due to its implicit meaning of "expensive."

## 5. Develop Rules for Coding Your Texts

After taking the generalization of concepts into consideration, a researcher will want to create translation rules that will allow him/her to streamline and organize the coding process so that he/she is coding for exactly what he/she wants to code for. Developing a set of rules helps the researcher insure that he/she is coding things consistently throughout the text, in the same way every time. If a researcher coded "economically challenging" as a separate category from "expensive" in one paragraph, then coded it under the umbrella of "expensive" when it occurred in the next paragraph, his/her data would be invalid. The interpretations drawn from that data will subsequently be invalid as well. Translation rules protect against this and give the coding process a crucial level of consistency and coherence.

## 6. Decide What to Do with "Irrelevant" Information

The next choice a researcher must make involves irrelevant information. The researcher must decide whether irrelevant information should be ignored (as Weber, 1990, suggests), or used to re-examine and/or alter the coding scheme. In the case of this example, words like "and" and "the," as they appear by themselves, would be ignored. They add nothing to the quantification of words like "inexpensive" and "expensive" and can be disregarded without impacting the outcome of the coding.

## 7. Code the Texts

Once these choices about irrelevant informations are made, the next step is to code the text. This is done either by hand, i.e. reading through the text and manually writing down concept occurrences, or through the use of various computer programs. Coding with a computer is one of contemporary conceptual analysis' greatest assets. By inputting one's categories, content analysis programs can easily automate the coding process and examine huge amounts of data, and a wider range of texts, quickly and efficiently. But automation is very dependent on the researcher's preparation and category construction.

### 8. *Analyze of Results*

Once the coding is done, the researcher examines the data and attempts to draw whatever conclusions and generalizations are possible. Of course, before these can be drawn, the researcher must decide what to do with the information in the text that is not coded. One's options include either deleting or skipping over unwanted material, or viewing all information as relevant and important and using it to reexamine, reassess and perhaps even alter one's coding scheme. Furthermore, given that the conceptual analyst is dealing only with quantitative data, the levels of interpretation and generalizability are very limited. The researcher can only extrapolate as far as the data will allow. But it is possible to see trends, for example, that are indicative of much larger ideas. Using the example from step three, if the concept "inexpensive" appears 50 times, compared to 15 appearances of "coverage for everyone," then the researcher can pretty safely extrapolate that there does appear to be a greater emphasis on the economics of the health care plan, as opposed to its universal coverage for all Americans

## Steps in Relational Analysis

### 1. *Decide the Level of Analysis*

First, the researcher must decide upon the *level of analysis*. With the health care speeches, to continue the example, the researcher must decide whether to code for a single word, such as "inexpensive," or for sets of words or phrases, such as "coverage for everyone."

### 2. *Choose a Sample or Samples for Analysis*

Once the question has been identified, the researcher must select sections of text/speech from the hearings in which Bill Clinton may have not told the entire truth or is obviously holding back information. For relational content analysis, the primary consideration is how much information to preserve for analysis. One must be careful not to limit the results by doing so, but the researcher must also take special care not to take on so much that the coding process becomes too heavy and extensive to supply worthwhile results.

### 3. *Determine the Type of Relationships to Examine*

Once the sample has been chosen for analysis, it is necessary to determine what type or types of relationships you would like to examine. There are different subcategories of relational analysis that can be used to examine the relationships in texts.

### 4. Reduce the Text to Categories and Code for Words or Patterns

At the simplest level, a researcher can code merely for existence. This is not to say that simplicity of procedure leads to simplistic results. Many studies have successfully employed this strategy. For example Palmquist (1990) did not attempt to establish the relationships among concept terms in the classrooms he studied; his study did, however, look at the change in the presence of concepts over the course of the semester, comparing a map analysis from the beginning of the semester to one constructed at the end. On the other hand, the requirement of one's specific research question may necessitate deeper levels of coding to preserve greater detail for analysis.

### 5. Explore the Relationships Between Concepts

Once words are coded, the text can be analyzed for the relationships among the concepts set forth. There are three concepts, which play a central role in exploring the relations among concepts in content analysis.

(a) *Strength of Relationship*: Refers to the degree to which two or more concepts are related. These relationships are easiest to analyze, compare, and graph when all relationships between concepts are considered to be equal. However, assigning strength to relationships retains a greater degree of the detail found in the original text. Identifying strength of a relationship is key when determining whether or not words like unless, perhaps, or maybe are related to a particular section of text, phrase, or idea.

(b) *Sign of a Relationship*: Refers to whether or not the concepts are positively or negatively related. To illustrate, the concept "bear" is negatively related to the concept "stock market" in the same sense as the concept "bull" is positively related. Thus "it's a bear market" could be coded to show a negative relationship between "bear" and "market". Another approach to coding for strength entails the creation of separate categories for binary oppositions. The above example emphasizes "bull" as the negation of "bear," but could be coded as being two separate categories, one positive and one negative. There has been little research to determine the benefits and liabilities of these differing strategies. Use of Sign coding for relationships in regard to the hearings my be to find out whether or not the words under observation or in question were used adversely or in favour of the concepts (this is tricky, but important to establishing meaning).

### Direction of the Relationship

Refers to the type of relationship categories exhibit. Coding for this sort of information can be useful in establishing, for example, the impact of new information in a decision making process. Various types of directional relationships include, "X implies Y," "X occurs before Y" and "if X then Y," or quite simply the decision whether concept X is the "prime mover" of Y or *vice versa*. In the case of the 1998 hearings, the researcher might note that, "maybe implies doubt," "perhaps occurs before statements of clarification," and "if possibly exists, then there is room for Clinton to change his stance." In some cases, concepts can be said to be bi-directional, or having equal influence. This is equivalent to ignoring directionality. Both approaches are useful, but differ in focus. Coding all categories as bi-directional is most useful for exploratory studies where pre-coding may influence results, and is also most easily automated, or computer coded.

### 6. Code the Relationships

One of the main differences between conceptual analysis and relational analysis is that the statements or relationships between concepts are coded. At this point, to continue our extended example, it is important to take special care with assigning value to the relationships in an effort to determine whether the ambiguous words in Bill Clinton's speech are just fillers, or hold information about the statements he is making.

### 7. Perform Statistical Analyses

This step involves conducting statistical analyses of the data you've coded during your relational analysis. This may involve exploring for differences or looking for relationships among the variables you've identified in your study.

### 8. Map the Representations

In addition to statistical analysis, relational analysis often leads to viewing the representations of the concepts and their associations in a text (or across texts) in a graphical—or map—form. Relational analysis is also informed by a variety of different theoretical approaches like linguistic content analysis, decision mapping, and mental models.

## Practical Applications of Content Analysis

Content analysis can be a powerful tool for determining authorship. For instance, one technique for determining authorship is to compile a list of suspected authors, examine their prior writings, and correlate the frequency of nouns or function words to help build a case for the probability of each person's authorship of the data of interest. A Bayesian technique based on word frequency was used to show that Madison was indeed the author of the Federalist papers; recently, a more holistic approach was used to determine the identity of the anonymous author of the 1992 book Primary Colors.

Content analysis is also useful for examining trends and patterns in documents. For example, Stemler and Bebell (1998) conducted a content analysis of school mission statements to make so inferences about what schools hold as their primary reasons for existence. One of the major research questions was whether the criteria being used to measure program effectiveness (e.g., academic test scores) were aligned with the overall program objectives or reason for existence.

### Conducting a Content Analysis

According to Krippendorff (1980), six questions must be addressed in every content analysis:

(a) Which data are analyzed?
(b) How are they defined?
(c) What is the population from which they are drawn?
(d) What is the context relative to which the data are analyzed?
(e) What are the boundaries of the analysis?
(f) What is the target of the inferences?

At least three problems can occur when documents are being assembled for content analysis. First, when a substantial number of documents from the population are missing, the content analysis must be abandoned. Second, inappropriate records (e.g., ones that do not match the definition of the document required for analysis) should be discarded, but a record should be kept of the reasons. Finally, some documents might match the requirements for analysis but just be uncodable because they contain missing passages or ambiguous content.

### Analyzing the Data

Perhaps the most common notion in qualitative research is that a content analysis simply means doing a word—frequency count. The assumption made is that the words that are mentioned most often are the words that reflect the greatest concerns. While this may be true in some cases, there are several counterpoints to consider when using simple word frequency counts to make inferences about matters of importance.

One thing to consider is that synonyms may be used for stylistic reasons throughout a document and thus may lead the researchers to underestimate the importance of a concept (Weber, 1990). Also bear in mind that each word may not represent a category equally well. Unfortunately, there are no well-developed weighting procedures, so for now, using word counts requires the researcher to be aware of this limitation. Furthermore, Weber reminds us that, "not all issues are equally difficult to raise. In contemporary America it may well be easier for political parties to address economic issues such as trade and deficits than the history and current plight of Native American living precariously on reservations" (1990, p. 73). Finally, in performing word frequency counts, one should bear in mind that some words may have multiple meanings.

For instance the word "state" could mean a political body, a situation, or a verb meaning "to speak". A good rule of thumb to follow in the analysis is to use word frequency counts to identify words of potential interest, and then to use a Key Word In Context (KWIC) search to test for the consistency of usage of words. Most qualitative research software (e.g., NUD*IST, Hyper RESEARCH; see further information at the end of this Digest) allows the researcher to pull up the sentence in which that word was used so that he or she can see the word in some context. This procedure will help to strengthen the validity of the inferences that are being made from the data.

### Emergent *vs.* a Priori Coding

There are two approaches to coding data that operate with slightly different rules. With emergent coding, categories are established following some preliminary examination of the data. The steps to follow are outlined in Haney, Russell, Gulek, & Fierros (1998) and will be summarized here. First, two people independently review the material and come up with a set of features that form a checklist. Second, the researchers compare notes and reconcile any differences that show up on their initial checklists. Third, the researchers use a consolidated checklist to independently apply coding. Fourth, the researchers check the reliability of the coding (a 95% agreement is suggested; .8 for Cohen's kappa). If the level of reliability is not acceptable, then the researchers repeat the previous steps. Once the reliability has been established, the coding is applied on a large-scale basis. The final stage is a periodic quality control check.

When dealing with a priori coding, the categories are established prior to the analysis based upon some theory. Professional colleagues agree on the categories, and the coding is applied to the data. Revisions are made as necessary, and the categories are tightened up to the point that maximizes mutual exclusivity and exhaustiveness (Weber, 1990).

### Coding Units

There are several different ways of defining coding units. The first way is to define them physically in terms of their natural or intuitive borders. The second way to define the recording units syntactically, that is, to use the separations created by the author, such as words, sentences, or paragraphs. A third way to define them is to use referential units. Referential units refer to the way a unit is represented. A fourth method of defining coding units is by using propositional units. Propositional units are perhaps the most complex method of defining coding units because they work by breaking down the text in order to examine underlying assumptions.

Typically, three kinds of units are employed in content analysis:

Sampling units,
Context units, and
Recording units.

Sampling units will vary depending on how the researcher makes meaning; they could be words, sentences, or paragraphs. In the mission statements project, the sampling unit was the mission statement. Context units neither need be independent or separately describable. They may overlap and contain many recording units. Context units do, however, set physical limits on what kind of data you are trying to record. In the mission statements project, the context units were sentences. This was an arbitrary decision, and the context unit could just as easily have been paragraphs or entire statements of purpose. Recording units, by contrast, are rarely defined in terms of physical boundaries. In the mission statements project, the recording unit was the idea(s) regarding the purpose of school found in the mission statements (e.g., develop responsible citizens or promote student self-worth). Thus a sentence that reads, "The mission of Jason Lee School is to enhance students' social skills, develop responsible citizens, and foster emotional growth" could be coded in three separate recording units, with each idea belonging to only one category (Krippendorff, 1980).

## USES OF LIBRARY IN RESEARCH

A researcher should make the maximum use of the Library information sources as there are wealth of information and materials in the Libraries. The researchers should not hurry into their research field without first consulting the necessary books, periodicals, past and present investigations of relevance official reports and statistics and records of institutions.

Consulting the available library information resources will be useful to a researcher in many ways as given below:

- Library resources provides the necessary background knowledge of the problem to be investigated and develops the insight of the researcher
- The knowledge secured from Library reading will also help a researcher understand the writing style and interpretation of findings.
- Secondary sources of data gathered from library serve as base for analysis and comparative study. It is more useful for interpretation.
- Library literature provides an opportunity of understanding the method, techniques, measures and approaches employed by other research scholars and thus lead to significant improvement of his design.
- Library helps the Research scholar to review the literature to find out the research gap which is the basis for most of the research projects.

### Sources available in the Library for Research purpose

A researcher must have knowledge of the sources of data which are kept in the reference shelves of the Library. Some of the important information sources are listed below.

- Dictionaries
- Encyclopaedias
- Handbooks
- Tables
- Formulas
- Manuals
- Textbooks
- Bibliographies
- Directories
- Gazetteers
- News Summaries and Newspaper Indexes
- Yearbooks

### *Dictionaries*

A Dictionary is a book, which deals with words of a language or of some special subjects, author, etc. Thus a dictionary is a wordbook. Although a dictionary is supposed to deal with words but often it may go beyond this.

### *Examples*

Websters "Third New International Dictionary of the English Language, unabridged with seven language dictionary. Springfield, Mass, Merriam, 1961.

### *Encyclopaedias*

An Encyclopaedia is a book giving information on all branches of knowledge or a specific subject. It is an ideal book, which deals with concepts. An encyclopaedia is a store-house of knowledge giving all information of significance. However, it is best used for finding answers to background questions related to general information and self-education. One often turns to encyclopaedias for one's every day information requirements. This is also true of scientist and technologists.

### *Examples*

Encyclopaedia Americana, New York.

### *Encyclopædia Britannica*

The Encyclopædia Britannica was first published in 1768-71 as Encyclopædia Britannica, or, A dictionary of arts and sciences, compiled upon a new plan. The Britannica was an important early English-language general encyclopaedia and is still regarded as one of the most important reference books in the English language. It is published today by Encyclopædia Britannica Inc., a privately held company.

From the late 18th century to the early 20th century, the Britannica's articles were often judged as the foremost authority on a topic, and sometimes included new research or theory intended for a scholarly audience. During this era, the Britannica gained its reputation and had a unique position in English-speaking culture.

### Hand Books

A handbook is a compilation of miscellaneous information in a compact and handy from. It contains data, procedure, principles, etc. Tables, graphs, Diagrams and illustration are provided. Scientists and technologists use handbook in their fields rather frequently.

#### Examples

Hand Book of Chemistry and Physics: A ready reference book of chemistry and physical data, 52nd ed., Cleveland Ohio, Chemical Rubber, 1971.

### Tables

Many of the handbooks contain data in the from of tables. Some of the handbooks devote substantial portion of the work to tables as compared with text. Tables are a convenient from to present data (e.g. extremely useful in science; especially physical sciences and technology.

#### Examples

International Critical Tables New York, McGraw Hill 1226-33, 7 vols. annex.

### Formulas

The practicing scientist or technologist turns more readily to and it is these that make up the bulk of titles in descriptive list such as W.R. Turnbull Scientific and Technical Dictionaries. It is common of such dictionaries to go beyond their basic function of defining works and examples. Abound of dictionaries are with substantial appendices of table, formulate and other non-dictionary data.

Pharmacopoeias are drug Handbooks. The British Pharmacopoeias appears every five years on the recommendations of Medicine commission under Act of Parliament. Supplementing pharmacopoeias are formularies such as British National Formulary, which are usually receipt books. Formularies other than pharmaceutical make a category of reference books that could be well studied with Hand.

#### Examples

The chemical Formulary (N.Y.) chemical publishing G, 1933.

### Manuals

In the common practice, a manual is an instruction book, which instructs how to do something by specific and clear directions.

### Examples

Manual for writers of term papers, theses, dissertations, revered, Chicago University of Chicago Press, 1955.

Professional investor's manual, by R.S. Greenly, London, Greenly, 1974.

### Text Books

A textbook is a book of information. Its primary aim is not to impart information about a specific subject but to enable one to develop proper understanding of the subject. Presentation is extremely important and it is prepared to serve a particular level of readership. It cannot be comprehensive. Often presentation is colourful and attractive giving plenty of illustrations and diagrams. A good textbook takes into consideration the method of teaching and the level of readership. It is revised, keeping iv view the new development and changing methodology of teaching. There is a difference of opinion about the place of textbooks as tertiary sources.

### Examples

Theory of Cataloguing by Girjakumar and Krishna Kumar, 2ne ed., Delhi, Vikas, 1977.

Text book of Cytology by Waiter V. Brown and Eldridge, M. 2nd ed., Berthe, St. Lovis Mosby, 1974

### Bibliographies

A bibliography is an organized list of primary or other sources relating to a given subject(s) or person. It is usually arranged alphabetically by author or chronologically or topic-wise. It may be comprehensive or selective. Sometimes, it may be provided with annotations. It may be published as a part of a larger work or as a separate work. The basic aim of a bibliography is to assist the users in locating the existence of or identifying a book or any other material, which may be of interest to him. A well prepared bibliography provides a definitive coverage of documents over a period of time within specified limits. Thus, it also serves the purpose of retrospective searching of literature.

### Examples

Dudley David Criffith, Bibliography of Chavcer, 1908-53 Scattle, University of Washington Press, 1955.

ASLIB book list, A monthly list of recommended scientific and technical books with annotations, London ASLIB, Vol. 1..... 1935, Monthly.

Indian National Bibliography (INB).

British National Bibliography (BNB).

### Directories

Directories form the largest category of reference sources. Directories provide information about organizations of different kinds covering learned bodies, scientific societies, professional bodies, trade associations etc. A directory is a list of persons, organizations, professions, industries or trades. The list is systematically arranged, either in alphabetical or in classified order. Because the information in directories becomes out-of date fairly rapidly they are published annually or new editions are brought out in every two three years.

## Types of Directories

### *(1) Local Directories*

Usually for the large towns and cities only. These normally include:

(a) A list of private residents, arranged alphabetically by surname.
(b) An alphabetical list of streets, giving the name of the occupier of each property in each street.
(c) A classified list of trades-similar to the "Yellow pages" in a telephone directory.
(d) List of establishments such as places of worship, places of entertainment, etc. e.g. Kelly's Post office London Directory.

### *(2) Professional Directories*

These are list of qualified practitioners in particular in professional, and include brief biographical details and sometimes information about the profession itself. For example:

(a) Crockfrod's Clerical Directory—published every other year,
(b) Law List—annual,
(c) Library Association Year Book—annual, and
(d) Medical Directory—annual,

### *(3) Trade Directories*

(a) General and National—i.e. All trades and industries of a particular country. Arrangement is usually classified or alphabetical; by the type of trade or industry; with an additional alphabetical list of individual firms, e.g. Kelly's Directory of Manufactures and Merchants; Kompass UK.
(b) Specialist and National—i.e., concerned with one field of industry in a particular country, e.g., British Plastics year Book.

### *(4) Telephone Directories*

Each telephone directory covers the subscribers in a defined geographical area. The main list is alphabetical by name of subscriber, but the "yellow pages" section, which is separately published, contains classified list of subscribers arranged by type of industry or service.

### Gazetteers

A Gazetteer is a directory of geographical places in addition to geographical location; it gives historical, statistical, cultural and other relevant information, such as pronunciation. Because they provide a variety of factual material about places, gazetteers are important reference sources. Recent editions describe a place as it is now; old editions give historical information about it. The economic growth or decline of give historical information about it. The economic growth or decline of a town or city as indicated by data on population, type of industries, schools and so on; will often be shown by the brief facts given in gazetteers over a period of years. Some gazetteers include entries for rivers, capes and other geographical features.

### News Summaries and Newspaper Indexes

Whenever reference queries on significant news or specific events, both current and retrospective are to be answered. "Index to Newspapers and News Summaries are used as dependable tools. They record incidents, events and facts from local, national and international Newspapers in a condensed from. Usually they are published in loose leaf from, so to be filed in libraries every week.

*Kissing's Contemporary Archives*: Weekly Diary of World Events, 1931— Bristol, Keesing.
*Facts on File*: The index of world events, 1940, New York.
*Africa Diary*: Weekly record of events in Africa with Index, 1961, New Delhi, Africa Press.
*Asian Recorder*: A weekly digest of outstanding Asian events with Index, 1955, Delhi, Sankaran.

### Year books

The current information and latest data on different subjects can be found in the yearbooks.

(a) Year book of Agricultural co-operation b. Year book of International organization.

## USES OF BIBLIOGRAPHIC DATABASES IN RESEARCH

A database is a set of information formatted into defined structures. In this context information is likely to be text. The text can be a basic bibliographic citation including author's names and identifying the source, it can be an enhanced citation including subject headings and abstracts or it could be a complete text of the article or report. The basic elements of a bibliographic database includes a variety of items or data elements such as author, title, journal title, publisher, collation, etc.

## CD-ROM Databases

The enormous storage capability of CD-ROM technology in small containers of disks has made the storage medium very attractive. This technology has made it possible to store enormous data in an unbelievable little space for any purpose, alphabets, digits, image, colour audio, graphics, multimedia, and the like. During the early phase of CD-ROM technology, as early as mid-1980's, bibliographic databases were stored. Now a major CD-ROM market is held by bibliographic and nonbibliographic databases for library and information areas. During last two decades a large number of CD-ROM manufacturers have produced enormous organized databases for access to information and full-texts in all branches of human knowledge and these are ongoing projects by large database producers.

The data stored on such disks can be retrieved, displayed, manipulated and printed in many ways but the users cannot alter the data on the disks. New updates are periodically added to the already existing core of data, with each new disk replacing each previous disk. In addition to its huge storage capability, there are several other features of CD-ROM that make it especially useful for libraries and information centre. The data on CD-ROM are permanently and physically encoded and cannot therefore, be lost by power cuts or surges. The physical elements of the disk containers and the 'print' on them is almost permanent and cannot be damaged ordinarily in adverse atmospheric and handling conditions. These disks cannot be affected by magnetic or microwave scanning. Another advantage of CD-ROM is that users can spend as much time of escalation of cost for the time consumed as in case of online search.

## ERIC

Established by the US government, ERIC acquires, indexes and distributes the most important and comprehensive collection of education materials available today. The search CD 450 Education Series consists of three valuable databases on five discs with in-depth information on the entire field of education.

ERIC's current files contain citations to education data complied related from 1982 to the present and consist of two separate files on one disc:

1. Current Index to Journals in Education (CIJE) lists over 10,000 citations and abstracts for articles in over 750 education-related journals.
2. Resources in Education (RIE) contains more than 79,000 annotated citations to technical and research reports, conference papers, government documents and other unique materials.

Both files allow the user to access information on thousands of subjects. ERIC users can easily locate information in the database using controlled vocabulary from the theasaures of ERIC Descriptions or free text terms.

ERIC-Retrospective Files provide comprehensive retrospective files for access to additional information on published and unpublished documents pertaining to education. The files are subjects of the ERIC database.

### Silver Platter CD-ROM Products

MEDLINE on silver platter is the entire MEDLINE database of the US National Library of Medicine from 1966 to present on compact disc. It contains bibliographic citations and abstracts of biomedical literature, and includes all foreign languages, all data elements, and fully indexed.

CANCER-CD contains references, abstracts and commentaries of the worlds literature in Cancer and related subjects from Elsevier Science Publishers, year book Medical Publishers and the complete CANCERLIT file from the National Cancer Institute in conjunction with the US National Library of Medicine. Silver Platter has merged duplicate citations into one record while preserving information that is unique to each information provider. Coverage is from 1985 to present.

CHEM-BANK is a collection on CD format of three major data banks of potentially hazardous chemicals: Registry of Toxic Effects of Chemical Substances (RTECS) from the US National Institute for Occupational safety and health; oil and hazardous materials technical assistance data system (OHMTADS) from the US environment protection agency; and chemical hazard response information system (CHRIS) from the US department of transportation (Coast Guard).

OSH-ROM is a collection of occupational health and safety information. It contains three complete bibliographic databases:

NIOSHTIC, database of the National Institute for Occupational Safety Health (USA),

HSELINE, database of the International safety executive (UK),

CISDOC, database of the International Labour Organization (UN),

Collectively these databases contain over 3,00,000 citations taken from over 500 journals and 1,00,000 monographs and technical reports.

PsycLIT contains journal citations with abstracts in psychology and behavioural sciences from the PsycINFO department of the American Psychological Association. Coverage is from 1974 to present.

Socio file is an index of sociological abstracts of world journals. It has published since 1974 and the enhanced bibliographic citations for dissertations in sociology and related disciplines that have been added to the database since 1986.

LISA contains abstracts of the worlds literature in library science, information science, and related discipline as compiled by the library association publishing ltd.

POPLINE is a bibliographic database containing more than 1,50,000 citations on population, family planning and related health care, law and policy issues. The database reaches as far back as 1886 and includes citations and abstracts to journal articles, monographs, technical reports, and unpublished works. POPLINE is maintained by the population information programme at John Hopkins University, USA.

OXLINE is a collection of toxicological information from the US National Library of medicine, containing references to published materials and research in progress in the areas of adverse drug reactions, air pollution, carcinogenesis via chemicals drug toxicity, food contamination, occupational hazards, pesticides and herbicides, toxicology analysis, water treatment, and more.

### UMI Data Base On Disc

The UMI CD-ROM products are ABI/INFORM, Dissertation abstracts, newspaper abstracts, periodical abstracts and resource/one. These are fully integrated and complementary resource for access to a broad range of sources, yet each database is also an independent reference, targeted to specific user needs. The basic record format is common to all UMI databases.

ABI/INFROM CD-ROM version provides bibliographic citations and 150 word abstracts for articles from more than 800 business and management periodicals. Dissertation abstracts provides indexing to nearly one million doctoral dissertations and masters theses from almost 500 north American and 50 British Universities. Two archival discs contains citations, in many cases, abstracts to some of the worlds most valuable original research accepted for advanced degrees from 1861 to 1984. Current disc includes citations and 350 word abstracts.

Newspaper abstracts indexes a number of reputed new papers of North America, with abstracts of about 25 words. Periodical Abstracts contains virtually cover-to-cover indexing of 300 current general interest periodicals, beginning with January 1988 issues, with abstracts is about 25 words. The most frequently used titles are cited, and all readers guide titles plus over a hundred more with periodical abstracts, users can research current topics in consumer affairs, the arts, policies, science, and other subject areas of general concern. Resource/One, the information access tool, is ideal from small libraries. All UMI On Disc databases are supported by full text services.

# 7

# Role of Information Technology in Research

## DEFINITION

Information technology means a variety of technological applications in the process of communication of information. The term Information technology has been used as collective term for the whole spectrum of technologies providing the ways and means to acquire, store, transmit, retrieve and process information. According to Webster's New Encyclopaedia, information technology is the collective term for the various technologies involved in the processing and transmission of information. Thus information technology includes computer technology, communication technology, multimedia technology, optical technology, networking technology, etc.

Information technology has wider connotations for librarians that include in addition technologies like repro-micrographic technology, technical communication technologies and database creation and use.

According to Dr. S.S. Murthy Information Technology is operative in the following environments:

(a) Classification, cataloguing, indexing, database creation, CAS, SDI, etc.
(b) Organizing databases and automating library housekeeping operations.
(c) Resource sharing and information dissemination.
(d) Photography, microfilms, microfiche, etc.

(e) Technical writing editing publishing and DTP.

## Areas of Information Technology

(a) *Methods of communicating Information:* Electronic mail, facsimile transmission, electronic journals, teleconferencing and data communication network.
(b) *Methods and Tools for recording of Knowledge:* Computer storage media, optical storage media allowed focus of activities to shift to the transaction recorded in the computers and the people making decisions and performing various tasks.
(c) *Methods of keeping Records:* Computer hardware, software, designing, creating and editing databases, etc
(d) *Methods of Indexing Documents and Information:* Computerized indexes and index files; large machine readable catalogues, network of libraries.

## COMPUTER

An electronic device that stores and manipulates information. A device capable of accepting data in the form of facts and figures, manipulating them in a prescribed way, and supplying the results of these processes as meaningful information. This device usually consists of input and output devices, storage, arithmetic and logic units, and a control unit. Usually an automatic, stored-program machine is implied.

### Characteristics of Computers

Computer performs various information processing operations in a much faster, accurate and efficient way. It gives a lot of ways and means to use in matters involving creativity and judgement. Independent of other factors of a computer, its characteristics are as follows:

Speed
Accuracy
Reliability
Capability
Storage Capacity
Diligence
Automation

### *Speed*

A computer can do arithmetic, geometric and such other mathematical functions. It can

Add and subtract numbers,
Compare letters to determine alphabetic sequence,

Move and copy numbers and letters, and
And perform scientific calculations at greater speed.

The significance is the speed with which computers carry out these operations. This *speed varies from a few microseconds (millionth of a second) to nanoseconds (billionth of a second)*. For instance, a microcomputer can evaluate investment decisions by performing hundreds of thousands of machine operations in a second.

### Accuracy

Computers are very accurate. They produce accurate results. They can *perform* their *innumerable operations with great accuracy*. Their circuits have no mechanical parts to wear any malfunctions. They can run continuously for days at a stretch without any error. Errors in hardware can occur, but error detecting techniques will prevent false results.

### Reliability

Computer output is generally very much reliable. One condition is that the input data and the program of instructions entering the computer should be relevant and correct.

### Capability

Computers are capable of doing anything that may challenge human brains. They can operate on data at phenomenal speeds. They can produce perfect results that would simply not be feasible otherwise. Computers can be used to provide management with up-to-the-minute figures on all aspects of its business. With that information, managers and policy-makers can make more meaningful decisions.

### Storage Capacity

Various computer media can store millions of characters of data in condensed form. Hence, a tremendous storage is possible to maintain the vital records necessary in a library/business environment. The storage capacity of hard disks in computers have gone beyond 80 GB. It is growing in terms of TBs (Tera Bytes). Banks, Libraries and very big organizations can store their thousands of records with their profiles on a computer very easily.

### Diligence

Diligence means being constant and earnest in effort and application. Human beings suffer from tiredness, lack of concentration and the like. Hence, they may not be able to repeat a work with the same or uniform spirit, energy and enthusiasm. Being a machine, computers do not have any of the weakness suffered by human beings. Whether it is the first time or the millionth time, computers work with the same diligence (speed and accuracy).

### Automation

The level of automation achieved with the computer is phenomenal. Automated systems have simplified the work as well as reduced the human strain. In an automated environment, computers execute the programs in correct sequences flawlessly. Libraries automate their services leading to user satisfaction.

Automation encompasses fields from designing to manufacturing, Road upto Air travel services, Restaurant to recreation, Education, Therapies, Administration and what not. Computer can switch on/off automatically at the desired/appropriate time. Computers, because of their human friendly characteristics, have become all pervasive. Their role has become inevitable.

### Five Generations of Computer

The development of electronic computer technology began in the early 1940s. During the 1980s and 90s, progress was towards more advanced systems and technologies. From the early 1940s to the present, there have been stages of development of computer technology and systems. Those stages have been named 'generations'.

Each computer generation had unique characteristics or properties. Four generations of computers have been identified so far and the race is on for the fifth generation. The different generations and the period they belonged to have been categorized as follows:

1. First Generation (1945-55)
2. Second Generation (1955-65)
3. Third Generation (1965-75)
4. Fourth Generation (1975-85)
5. Fifth Generation (1986- )

### Components of a Computer

A 'computer system' consists of three main functional components or sub-systems namely, the central processing unit (CPU); the input/output, and the internal memory.

### Central Processing Unit (CPU)

The CPU is generally referred to as the brain of the computer system. The CPU is composed of three units:

(I) Control unit,
(II) The Arithmetic Logic Unit (ALU), and
(III) The primary storage unit.

### The Control Unit

- Maintains order and controls activity in the CPU,

- Directs the sequence of operations,
- Interprets the instructions of a program in storage, and
- Produces signals that act as commands to circuits to execute the instructions.

## How Computer Works

A general purpose computer has four main sections: the arithmetic and logic unit (ALU), the control unit, the memory, and the input and output devices (collectively termed I/O). These parts are interconnected by busses, often made of groups of wires.

The control unit, ALU, registers, and basic I/O (and often other hardware closely linked with these) are collectively known as a central processing unit (CPU). Early CPUs were composed of many separate components but since the mid-1970s CPUs have typically been constructed on a single integrated circuit called a *microprocessor*.

### Control Unit

The control unit (often called a control system or central controller) directs the various components of a computer. It reads and interprets (decodes) instructions in the program one by one. The control system decodes each instruction and turns it into a series of control signals that operate the other parts of the computer. Control systems in advanced computers may change the order of some instructions so as to improve performance.

A key component common to all CPUs is the program counter, a special memory cell (a register) that keeps track of which location in memory the next instruction is to be read from.

The control system's function is as follows—note that this is a simplified description, and some of these steps may be performed concurrently or in a different order depending on the type of CPU:

1. Read the code for the next instruction from the cell indicated by the program counter.
2. Decode the numerical code for the instruction into a set of commands or signals for each of the other systems.
3. Increment the program counter so it points to the next instruction.
4. Read whatever data the instruction requires from cells in memory (or perhaps from an input device). The location of this required data is typically stored within the instruction code.
5. Provide the necessary data to an ALU or register.
6. If the instruction requires an ALU or specialized hardware to complete, instruct the hardware to perform the requested operation.

7. Write the result from the ALU back to a memory location or to a register or perhaps an output device.
8. Jump back to step (1).

Since the program counter is (conceptually) just another set of memory cells, it can be changed by calculations done in the ALU. Adding 100 to the program counter would cause the next instruction to be read from a place 100 locations further down the program. Instructions that modify the program counter are often known as "jumps" and allow for loops (instructions that are repeated by the computer) and often conditional instruction execution (both examples of control flow).

It is noticeable that the sequence of operations that the control unit goes through to process an instruction is in itself like a short computer program—and indeed, in some more complex CPU designs, there is another yet smaller computer called a micro sequencer that runs a micro-code program that causes all of these events to happen.

### *Arithmetic Logic Unit (ALU)*

The ALU is capable of performing two classes of operations: arithmetic and logic. The set of arithmetic operations that a particular ALU supports may be limited to adding and subtracting or might include multiplying or dividing, trigonometry functions (sine, cosine, etc.) and square roots. Some can only operate on whole numbers (integers) whilst others use floating point to represent real numbers—albeit with limited precision. However, any computer that is capable of performing just the simplest operations can be programmed to break down the more complex operations into simple steps that it can perform. Therefore, any computer can be programmed to perform any arithmetic operation—although it will take more time to do so if its ALU does not directly support the operation. An ALU may also compare numbers and return Boolean truth values (true or false) depending on whether one is equal to, greater than or less than the other. Logic operations involve Boolean logic: AND, OR, XOR and NOT. These can be useful both for creating complicated conditional statements and processing Boolean logic. Super scalar computers contain multiple ALUs so that they can process several instructions at the same time. Graphics processors and computers with SIMD and MIMD features often provide ALUs that can perform arithmetic on vectors and matrices.

## Classification of Computers

Computers belong to various capacity categories and sizes. They differ according to their function and purposes. Computers, normal in size, are found on table tops (Desktop) while some may carry one in a brief case (laptop). Computers with a size of a palm (Palmtop) or that of a diary (notebook) have also been there.

Classification of computers varies according to different criteria. In general, computers can be classified according to the input of signals, they accept or on the computing power.

## Classification Based on Input Signals

Computers can basically be divided into two types, namely,

1. Analog computers, and
2. Digital computers.

### 1. *Analog Computers*

An analog computer operates by measuring rather than by counting. In other words, an analog computer operates on inputs of signals, continuously varying quantities or physical magnitudes such as temperature, pressure, and the like.

Analog computers are used for scientific and engineering purposes. A slide rule and a car speedometer are examples for analog devices.

### 2. *Digital Computers*

A digital computer operates essentially by counting. It operates on electronic inputs that are on-off or incrementally-stepped quantities represented by numerical digits.

In other words, all quantities are expressed as numbers (binary) and the computer operates on discrete numbers. Digital computers are used in data or information processing activities.

## Classification Based on Computing Power

Based on computing power, the present day computers may be grouped into different classes such as :

- Super computers,
- Mainframes,
- Mini computers,
- Microcomputers
- Personal computers.
- Network computers

## Input Devices

Before computer processing, data must be entered into the computer by an input device so that they can be translated into a machine-readable form. Input devices are categorized into two namely, Transcriptive data entry and Source data entry.

## Transcriptive Data Entry

Punched cards and Card readers (Outdated now)

Keyboards
Mouse
Joystick
Track ball
Touch screen

### *Punched Cards and Card readers*

Punched card is a rigid piece of paper containing rows and columns of numbers. Required components are :

Punched cards
Keypunch machine
Hollerith code
A card reader

These cards are put into a keypunch machine, which places holes in the card to represent the data. This pattern of punched holes used to represent characters on the card is called the Hollerith code. A card reader that translates the punched information into a machine-readable code and then sends it to the CPU for processing to interpret these holes. Now-a-days, this system is not in practice.

The punched card had numerous uses in industry. It was a widely used file in small-scale computer installations. Today it is outdated.

### Source Data Input Devices

There are devices for entering data directly into a computer system without a transcription process is referred to as source data. Source data input are:

Magnetic ink character recognition (MICR)
Magnetic strips
Optical recognitions
Optical character recognition (OCR)
Optical bar recognition (OBR)

### *Magnetic Ink Character Recognition (MICR)*

MICR is the interpretation by a computer of a line of characters written in special magnetic ink. Humans can read these characters as well. For example in a bank cheque, there is a line of numbers and some odd-shaped characters. Cheque number amount of the cheque are all printed in magnetic ink. These cheques are sent through a MICR reader to interpret the information, update the appropriate accounts and in some cases, sort the cheque afterwards.

There are several advantages associated with the use of MICR:

- Cheques may be roughly handled, folded, smeared and stamped, but they can still be read with a high degree of accuracy.

- Processing is speeded because cheques can be fed directly into the input device.
- People can easily read the magnetic ink characters.

The main limitation of MICR is that only the 10 digits and 4 special characters needed for bank processing are used. No alphabetic characters are available.

### Magnetic Strips

They are thin bands of magnetically encoded data that are found on the back of credit cards. The data stored on the card vary from one application to another, but they include account numbers or special access codes. Data in the form of magnetic strips cannot be seen or interpreted by simply looking at the card and so it can be highly sensitive or personal.

### Optical Recognitions

Optical recognition occurs when a device scans a printed surface and translates the image the scanner sees into a machine-readable format that is understandable by the computer. Optical recognition can be of the following types:

#### (a) Optical Mark Recognition (OMR)

It employs marks sensing to scan and translate, based on its location which is a series of pen or pencil marks into computer readable form. For instance, the objective type multiple choice question paper we get in the bank recruitment exam. A computerized optical mark reader scores the tests by identifying the position of the mark.

#### (b) Optical Bar Recognition (OBR)

This is a slightly more sophisticated type of optical recognition. Have you seen a series of thin black bars and spaces on the back of the books? They are bar codes or product codes that are arranged to represent data, such as the name of the manufacture type of product, etc. An optical bar reader recognizes and interprets them on the basis of width of the lines. A scanner reads the bar code and the price and product are then matched by the mark.

#### (c) Optical Character Recognition (OCR)

This is the most sophisticated type of optical recognition. An optical card reader works in the same way as the human eye. It recognizes specially shaped numeric and alphabetic characters.

A set of optical characters may be used to print merchandise tags that can be read using an OCR Reader. To process the sales transaction, the information on the tag such as item price and the inventory number can be automatically entered at a point of sale terminal. Pertinent data can be saved and transferred to the company's main computer system.

The primary advantages of OCR is that it eliminates some of the duplication of human effort for inputting data into the computer. This reduction in effort can improve data accuracy. It can increase the timeliness of the information processed.

Apart from the above, there are devices which serve as input as well as output devices. They include floppy disks and CDs.

## INTERNET

### History of the Internet

The Internet was created as a result of the Cold War. In the mid-1960s it became apparent that there was a need for a bomb-proof electronic communication system. A concept was devised to link computers by cable or wire throughout the country in a distributed system so that if some parts of the country were cut-off from other parts, messages could still get through. In the beginning, only the federal government and a few universities were linked because the Internet was basically an emergency military communication system, operated by the Department of Defense's Advanced Research Project Agency (ARPA). The whole operation was referred to as *ARPANET*.

*ARPA* was linked to computers at a group of top research universities receiving ARPA funding. The first four universities connected to ARPANET were the University of California-Los Angeles, Stanford University, the University of California-Santa Barbara, and the University of Utah. Thus, the Internet was born. Because of a concept developed by Larry Roberts of ARPA and Glen Kleinrock at UCLA, called packet switching, the Internet was able to become a decentralized system, which would prevent large-scale destruction of any centralized system. The system allowed different types of computers from different manufacturers to send messages to one another. Computers merely transmitted information to one another in a standardized protocol packet. The addressing information in these packets told each computer in the chain where the packet was supposed to go.

As the Internet grew, more capability was added. A program called *Telnet* allowed remote users to run programs and computers at other sites. The File Transfer Protocol (FTP) allowed users to transfer data files and programs. Gopher programs, developed at the University of Minnesota and named after the university's mascot, allowed menu-driven access to data resources on the Internet. Search engines such as Archie and Wide Area Index Search (WAIS) gave users the ability to search the Internet's numerous libraries and indices. By the 1980s people at universities, research laboratories, private companies, and libraries were aided by a networking revolution. There were more than thirty thousand host computers and modems on the Internet. The forerunner of the Internet was the Bitnet, which was a network of virtually every major university in the world. E-mail became routine and inexpensive, since the Internet is a *parasite* using the existing multibillion-dollar telephone networks of the world as its carriers.

In 1972 Ray Tomlinson invented network e-mail, which became possible with the FTP. With e-mail and FTP, the rate at which collaborative work could be conducted between researchers at participating computer science departments was greatly increased. Although it was not realized at the time, the Internet had begun. *TCP* (Transmission Control Protocol) breaks large amounts of data down into packets of a fixed size, sequentially numbers them to allow reassembly at the recipient's end, and transmits the packets over the Internet using the Internet protocol.

After the invention of e-mail, it wasn't long before mailing lists were invented. This was a technique by which an identical message could be sent automatically to large numbers of people. The Internet continues to grow. In fact, it is estimated that almost 65 million adults go online on the Internet in the United States every month. Presently, no one operates the Internet. Although there are entities that *oversee* the system, "no one is in charge." This allows for a free transfer and flow of information throughout the world.

In 1984 the National Science Foundation (NSF) developed NSFNET. Later NASA, the National Institutes of Health, and others became involved, and nodes on the Internet were divided into basic varieties that are still used today. The varieties are grouped by the six basic Internet domains of GOV, MIL, EDU, COM, ORG, and NET. The ARPANET itself formally expired in 1989, a victim of its own success, and the use of TCP/IP (Transfer Control Protocol/Internet Protocol) standards for computer networks is now global.

If Internet invention had stopped at this point, we would probably still be using the Internet primarily just for e-mail. However, in 1989 a second miracle occurred. Tim Berners-Lee, a software engineer at the *CERN* physics lab in Switzerland, developed a set of accepted protocols for the exchange of Internet information, and a consortium with users was formed—thus creating the World Wide Web, the standard language for encoding information. *Hypertext Markup Language* (HTML) was adopted. Berners-Lee proposed making the idea global to link all documents on the Internet using hypertext. This lets users jump from one document to another through highlighted words. Other web standards, such as URL (Universal Resource Language) addresses on the Web page and HTTP (Hypertext Transfer Protocol), are also Berners-Lee's inventions. Berners-Lee could have been *exceedingly* rich based on his invention, but he left the fortune building to others because he "wanted to do the revolution right."

As a result of Berners-Lee's invention, in 1993 a group at the University of Illinois, headed by Mark Andreesen, wrote a graphical application called Mosaic to make use of the Web easier. The next year a few students from that group, including Andreesen, co-founded Netscape after they graduated in May and released the browser for the World Wide Web in November 1994. The World Wide Web is making the Internet easier to use and has brought two giant advantages. Until the Web, the Internet communicated text only, but the Web permits exchange of un coded graphics, color-coded graphics, color photographs and designs, even video and sound; and it formats typed copy into flexible typographic pages. The Web also permits use of hyperlinks, whereby users can click on certain words or phrases and be shown links to other information or pictures that explain the key words or phrases. As a result of the World Wide Web and Web browsers, it became easy to find information on the Internet and the Web. Various search engines have been developed to index and retrieve this information.

## Concept

Internet is the world's largest computer network, the network of networks, scattered all over the world. It was created nearly 30 years ago as a project for the U.S. Department of Defence. Its goal was to create a method for widely separated computers to transfer data efficiently whether war or peace. From a handful of computer and users in the 1960s.

Today the Internet has grown to thousands of regional networks that connect millions of users round the earth. Any single individual, company, or country does not own this global network.

A network of networks, or Internet, is a group of networks that are:

- Interconnected physically.
- Capable of communicating and sharing data with each other.
- Able to act together as a single network.

Machines on one network can communicate with machines on other networks send data, files, and other information back and forth.

For this to work, the networks and machines that are part of the Internet have to agree either to speak the same "language" when they are communicating or to use an "interpreter." This "language" is known as software that enables the different types of machines on separate networks to communicate and exchange information.

To be used by different types of machines and yet be understood by all of them, the software must follow a set of rules. Those set of rules are called protocol. The Internet, with a capital "I," is the network of networks, which either uses the TCP/IP protocol or interacts with TCP/IP networks via gateways (the interpreters). The Internet presents these networks as one, seamless network for its users.

Internet covers the globe and includes large, international networks as well as many smaller, local-area networks (LANs).

Internet offers access to data, graphics, voice, sound, software, text, and people through a variety of services and tools for communication and data exchange. The value of Internet is highly commendable due to three obvious reasons.

Internet is the cheapest and fastest means to :

- Get information

- Provide information
- Compile information

Given below is a list of activities that one could do with a web browser:

- Visit websites
- Send and receive electronic mail
- Read and post articles in newsgroups
- Download files to your PC
- Chat with other users online
- Play games with others online
- Access on-line multimedia including radio and video broadcasts
- Search the Internet for information
- Subscribe to electronic newsletters
- Join contests
- Contribute articles and other materials
- Do online shopping and find jobs
- Post one's resume on the Internet
- Create your own websites
- Create an Email account
- Use the Email reminder service
- Find a person's details
- Send greetings to others.

The above list is by no means a complete and comprehensive one. There are a lot of other things that one can do on the Internet. The rise of the Internet has not only opened the door to the developing conventional research techniques such as surveys, questionnaires, experiments and interviews, but also enabled researchers to use literature search and retrieval techniques to locate and return materials from the web at an exponential rate in terms of size and rapidity.

## WORLD WIDE WEB (WWW)

World Wide Web and the Internet are not the same, but they are related and inter-dependent. The Web resides "on top of " the Internet. World Wide Web is a huge collection of "Pages" of information linked to each other around the globe. Each page can be a combination of text, pictures, audio clips, video clips, animations and other electronically presentable material.

Before the World Wide Web, the Internet was very difficult to navigate. Much of the information on it was tough to find and just as difficult to make use of. Locating and downloading files residing on the Internet needed some UNIX skills and specilised tools to get the job done.

Tim Berners-Lee is widely known as the father of the World Wide Web. Berners was a physicist at the European Organization for Nuclear Research (CERN), a highly esteemed particle physics loboratory in Switzerland. He became frustrated with the difficulty of navigating the Internet and the lack or common, easy to use interface for accessing the information residing on it.

## Advantages of Internet-based Surveys in Research

The most widely used data collection instrument for Internet surveys is the questionnaire. There are several claimed advantages to using an Internet questionnaire in comparison to a paper questionnaire.

- It reduces costs (e.g. of postage, paper, printing, keying in data).
- It enables a wider and much larger population to be accessed.
- It enables researchers to reach difficult populations under the cover of anonymity and non-traceability.
- It reduces the time take to distribute, gather and process data.
- Reduction of researcher effects.
- Human error is reduced in entering and processing online data.
- Additional features may make the survey attractive (e.g. graphics, colour, fonts).
- Greater generability may be obtained as Internet users come from a wide and diverse population.

## Searching for Research Materials on the Internet

The storage and retrieval of research data on the Internet play an important role not only in keeping researchers abreast of developments across the world, but also in providing access to data which can inform literature searches to establish construct and content validity in their own research. Online journals, abstracts and titles enable researchers to keep up with the cutting edge of research and to conduct a literature search of relevant materials on their chosen topic. Websites and email correspondence enable networks and information to be shared.

With regard to searching libraries, there are several useful web sites:

*www.loc.gov* (the united States Library of Congress).

*www.lcweb.loc.gov/z3950(*links to US libraries).

*www.lindex.com/*(the Library Index web site, linking to 18,000 Libraries).

*www.copac.ac.uk.copac* (This enables researchers to search major UK libraries).

*http://vlib.org/* (the Virtual Library, and provides online resources).

For theses, Aslib Index to Theses is useful (*http://www.theses.com*) and the Networked Digital Library of Theses and Dissertations can be located at *www.theses.org*.

## SEARCH ENGINES

Researchers who do not know a web site address have at their disposal a variety of search engines to locate it. At the time of writing some widely used Search Engine are:

*www.google.com* *www.msn.com*
*www.netscape.com* *www.search.aol.com*
*www.altavista.com* *www.directhit.com*
*www.excite.com* *www.askjeeves.com*
*www.northernlight.com* *www.yahoo.com*
*www.hotbot.com* *www.goto.com*
*www.cyber411.com* *www.lycos.com*
*www.infoseek.com* *www.webcrawler.com*
*www.khoj.com*—a search engine for Indian web sites.

All of these search engines enable researchers to conduct searches by keywords. Some of these are parallel search engines and some are file search engines. Finding research information, where not available from databases and indices on CD-Roms, is often done through the Internet by trial and error and serendipity, identifying the key words singly or in combination.

## USEFUL RESOURCES FOR LIBRARY AND INFORMATION PROFESSIONALS

### Free E-Journals/Newsletters

- Issues in Science and Technology Librarianship (*http://www.library.ucsb.edu/istl/*)—A quarterly publication of the Science and Technology Section, Association of College and Research Libraries, USA.
- ITPapers.com (*http://www.itpapers.com/*)—Yellow pages of white papers. Covers several categories, including libraries.
- Australian Academic & Research Libraries (*http://www.alia.org.au/sections/ucrls/aarl/*)—Quarterly journal devoted to all aspects of librarianship in university and college libraries.
- THE INFORMED LIBRARIAN ONLINE (*http://www.infosourcespub.com/*) THE INFORMED LIBRARIAN is a monthly compilation of the most recent tables of contents from over 180 valuable domestic and foreign library and information-related journals, e-journals, magazines-magazines, newsletters and e-newsletters.
- Bulletin of the American Society for Information Science and Technology (*http://www.asis.org/Bulletin/index.html*).
- Information Today (*http://www.infotoday.com/it/itnew.htm*)

Information industry news services for the information professional.

- LIBRES—Library and Information Science Research Electronic Journal (*http://libres.curtin.edu.au/*).
- Journal of Information, Law and Technology (*http://elj.warwick.ac.uk/jilt/*).
- D-Lib Magazine (*http://www.dlib.org/*)—D-Lib Magazine is a monthly magazine about innovation and research in digital libraries.
- Journal of Digital Information (*http://jodi.ecs.soton.ac.uk/*)—E-journal publishing papers on the management, presentation and uses of information in digital environments
- Information Research: An international electronic journal (*http://informationr.net/ir/*)—Information Research is a free, international, scholarly journal, dedicated to making freely accessible the results of research across a wide range of information-related disciplines.
- Journal of Electronic Publishing. (*http://www.press.umich.edu/jep*)—The Journal of Electronic Publishing is for the thoughtful forward-thinking publisher, librarian, scholar, or author—in fact, anyone in this new business—facing those challenges.
- Current Cites (*http://sunsite.berkeley.edu/CurrentCites/*)—monitors information technology literature in both print and digital forms, each month selecting only the best items to annotate for a free publication.
- Ariadne (*http://www.ariadne.ac.uk/*)—The Ariadne newsletter is aimed at working librarians in academic libraries in the UK.
- First Monday (*http://www.firstmonday.dk/*)—One of the first peer-reviewed journals on the Internet, about the Internet and the Global Information Infrastructure.
- Free Online Scholarship Newsletter (*http://www.earlham.edu/~peters/fos/index.htm*)—The purpose of the newsletter is to share news and discussion on the migration of print scholarship to the Internet and efforts to make it available to readers free of charge.
- Free Pint (*http://www.freepint.com/*)—Free Pint is a free email newsletter giving you tips, tricks and articles on how and where to find reliable Web sites and search more effectively.
- Information Today and Tomorrow (ITT) (*http://itt.nissat.tripod.com*)—Quarterly newsletter from NISSAT.
- *Digital libraries*—a column in *Library Journal* by Roy Tennant, Manager, eScholarship Web & Services Design, California Digital Library.

Bibliozine—the e-magazine for librarians. (*http://www.bibliozine.com/index.shtml*)

RLG DigiNews. Produced for RLG by the Cornell University Libraries Department of Preservation and Conservation, RLG DigiNews is a bimonthly Web-based newsletter focused on issues of vital interest to managers of digital initiatives. (*http://www.rlg.org/preserv/diginews/*)

For other free/partially free e-journals and newsletters in the information field, consult the list maintained by Prof. Tom Wilson at Information R.Net

## Indian Discussion Forums and List Services

- LIS-Forum—Discussion forum for library and information professionals in India

Submissions: lis-forum@ncsi.iisc.ernet.in
List info: *http://ncsi.iisc.ernet.in/mailman/listinfo/lis-forum*

- IATLIS—Indian Association for Teachers in Library and Information Science discussion forum

Submissions: iatlis@yahoogroups.com
List info: *http://groups.yahoo.com/group/iatlis/*

- Corporatelibrns ? An interactive forum for corporate librarians

Submissions: corporatelibrns@yahoogroups.com
List info: *http://groups.yahoo.com/group/corporatelibrns/*

- Digital Libraries: India

Submissions: digilib_india@yahoogroups.com
List info: *http://groups.yahoo.com/group/digilib_india/*

## L&I Websites and Portals

- NMLIS - New Millennium LIS Professionals

Submissions: nmlis@yahoogroups.com
List info: *http://groups.yahoo.com/group/nmlis/*

- INDIA-LIS—The INDIA-LIS is a Library and Information Science in India Mailing List

Submissions: india-lis@infoserv.inist.fr
List info: *http://infoserv.inist.fr/wwsympa.fcgi/info/india-lis*

- Aeroinfo (*http://www.cmmacs.ernet.in/nal/icast/*)—Information portal for aerospace engineering
- Delnet (*http://www.delnet.nic.in/*) - Delhi Library Network

- Inflibnet (*http://www.inflibnet.ac.in/*)—Information & Library Network Centre
- Infolibrarian (*http://www.infolibrarian.com/*)—infolibrarian.com gives all possible information required by the library professionals in India and abroad
- MylibNet (*http://www.mylibnet.org/*)—Mysore Library Network
- SciGate (*http://www.ncsi.iisc.ernet.in/*)—The IISc Science information portal
- Unesco Libraries Portal (*http://www.unesco.org/webworld/portal_bib*)—An international information gateway for librarians and library users.
- Vidyanidhi (*http://www.vidyanidhi.org.in/*)—Digital library of Indian theses and dissertations.

## Resource Lists

- Scholarly Electronic Publishing Bibliography (*http://info.lib.uh.edu/sepb/sepb.html*)

This selective bibliography presents over 1,500 articles, books, and other printed and electronic sources that are useful in understanding scholarly electronic publishing efforts on the Internet.

- Electronic Resources for Information Research Methods (*http://informationr.net/rm/*)
- World List of Departments and Schools of Information Studies, Information Management, Information Systems, etc. (*http://informationr.net/rm/*)
- Digital Information Services in Enterprises: A Resource List of Case Studies, Best Practices, White Papers, Guides and Standards (*http://scigate.ncsi.iisc.ernet.in/raja/is214/214-2001-2002/resources.htm*)

## Free Software

- Open Source Systems for Libraries (*http://www.oss4lib.org/*)—"Our mission is to cultivate the collaborative power of open source software engineering to build better and free systems for use in libraries. Toward this end, we maintain a listing of free software and systems designed for libraries".
- Greenstone Digital Library Software (GSDL) (*http://www.greenstone.org/*)
- E-Prints Archive Software (*http://www.eprints.org/*)
- Free/Open Source Software for Library and Information Management (listing) (*http://scigate.ncsi.iisc.ernet.in/raja/opendl/free-software.htm*)

## Licensing, IPR, Consortia

International Coalition of Library Consortia—ICOLC (*http://www.library.yale.edu/consortia/*)

Copyright related resources maintained at the Copyright Clearance Center Inc. (*http://www.copyright.com/CopyrightResources/default.asp*)

Liblicense—Licensing digital information: A resource for librarians (*http://www.library.yale.edu/~llicense/index.shtml*)

## Resources for Library and Information Science

➢ *http://acqweb.library.vanderbilt.edu/acqweb/lis_gen.html*

Library and Information Science Resources—general sites

➢ *http://bubl.ac.uk*

Free user friendly access to selected internet resources covering all subject areas with a special focus on Library and Information Science

➢ *http://copac.ac.uk/copac*

National Online Public-Access Catalogue (COPAC)

➢ *http://drtc.isibang.ac.in/DRTC/Consortia*

Indian Coalition of Library Consortia (ICLIC)

➢ *http://iris.emeraldinsight.com*

Library Link—Current awareness for the information professional

➢ *http://lib.mansfield.edu/digital.html*

Digital library resources

➢ *http://lib.mansfield.edu/library.html*

Library Science internet resources

➢ *http://members.lycos.co.uk/bluedolphinprint/libraryworld.libworld.html*

Library World-Web tools for the Librarian

➢ *http://sunsite.berkeley.edu/libweb/index/html*

Libweb-Library servers via World Wide Web. Currently lists over 6600 pages from libraries in over 115 countries

➢ *http://http://www.lib.umi.com/disertations/intrial/gateway*

Proquest digital dissertations

➢ *http://www.bl.uk/services/information/librarianship.html*

British Library—Librarianship and Information Sciences Service

➢ *http://www.burioni.it/news/novita/isi.htm*

The Web of Science for access to ISI citation databases

➢ *http://www.curl.ac.uk/database*

Consortium of University Research Libraries (CURL) database

➢ *http://www.infolibrarian.com/dlib.htm*

Digital library resources and projects

➢ *http://www.itcompany.com/inforetriever*

Internet Library for Librarians

➢ *http://www.lib.berkeley.edu/Teachinglib/Guides/Internet/FindInfo.html*

Finding information on the internet: a tutorial

➢ *http://www.library.ucsb.edu/istl*

Issues in Science and Technology Librarianship

➢ *http://www.libraryhq.com*

Resources for the Wired librarians
➢ *http://www.lii.org*
Librarian's index to the internet
➢ *http://www.soc.soton.ac.uk/LIB/infoskills*
Library and Information Services-Information skills
➢ *http://www.theses.org*
Digital Library of ETDs (Electronic Theses and Dissertations)

## Reference Sources

➢ *http://lib.mansfield.edu/libstaff.html*
Reference resources for Librarians
➢ *http://lib.mansfield.edu/mer-ref.html*
Reference resources online
➢ *http://www.dekker.com/servlet/product/productid/E-ELIS*
Encyclopedia of Library and Information Science
➢ *http://www.ipl.org/div/subject/browse/ref00.00.00*
Internet Public Library
➢ *http://www.lib.uchicago.edu/e/reg/using/reference/socsciref.html*
Social Sciences reference sources
➢ *http://www.lib.usf.edu/ref/bibs/libscience.html*
Library Science reference sources
➢ *http://www.libraryspot.com*
Reference links
➢ *http://www.nlc-bnc.ca/vrc-rvc*
Virtual Reference Canada (VRC)
➢ *http://www.um.ac.ir/~fattahi/Refere~/htm*
Reference sources for Librarians
➢ *http://www.vrd.org*
Virtual reference desk
➢ *http://www.vrd.org/pubinfo/proceedings99_bib.shtml*
Digital reference resources

## Open Sources

➢ *http://bubl.ac.uk*
Selected internet resources in Library and Information Science
➢ *http://eprints.rclis.org*
E-Prints in Library and Information Science
➢ *http://www.academicinfo.net/infoscilibraryj.html*
Library and Information Science—Digital Library—Online journals
➢ *http://www.asiaosc.org/topic_9.html*
Asian open source centre—promoting open source and free software in Asia
➢ *http://www.biomedcentral.com/openaccess/oanews*
Open Access Now—Campaigning for freedom of research information
➢ *http://www.doaj.org*

Directory of open access journals

➢ *http://www.istl.org/00-fall/internet.html*

Free scholarly electronic journals: an annotated webliography

➢ *http://www.plos.org*

Public Library of Science—premier open-access journals in Biology and Medicine

## E-Journals and Databases

➢ *http://www.dlib.org*

Digital Library magazine

➢ *http://www.elseviersocialsciences.com/libraryscience*

Elsevier Social Sciences—Library and Information Sciences

➢ *http://www.libdex.com/journals.html*

Library journals, newsletters

➢ *http://www.librarysupportstaff.com/libjourn.html*

Library and Information Science and Education—Online journals

➢ *http://www.plos.org*

Library and Information Science journals by title

➢ *http://bubl.ac.uk/journals/bycat.htm*

Library and Information Science journals by category

➢ *http://db.arl.org/dsej/start.html*

ARL Directory of Scholarly e-journals and academic discussion lists

➢ *http://www.britishcouncil.org/info@uk/links5.htm*

International Library and Information journals and websites

➢ *http://www.crossref.org*

Citation linking backbone—a collaborative reference linking service that allows the user to click on a citation and be taken directly to the target content

## LIS e-groups

➢ *http://ncsi.iisc.ernet.in/mailmar/listinfo/lis-forum*

Library and Information Science forum—Discussion forum for Library and Information Professionals in India

*libraryphorum@yahoogroups.com*

Library phorum—Forum for Library and Information Science Professionals in India

➢ *tadilnet@yahoogroups.com*

TADILNET (Tamil Digital Library Network) is an informal discussion group to

co-ordinate scattered world wide efforts in Tamil Digital Library area

➢ *http://www.vrd.org/Dig_Ref/dig_ref.shtml*

A list serve for Digital reference services

➢ *emala@yahoogroups.com*

Madras Library Association e-group

➢ *https://drtc.isibang.ac.in/index.jsp*

Librarian's Digital Library—Digital Library discussion forum - (DLRG) at DRTC, Bangalore

## TYPES OF NETWORKS

There are many different types of networks. However from an end users point of view there are two basic types:

*Local Area Networks (LAN)*—The computers are geographically close together (that is, in the same building).

*Wide-area networks (WANs)*—The computers are farther apart and are connected by telephone lines or radio waves.

In addition to these types, the following characteristics are also used to categorize different types of networks.

*Topology*—The geometric arrangement of a computer system. Common topologies include a bus, star, and ring.

*Protocol*—The protocol defines a common set of rules and signals that computers on the network use to communicate. One of the most popular protocols for LANs is called Ethernet. Another popular LAN protocol for PCs is the IBM token-ring network.

*Architecture*—Networks can be broadly classified as using either peer-to-peer or client/server architecture. Computers on a network are sometimes called nodes. Computers and devices that allocate resources for a network are caned servers.

### Local Area Network (LAN)

LAN is a computer network that spans a relatively small area. Most LANs are confined to a single building or group of buildings. However, one LAN can be connected to other LANs over any distance via telephone lines and radio waves.

A system of LANs connected in this way is called a wide-area network (WAN). Most LANs connect workstations and personal computers. Each node (individual computer) in a LAN has its own CPU with which it executes programs, but it is also able to access data and devices anywhere on the LAN. This means that many users can share expensive devices, such as laser printers, as well as data. Users can also use the LAN to communicate with each other, by sending Email or engaging in chat sessions.

There are different types of LANs—token-ring networks, Ethernets, and ARCnets being the most common for PCs.

## METROPOLITAN AREA NETWORK (MAN)

Attempts are being made to develop this type of network in metropolitan areas such as Delhi, Bangalore, Chennai, etc.

### Wide Area Network (WAN)

A WAN is a computer network that spans a relatively large geographical area. Typically, a WAN consists of two or more local-area networks (LANs).

Computers connected to a wide-area network are often connected through public networks such as the telephone system. They can also be connected through leased lines or satellites. *The largest WAN in existence is the Internet.*

## LIBRARY AND INFORMATION NETWORK

In the field of Library and information science, the term "network" has been used broadly to mean anything from the organizational resource sharing arrangements established among nearby libraries to automated networks such as those operated by bibliographic utilised.

Library networks can be characterized in the following way:

(1) They are developed specifically to support library technical processes such as shared cataloguing.
(2) They provide a particular set of services and are operated by single Organisation.
(3) They are largely terminal to host networks.

In the year 1963, Ohio college was the first library to establish library network. The sources of OCLC (Online Computer Library Centre) led many library networks to grow in different part of the world during the last two decades.

The U.S. National Commission on Library and Information Sciences (NCLIS) in its National Programme Document (1975) defines a library network as:

> "Two or more libraries engaged in a common pattern of information exchange, through communications, for some functional purposes. A network usually consists of a formal arrangement whereby materials, information and services provided by a variety of libraries are available to all potential users. Libraries may be in different jurisdictions but agree to serve one another on the same basis as each serves its own constituents. Computers and telecommunication may be among the tools used for facilitating communication among them".

The pressure for resource sharing due to the devaluation of the rupee, rising costs of published materials, increase in the number of published materials and limited financial resources, resulted in switching over to automation in libraries. The library and Information Networks aim at:

(i) Research sharing which may include sharing documents, information, manpower and cost:

(ii) Bibliographic control through shared, distributive or cooperative acquisition, storage retrieval and distribution of information sources of documents.

In India, the number of libraries turning to automation has increased at a reasonably good pace. Many libraries and Information centre get their catalogue and bibliographies prepared in machine readable form to provide computer information service to users, and also to participate in library network.

## Characteristics of L&I Networks

Library networks have the following characteristics:

| | | |
|---|---|---|
| Data | : | Bibliographic records (MARC) |
| Retrieval | : | Author/title/number (subject) keyword/code |
| Access | : | Telecommunication network/private network/ Hard Wired network |
| Users | : | Librarians and Library clientele |

The various characteristics of L&I networks can be identified:

- *Equal opportunity of access*: to total information resources to every individual regardless of location, social status or physical condition. The access to network is for all those who are connected through communication links.
- *Interdependence*: Libraries are no longer self sufficient in terms of collection, personnel or services libraries are dependent on one another for sharing their resources. Accordingly interdependence has become a characteristic of L&I network concept, several L&I networks can works in collaboration and derive benefits of inter-dependence.
- Large data bases networks can control and provide access on cooperative basis to very large scale bibliographic data bases.
- *Standards and quality*: networks develop, use and propagate the use of well individual library or information centre.
- Shared decision-making policy decision are arrived on mutual benefits and collective agreements among participants.
- All library services networks are generally designed to provide whole range of library services.
- *Integration and coordination*: of efforts, collection, money, manpower, and expertise of participants. Earlier it was felt that an integration by merging specialized information centers and services would from the basis of networking. Things did not happen in the expected way and specialized information centres became more specialized remaining as independent L&I network development has emerged as consisting of separate operations

largely different from those offered by specialized information centers.

- *Centralization*: the network activities are centralized, large bibliographic databases centrally stored and monitored, at times a national apex body holds the responsibility of network management.
- *Cost and productivity:* cost involved is distributed over several participants and the productivity is increased in terms of total information services or information products.
- *Research and development:* networks provide opportunity for research and development work in the field of L&I services through exhaustive, comprehensive, multiaccess data bases, their online use, feedback, etc.
- *Internationalism:* network may have gateways to access other networks and database and global level and hence work to achieve internationalism.
- *Top up/Bottom down:* the national scientific panels, generally, advocated, the development of L&I network staffing at the national level. However, this approach was not considered as essential to network concept. (e.g., OCLC) and in theory (e.g., NCLIS programme statement of USA) the approach form the grasz root level was accepted. Hence, building a network from the bottom-up-based libraries, their willingness to support and sustain the network activities was desirable.

To understand the dimensions of library co-operations one has to be conversant with modern developments in online catalogues, multi-dimentional searching and serials control.

CALIBNET (Calcutta Library Network)
DELNET (Delhi Library Network)
Ahmedabad Library Network (ADINET)
Tamil Digital Library Network (TADILNET)
Madras Library Network (MALIBNET)
INFLIBNET (Information and Library Networks)

Above are the important proposed library networks to promote sharing of resources among the libraries in India

### Calibnet

To promote sharing of resources among the libraries in calcutta by developing a network of libraries, by collecting, storing and dissimination information and offering computerised services to the users and fund accounting.

(1) Acqusition and fund accounting
(2) Serials control
(3) Cataloguing
(4) Circulation
(5) User services

## DELNET

In order to provide efficient services to users in earth library in Delhi and enhance scope of the services, DELNET stands for significantly improving resource sharing among the libraries in Delhi and its plans provided automation facilities in the following areas.

(a) Acquisition and fund accounting
(b) Serials control
(c) Books and journals maintenance
(d) Circulation
(e) User services
(f) Creation and Maintenance of bibliographic database
(g) Inter-Library user services
(h) Document copy and transfer facilities
(i) Access to national and international database
(j) Union catalogue
(k) Current awareness and SDI
(l) Authority data
(m) Subject profiles
(n) Abstracts

## Ahmedabad Library Network (ADINET)

ADINET is an Information Network of Libraries in and around Ahmedabad. ADINET was registered as a Society in October 1994. Initially it was sponsored by National Information System for Science and Technology (NISSAT), Department of Scientific and Industrial Research, Government of India.

## Tamil Digital Library Network (TADILNET)

TADILNET is an Internet-based networking group of individuals and institutional representatives engaged in or interested in building digital Tamil collections. It is a voluntary forum to share information on the content of individual collections, location of primary resources, sharing of experience in Tamil digitization efforts, build common standards and protocols that lead to efficient comprehensive catalogue of e-archives, search engines, etc.

Currently the TADILNET forum consists of ca. 30 individuals from many of the leading academic institutions (academicians, librarians in charge of libraries with major Tamil resource collections and software professionals interested in Tamil Digital Library development) and they come from India, Sri Lanka, Singapore, Malaysia, Europe and North America. The group uses *net-based mailing list at Yahoo groups* for continuous dialogue. Subscription is open to anyone interested in Digital Tamil Library Development.

## Madras Library Network (MALIBNET)

MALIBNET—a registered society (non-government organisation) was formed in 1993. Through an MOU, Indian National Scientific Documentation Center (*INSDOC*) has been entrusted the responsibility of setting up and provides technical support for operating the network. Presently, nearly 50 libraries in Madras are contributing actively to the creation of various databases on Malibnet. With the help of communication links and sophisticated information technology, the resources of the member libraries are shared and made available to the users. Presently 17 major educational/research institutions have joined as *member institutions* of MALIBNET.

## INFLIBNET

Information and Library Network (INFLIBNET) Centre is an Autonomous Inter-University Centre (IUC) of University Grants Commission (UGC) involved in creating infrastructure for sharing of library and information resources and services among Academic and Research Institutions. INFLIBNET works collaboratively with Indian university libraries to shape the future of the academic libraries in the evolving information environment.

The project on information and library networking aims at the establishment of a national network of libraries and information centers in universities, colleges, research and development organisation, etc in India.

The main objectives of INFLIBNET are:

(a) To evolve a national network of libraries and information centre in the country and to improve information handling capability.
(b) To provide reliable access to document collection through online union catalogue.
(c) To provide better access to bibliographic information sources with citation and abstracts through online accessing of international database held by international information networks and centers.
(d) To provide document service by establishing resource centers around libraries having a rich collection of documents.
(e) To provide information resource utilisation through shared cataloguing, inter-library loan service.
(f) To computerise operations of libraries and information centers in the country following a uniform standard.

(g) To facilitate communication among scientists, engineers, researchers, social scientists, academics, faculties and students through electronic mail.
(h) To enabler users regardless of location and distance, to access information.
(i) To create online information service.
(j) To encourage co-operation among libraries.
(k) INFLIBNET has introduced an Online Journals Service to University and College libraries in India.

## UGC-INFONET

*UGC-Infonet* is an ambitious programme of UGC to interlink all the Universities in the country with state-of-art technology. The Network will overlay on ERNET backbone and provide Internet and Intranet Services. It is providing Internet Connectivity to 150 Universities in first phase. Another 8 universities are being added in 2008. INFLIBNET is responsible for executing and monitoring the entire project.

### The Mission

- UGC-Infonet will become a vehicle for distance learning to facilitate spread of quality education all over the country.
- UGC-Infonet will be a tool distribute education material and journals to the remotest of areas.
- UGC-Infonet will be a resource for researchers and scholars for tapping the most up-to-date information.
- UGC-Infonet will form a medium for collaboration among teachers and students, not only within the country but all over the world.
- UGC-Infonet will be an Intranet for University Automation.
- UGC-Infonet will encompass entire University System for most efficient utilisation of precious network resources.
- UGC-Infonet will establish a channel for Globalisation of Education and facilitate the universities in marketing their services and developments.

The following are involved in the project:

- University Grants Commission (UGC)
- Information and Library Network Centre (INFLIBNET)
- Education Research Network (ERNET) on turnkey basis
- Universities

## E-Resources@UGC-Infonet Digital Library Consortium

The UGC-Infonet Digital Library Consortium subscribes to the following resources for its member institutions. All electronic resources subscribed are available from the publisher's Web site. Following is the list of E-Resources with link to their brief introduction.

## Full-Text E-Resources

- *American Chemical Society http://www.pubs.acs.org/*
- *American Institute of Physics http://scitation.aip.org/publications/myBrowsePub.jsp#AIP*
- *American Physical Society http://scitation.aip.org/publications/myBrowsePub.jsp#APS*
- *Annual Reviews http://arjournals.annualreviews.org/*
- *Blackwell Publishing http://www3.interscience.wiley.com/*
- *Cambridge University Press http://journals.cambridge.org/*
- *Elsevier Science http://www.sciencedirect.com/*
- *Emerald http://www.emeraldinsight.com*
- *Institute of Physics http://www.iop.org/EJ/*
- *J-STOR http://www.jstor.org/*
- *Nature http://www.nature.com/*
- *Oxford University Press http://www.oxfordjournals.org*
- *Portland Press http://www.portlandpress.com/pp/journals/default.htm*
- *Project Euclid http://projecteuclid.org/*
- *Project Muse http://muse.jhu.edu/*
- *Royal Society of Chemistry http://www.rsc.org/Publishing/Journals/*
- *SIAM http://epubs.siam.org/*
- *Springer Link http://www.springerlink.com/*
- *Taylor and Francis http://www.informaworld.com/*
- *SciFinder Scholar http://www.cas.org/SCIFINDER/SCHOLAR/index.html*
- *MathSciNet http://www.ams.org/mathscinet/*
- *Royal Society of Chemistry (6 Databases) http://www.rsc.org/Publishing/CurrentAwareness/index.asp*
- *ISID http://isid.org.in/*
- CCC *http://jccc-ugcinfonet.in* or *www.jccc-ugcinfonet.in*
- *About Open Access oaeresources.html*
- *Open Access E-Journals oaeresources.html#ejournals*
- *Open Access Directories oaeresources.html#directories*
- *IRs@member Institutions oaeresources.html#IRs*

Examples of free e-journals are :

1. *Open J-Gate (Informatics)* : The worlds largest open access e-journals portal launched informatics (India) Pvt. Ltd., Bangalore. Free service to any one across the globe.
   *www.open-gate.com*
2. Find Articles *www.findarticles.com*

3. The researching Librarian *www.researchinglibrarian.com*
4. INFO LIBRARIAN *www.infolibrarian*
5. INFORMATION RESEARCH *http://informationr.net/*
6. Free Encyclopadia through Internet *www.wikipedia.org*
7. WEBOPAC *www.tifr.res.in\library www.sjctni.edu*
8. ELECTRONIC THESIS DATABASE
   Networked Digital Library of Thesis and Dissertations
   *www.ndltd.org*
   *www.thesis.org*
   *www.dissertations.com*
   *www.umi.com*

## ERNET India

ERNET India, an autonomous society under Ministry of Information Technology, is providing Internet access to Education and Research community in the county for over 10 years. ERNET is a nation-wide terrestrial and satellite network with points of presence located at leading education and research institutions in major cities. ERNET infrastructure is a judicious mix of satellite and terrestrial networks ideally suited for the Education and Research community in the country.

ERNET has pioneered the Internet Revolution in the country. Way back in 1986 ERNET started as an R&D programme of the Government of India and UNDP with an objective of enhancing the national capabilities in the area of computer communication and networking. After successful completion of the R&D phase ERNET became an Autonomous Scientific Society under the then Department of Electronics (Now Department of Information Technology), to provide the best network resources to the Indian academic community. Marching towards this goal ERNET India is participating with UGC for implementation of the UGC-InfoNet.

Apart from providing Computer Network infrastructure for the academic community ERNET is playing a role of total service provider for the institutions. ERNET provides High End education in the area of computer networking, undertakes R&D for evolving newer solutions and also assist the universities in establishing their in-campus infrastructure, like campus LANs. Content provision is a major thrust area for ERNET. ERNET has designed and made operational many portals to supplement the information for students and teachers alike.

# 8

# Digital Library

Enabling technologies resulted in moving libraries and information centers into the computer age. The first part of this automation process was computerization of the circulation system which was perceived as a real need. A move towards authority retrieval and thereafter the catalogue card followed a few years later. Meanwhile, work had been underway in information retrieval in the database and online world.

Previously, libraries had to depend largely on their own staff to prepare in-house catalogue cards. The need for standardization, even in the manual age, led to AACR2 [Anglo-American Cataloguing Rules 2], and later to the ISBD [International Standard for Book Description] format.

## Computerisation—The beginning Point

Computerization of these bibliographic descriptions led to a further requirement for standards of bibliographic descriptions for Machine-Readable Catalogue formats (MARC). This requirement was borne for an "exchange" medium for bibliographic data.

## Need and Purposes of Computerisation

Computerisation initially took place in large libraries for management convenience. A centrally located store of bibliographic records in machine readable format could be used as a resource by many libraries.

Library automation systems became firmly established and recognized as a beneficial technology for the librarian. As computer power increased with a reduction in its prices, the automation providers increased the scope of the library automation functions. This led to the integrated library management system (ILS). These systems enable library staff to perform almost all of their functions "on-line", often meaning that data entered in one part of an integrated system can be used again elsewhere, thus saving time and money and further ensuring accuracy.

A typical ILS system provides a cataloguing module, OPAC, circulation control module, purchasing module, serials management module, import module and reports module. Others may also include facilities for inter-library loans.

## Improvement Over Computerised Environment

As the technology advanced, so did the library automation systems. The main focus was on improving the ability for the borrower to retrieve information from the library automation system. Command driven retrieval was replaced by menu-driven retrieval. OPAC terminals were set-up in libraries with options to perform simplified search strategies. The majority of systems were either on mainframe computers or on vendor specific hardware. Access to the database was through an OPAC terminal in the library.

The next advance was to enable desktop computer users access to the library over the organization-wide network. This meant that querying of the library database could be done remotely. Hitherto libraries had been running (and in some cases still are running) a suite of electronic online services for their patrons. There was access to the local catalogue. Online service provision was accessible by trained information scientists. Subject specialist libraries would often have a CD-ROM terminal set-up to enable users to perform more specific content searches.

The point is, that all of these services were in almost all cases being offered from different points of access. In fact, it has proved to be the system departments that have indirectly led to changes in the way the technology has affected libraries. Technology-led solutions gradually became popular and got widely used.

Librarians have not been slow to react to the enormous potential of the Internet as resource provider. Above all, librarians, like any other professionals, have to justify their service to their management in terms of quality and cost. Managing a library is no more about handling printed materials only.

Users are becoming much more demanding and sophisticated in their requirements. They require information in machine readable format, they require to access video information, sound, all sorts of digitized media.

Terms such as Electronic Library, Digital Library and Virtual Library, were defined separately in isolated compartments. Today, the technological advancements have made all three concepts more or less the same. Americans have popularized the term digital library to denote all the three concepts. Electronic Library is the first topic in the syllabus for this paper. In the lesson package, the term "Digital Library" and Electronic Library are used interchangeably.

Fundamentally, Information or documents remain digitized in all the three systems and binary.

## DEFINITION

A *digital library* is a library in which collections are stored in digital formats (as opposed to print, microform , or other media) and accessible by computers. The digital content may be stored locally, or accessed remotely via computer networks. A digital library is a type of information retrieval system.

The first use of the term *digital library* in print may have been in a 1988 report to the Corporation for National Research Initiatives. The term *digital libraries* was first popularized by the NSF/DARPA/NASA Digital Libraries Initiative in 1994. These draw heavily on As We May Think by Vannevar Bush in 1945, which set out a vision not in terms of technology, but user experience. The term *virtual library* was initially used interchangeably with *digital library,* but is now primarily used for libraries that are virtual in other senses (such as libraries which aggregate distributed content).

The *DELOS Digital Library Reference Model* defines a digital library as:

An organization, which might be virtual, that comprehensively collects, manages and preserves for the long-term rich digital content, and offers to its user communities specialized functionality on that content, of measurable quality and according to codified policies.

There are many definitions of a "digital library." Terms such as "electronic library" and "virtual library" are often used synonymously. The elements that have been identified as common to these definitions are:

- the digital library is not a single entity;
- the digital library requires technology to link the resources of many;
- the linkages between the many digital libraries and information services are transparent to the end users;
- universal access to digital libraries and information services is a goal; and
- Digital library collections are not limited to document surrogates: they extend to digital artifacts that cannot be represented or distributed in printed formats.

Leiner, B.M. (1998), The digital library is the collection of services and the collection of information objects that support users in dealing with information objects available directly or indirectly via electronic/digital means.

*Clifford Lynch (1995)*, a well-known expert on digital libraries and new technologies, defined digital library as "a system providing a community of users with coherent access to a large, organized repository of digital information and knowledge. The digital library is not just one entity, but multiple sources seamlessly integrated."

*Michael Lesk*, has predicted that half of the materials accessed in major libraries will be digital by the early 21st century. He defines digital libraries as "organized collections of digital information that combine the structuring and gathering of information, which libraries and archives have always done, with the digital representation that computers have made possible. Digital information can be accessed rapidly around the world, copies for preservation without error, stored compactly, and searched very quickly. A true digital library also provides the principles governing what is included and how the collection is organized" . His prediction have became true.

*Arms (2000)* defines digital libraries as "managed collection of information, with associated services, where the information is stored in digital formats and accessible over a network".

Hence digital libraries provide an organized and structured access to information contents in a distributed environment and assist users in searching, evaluating and utilizing resources irrespective of their format.

Digital libraries combine collection and expertise in a seamless interface, and therefore, require specialized staff to select, organize, evaluate, interpret, offer intellectual access, preserve the integrity and ensure the persistence over time of digital works so that they are readily and economically available for use by a defined community or set of communities (Waters, 1992).

Hence Digital Library or Electronic Library is a library which exists solely in electronic form or on paper. The building blocks required for such a library may not exist, and the chemical steps for such a library may not have been tested. These libraries are used in the design and evaluation of possible libraries.

These libraries provide access to electronic information in a variety of remote locations through a local online catalogue or other gateway, such as the internet. Electronic or digital library can also be called as an annotated, frequently updated subject guide to online resources. Information resources or information services that are available over the Internet. At BMCC, the Virtual Library site provides access to a large number of library resources (indexes, journals, and reference materials, for example) and online reference service via the campus computer network. Students access these resources through a browser on a workstation anywhere on campus or remotely from home.

***Purposes***

The purposes of a digital library system are:

- To expedite the systematic development of the means to collect, store, and organize information and knowledge in digital form; and of digital library collections;
- To promote the economical and efficient delivery of information to all sectors of society;
- To encourage co-operative efforts which leverage the considerable investment in research resources, computing and communications network;
- To strengthen communication and collaboration between and among the research, business, government, and educational communities;
- To take an international role in the generation and dissemination of knowledge in areas of strategic importance; and
- To contribute to the lifelong learning opportunities of all.

## OBJECTIVES OF THE DIGITAL LIBRARY

The main objectives of the digital library are:

- To capture, store, manipulate, and distribute information.
- To introduce and produce new services.
- To have large number of databases in CDs.
- To avoid routine and redundant activities.
- To provide facility for networking and resource sharing.
- To access national and international journals which are being published only in machine-readable form.
- To improve the cost effectiveness of library operations.
- To support library functions such as circulations, serial control, acquisition control, stock maintenance and other routine office works and developing in house databases.

## CHARACTERISTICS OF DIGITAL LIBRARY

Though digital libraries are still a concept they have certain special characteristics such as :

- A digital library is not a single entity, it may also provide access to digital material and resources from outside the actual confines of any one digital library;
- Digital libraries support quick and efficient access to a large number of distributed but interlinked information sources that are seamlessly integrated;

- ❖ Digital libraries have collections that: (i) are large and persist over time; (ii) are well-organized and managed; (iii) contain many formats; (iv) contain objects and not just their representations; (v) contain objects that may be otherwise unobtainable; and (vi) contain some objects that are digital ab origine; and
- ❖ Digital libraries include all the processes and services offered by traditional libraries though these processes will have to be revised to accommodate difference between digital and paper media.
  - Global infrastructure
  - Network accessibility
  - User friendly interface
  - Advanced search and retrieval
  - Supporting multimedia content
  - Accessibility from anywhere, home, school, libraries, etc.
  - 24/365 Accessibility
  - Greater opportunity for publishing
  - Equal opportunities of access
  - Reduce physical space
  - Break the time, space and language barriers
  - Searching and retrieval facilities
- ❖ Usage of electronic information will steadily increase, and usage of printed material will decrease;
- ❖ Access to the digital library is not bounded in space or time. It can be accessed from anywhere in any time; and
- ❖ Jobs, training and recruitment will be re profiled.

## FUNCTIONS OF DIGITAL LIBRARY

- Make information available for an longer time,
- Support advanced search and retrieved for enable greater access for information,
- Maintain other routine office works and developing in house database,
- Access national and international journal, which are being published only Machine readable form,
- Support all sorts of Library operations or functions,
- Digitize documents for preservation and for space saving,
- The basic functions of digital libraries are to,
- Capture, store, manipulate information and provide access to a large collection,
- Improve the cost effectiveness of library operations,
- Digitize documents for networking and resource sharing,
- Provide facilities for networking and resource sharing,
- Access national and international journal, which are being published only in Machine readable form,

## TYPES OF DIGITAL LIBRARY SERVICES

The research undertaken when reviewing the web pages revealed a range of terms that refer to similar conceptualised services: subject gateways, subject-based resource discovery systems, Internet resource guide, information gateways, hybrid libraries, virtual libraries, and SINs (Special Interest Networks). These are just a few of the synonyms used on the Internet to describe similar services.

Types of Digital Library services are discussed here under. They are:

WWW Virtual Library
Subject Gateway
Gateway
Portal
Vortal
Internet Resource Catalogue

### WWW Virtual Library

An early Web concept which reflects the scope of thinking in the mid 1990s, before the existence of standard metadata schemas for resource discovery. It was intended as an online catalogue of Web resources. Good examples still exist, such as the Australian Biological Research Network (also known as a Special Interest Network).

### Subject Gateway

A subject gateway has been defined by the Australian Subject Gateways Forum as: "a Web-based mechanism for accessing a collection of high quality, evaluated resources identified to support research in a particular subject discipline". It is a service which is accessed via a portal, through open standard protocols (such as Z39.50, Harvest Broker). What the end-user sees is a perfectly structured Web-base.

A simple definition of a subject gateway is:

> "An Internet accessible collection of descriptions and location details for a range of information, generally available electronically, organised by subject or discipline, and selected for inclusion based on a published set of quality criteria."

The IMesh Toolkit project provides the following definition:

> "A subject gateway is a web site that provides searchable and browsable access to online resources focused around a specific subject. Subject gateway resource descriptions are usually created manually rather than being generated via an automated process. Because the resource entries are generated by hand they are usually superior to those available from a conventional web search engine."

A further description of subject gateways as promoted by the DESIRE Project, funded by the European Commission, is:

> "Selective subject gateways on the Internet are characterised by their quality control. The core activities of resource selection and description rely on skilled human input (by librarians, academics and experts) and are not activities that lend themselves to automation."

## Characteristics of Subject Gateways

To summarise, subject gateways display the characteristics such as Resource Selection, Collection Maintenance, Resource Description and Subject Classification.

### A. *Resource Selection*

A human intermediary adds value by selecting appropriate Internet resources, usually according to rigid selection criteria. Resources are usually selected for their quality, authority, accessibility, currency and subject relevance. Other selection criteria may also apply such as language or geographic coverage.

### B. *Collection Maintenance*

Regular maintenance of the collection occurs, including the removal of resources that are no longer appropriate, are superseded or contain data entry errors. Regular link checks may also be carried out. These procedures may be automated or carried out manually through human intervention. A policy will exist that details these procedures.

### C. *Resource Description*

Selected resources are annotated by a human intermediary with a full description of the resource. The descriptions will be entered according to a predefined, structured metadata schema. The metadata is structured into separate fields. This enables the resource to be easily identified and located. It also facilitates structured searching. The descriptions may contain information about the content, author, publisher or publication date of the resource.

### D. *Subject Classification*

A human intermediary uses a subject classification schema to index all resources. This facilitate subject browsing.

Subject gateways are also often characterised by application of standards to allow interoperability with other services, and various value-adding features.

## Gateway

This term is used by the Resource Discovery Network in the UK as the preferred term for subject gateways. It is a generic term that is sometimes used interchangeably with the term subject gateway. The term is used to describe a "range of Internet sites that in some way provide access to other, predominantly Internet-accessible, resources." Renardus distinguishes between 'gateways', 'subject gateways' and 'quality-controlled subject gateways'.

### Portal

"In the library community, portals may be defined as an amalgamation of services to the patron. The amalgamation is achieved through seamless integration of existing services. It uses binding agents such as customisation and authentication services, search protocols (Z39.50), loan protocols (such as ISO10161), and e-commerce. The result is a personalised service which allows the individual to access the rich content of both print-based and electronic systems."

An addition to the portal definition end-users can also specify options which will push selected content to them on a pre-agreed basis.

Portals (also sometimes called Megaportals, Horizontal Enterprise Portals or HEPs) differ from *vortals*. They provide a broad range of services and content to a diverse range of customers. They do not target their services to a particular demographic group, industry or topical category. They can therefore be characterised as "horizontal" in scope.

They offer at least five features, including: web searching, news, reference tools, access to online shopping, and some communication capabilities such as free e-mail and chat.

### Vortal

Vertical portals are known as vortals. They provide content aggregation relevant to their industry, with links to related industry, supplier and even competitor sites. They may have community and collaboration capabilities, and e-commerce services for products and services relevant to its industry. Vertical portals also try to leverage branding and associated technologies in a focused way.

### Internet Resource Catalogue

An Internet Resource Catalogue is just one of the services offered by a gateway or portal. A database of Internet resource descriptions that is made accessible through a structured and/or unstructured network service. Sometimes used synonymously with 'portal' and 'gateway'.

### Components of Electronic/Digital Library

Electronic libraries not only cover text in machine readable from but also Graphics, Photographs, Videos and so on. Nowadays most of the text books are available in the electronic form. The three major components of electronic library are :

DOCUMENTS—In electronic libraries, collections contain fixed and permanent documents in electronic form

TECHNOLOGY—Electronic libraries are based on technology

WORK—Electronic libraries are to online or offline

## Issues in the Development of Electronic/Digital Libraries

The dramatic growth of the Internet in recent years has accelerated the pace of change and the debate over the role and future of the information intermediary has intensified.

There are five areas that need addressing before the electronic library can become a reality. They are:

Technical issues.

(a) Legal issues.
(b) Economic issues.
(c) Psychological issues.
(d) Educational issues.

The electronic library cannot become a reality until a number of technical issues are resolved. The electronic library cannot take effect unless issues to do with copyright privacy, etc. are dealt with. The question of how one should price, and charge for information in an electronic library has yet to be resolved. If the electronic library is to succeed, it must deliver information in the way that people feel most comfortable, rather than forcing people to read at PC terminal on a desk.

Print on paper is so common place that it almost appears natural to know what to do with the artefacts based on this technology. Methods of training and educating users have to be developed.

People also need to understand the implication of the electronic library for their life, their work, and their leisure.

## Advantages of Electronic Libraries

The advantages of digital libraries as a means of easily and rapidly accessing books, archives and images of various types are now widely recognized by commercial interests and public bodies alike.[11]

Traditional libraries are limited by storage space; digital libraries have the potential to store much more information, simply because digital information requires very little physical space to contain it. As such, the cost of maintaining a digital library is much lower than that of a traditional library.

A traditional library must spend large sums of money paying for staff, book maintenance, rent, and additional books. Digital libraries do away with these fees. Both types of library require cataloguing input to allow users to locate and retrieve material. Digital libraries may be more willing to adopt innovations in technology providing users with improvements in electronic and audio book technology as well as presenting new forms of communication such as wikis and blogs; conventional libraries may consider that providing online access to their OPAC catalogue is sufficient. An important advantage to digital conversion is increased accessibility to users. There in also availability to individuals who may not be traditional patrons of a library, due to geographic location or organizational affiliation.

*No physical boundary*. The user of a digital library need not to go to the library physically; people from all over the world can gain access to the same information, as long as an Internet connection is available.

*Round the clock availability*. A major advantage of digital libraries is that people can gain access to the information at any time, night or day.

*Multiple accesses*. The same resources can be used simultaneously by a number of institutions and patrons. This may not be the case for copyrighted material: a library may have a license for "lending out" only one copy at a time; this is achieved with a system of digital rights management where a resource can become inaccessible after expiration of the lending period or after the lender chooses to make it inaccessible (equivalent to returning the resource).

*Information retrieval*. The user is able to use any search term (word, phrase, title, name, subject) to search the entire collection. Digital libraries can provide very user-friendly interfaces, giving clickable access to its resources.

*Preservation and conservation*. Digitization is not a long-term preservation solution for physical collections, but does succeed in providing access copies for materials that would otherwise fall to degradation from repeated use. Digitized collections and born-digital objects pose many preservation and conservation concerns that analog materials do not. Please see the following "Problems" section of this page for examples.

*Space*. Whereas traditional libraries are limited by storage space, digital libraries have the potential to store much more information, simply because digital information requires very little physical space to contain them and media storage technologies are more affordable than ever before.

*Added value*. Certain characteristics of objects, primarily the quality of images, may be improved. Digitization can enhance legibility and remove visible flaws such as stains and discoloration. [12]

Electronic libraries(digital) are visualised as 'benchmark in the technology' and practicing knowledge dissemination. The action words for digital library are "do something, start getting involved and must participate".

(a) Accessibility from anywhere (home, school, libraries during travel, hotel etc.)
(b) Provide access to more information than possible to physically acquire and maintain.
(c) Support both formal and information learning.
(d) Media integration.
(e) Remote access to expensive and rare material.
(f) Greater opportunity for publishing.

## ELECTRONIC RESOURCES

One of the main resources available via the Electronic Library is electronic journals. Electronic journals or e-journals are an invaluable source of up-to-date scholarly information. Before we identify what e-journals are and the different types of e-journals available, it is useful to first look at journals in general

## Electronic Resources in Digital Libraries

Electronic Library is made up of different online resources from various vendors which may include: EBSCO, Gale, OCLC Collection, ProQuest, and netLibrary.

## EBSCO

Academic Search Premier contains indexing for nearly 8,050 publications, with full text for more than 4,600 of those titles. PDF back files to 1975 or further are available for well over one hundred journals, and searchable references are provided for more than 1,000 titles. Academic Search Premier contains full text coverage in biology, chemistry, education, engineering, humanities, physics, psychology, religion and theology, sociology, etc.

*Business Source Premier* offers indexing and abstracts for the 350 scholarly journals back to 1965 or the first published issue. This database includes searchable references for more than 1,170 journals. Journal ranking studies reveal that Business Source Premier is an excellent database for full text journals in all disciplines of business, including marketing, management, Marketing of Information System, Principles of Management, accounting, finance, econometrics and economics.

*Regional Business News* A supplemental database for customers of Business Source Premier. With daily updates, Regional Business News provides comprehensive full text for regional business publications (including titles from Crain Communications). Regional Business News has full text for more than 60 sources.

*Master FILE Premier* contains full text for 2,053 periodicals covering general reference, business, health, education, general science, multicultural issues and much more. This database also contains full text for more than 350 reference books, 84,074 biographies, 86,132 primary source documents, and an Image Collection of 107,135 photos, maps & flags. Master FILE Premier now offers PDF back files (as far back as 1975) for key publications including American Libraries, Foreign Affairs, History Today, Judaism, Library Journal, National Review, Saturday Evening Post, etc.

## OCLC Collection

*WorldCat* (The OCLC Online Union Catalog). (Approximately 2100 B.C.—present; Updated daily)

The world's most comprehensive bibliography, with more than 50 million bibliographic records representing 400 languages. Covers information back to 2100 B.C. Includes holdings information from libraries across the world. Bibliographic information only.

*Electronic Collections Online.* Access citations only from the full-image articles from Electronic Collections Online journals. Full-text/image articles from selected journals are available to their special group only.

### Proquest

*ProQuest Newspapers* is an accessible and thorough Web-based database with citations and abstracts from over 350 newspapers, over 250 of which provide full text, enabling users to search the latest news from around the world.

Coverage, updated daily, of local, state, regional, national, and international newspapers is available, including full-text access to 27 major newspapers: the Star Tribune, The Wall Street Journal, The Washington Post, The New York Times, the Chicago Tribune, the Los Angeles Times, Barron's, and USA Today, to name just a few. One can access a wide range of articles, not only top news stories, but arts, sports, and entertainment stories as well.

### MINITEX

The MINITEX Library Information Network is a publicly supported network of libraries in Minnesota, North Dakota, and South Dakota working cooperatively to improve library service.

MINITEX's mission is to enhance the effectiveness and efficiency of participating libraries by expanding their access to local, state, regional, national, and international information resources through conventional and innovative means.

### MnLINK Gateway

The MnLINK Gateway is a World Wide Web-based virtual library, providing access to multiple information resources, including open access to participating Minnesota library catalogs and secured access to available electronic databases. In addition, the MnLINK Gateway provides links to selected free Internet resources. *Click here to learn more about MnLINK.*

### Digital Library Performance Indicators

The electronic libraries can be evaluated on the basis of the following parameters:

- Percentage of the population reached by electronic library services.
- Number of sessions on each electronic library service per member of the target population.
- Number of remote sessions on electronic library services per member of the population to be served.
- Number of documents and entries (records) viewed per session for each electronic library service.

- Cost per session for each electronic library service.
- Cost per document or entry (record) viewed for each electronic library service.
- Percentage of information requests submitted electronically.
- Library computer workstation use rate.
- Number of library computer workstation hours available per member of the population to be served.
- Rejected sessions as a percentage of total attempted sessions.
- Percentage of total acquisitions expenditure spent on acquisition of electronic library services.
- Number of attendances at formal electronic library service training lessons per member of the population to be served.
- Library staff developing, managing and providing ELS and user training as a percentage of total library staff.
- User satisfaction with electronic library services.

## Librarian in the Electronic Age

Libraries mission is to work towards meeting the information needs of possible by providing high quality information systems, services, products, based on the recorded human knowledge of the world, through the utilisation of current and emerging information technologies, digital technology, to be an active player in the international information industry. To participate in educational training and development programmes that leads to better utilisation of information resources by the beneficiaries of our services at large.

As the arrival of digital libraries is imminent, Librarians are forced to re-educate themselves to meet this new challenge.

Librarians will continue to play a crucial role in collecting, Cataloguing, Indexing and retrieving of information, despite the pattern of information transfer and processing becoming complex. Further, it is foreseen that until such time as computers are capable of matching human intelligence and until such time as all the information required is delivered at an affordable price, the role of librarian will remain central.

## Challenges and Issues

The highest priority of a library, electronic (digital) or any other, is to serve the research needs of clientele. The development, maintenance and extension of its collection and its technologies must be supportive as well as subordinate to this primary objective.

The issues which should be dealt with before the implementation of digital libraries are information protection, property rights, privacy, relevance of information available in digital libraries as well as its value and data security.

In order to face the challenges in the present electronic environment there is a need to study and understand the transformation which are now taking place in the technology field.

- Co-operation and co-ordination among all segments of the information sector (Workers, information generators, processors, distributors, government and users.)
- Must develop mechanisms for sharing of information at local, national, regional and international level.
- Must implement a comprehensive and cohesive information technologies.

## ELECTRONIC RESOURCES—METADATA, METADATA STANDARDS

The explosive growth of interest in the Internet in recent years has created a digital extension of the academic research library for certain kinds of materials. Valuable collections of texts, images and sounds from many scholarly communities—collections that may even be the subject of state-of-the-art discussions in these communities—now exist only in electronic form and may be accessible from the Internet. Knowledge regarding the whereabouts and status of this material is often passed on by word of mouth among members of a given community. For outsiders, however, much of this material is so difficult to locate that it is effectively unavailable.

### What is Metadata?

Metadata is structured information that describes, explains, locates, or otherwise makes it easier to retrieve, use or manage an information resource. Metadata is often called data about data or information about information. The term metadata is used differently in different communities. Some use it to refer to machine understandable information, while others use it only for records that describe electronic resources. However, in the library environment, metadata is commonly used for any formal scheme of resource description, applying to any type of object, digital or non-digital. Traditional library cataloging is a form of metadata, and MARC 21 and the rule sets used with it such as AACR2 are metadata standards.

Other metadata schemes have been developed to describe various types of textual and non-textual objects such as archival materials, visual materials, geographic information, and science and social science datasets. There are several different types of metadata, including descriptive, administrative, and structural. Descriptive metadata describes a resource for purposes such as discovery and identification. It can include elements such as title, abstract, author, and keywords. Administrative metadata provides information to help manage a resource, such as when and how it was created, file type and other technical information, and who can access it. Rights management metadata is a form of administrative metadata dealing with intellectual property rights. Structural metadata indicates how compound objects are put together, for example, how pages are ordered to form chapters.

Metadata can describe resources at any level of aggregation. It can describe a collection, a unitary resource, or a component part of a larger resource (for example, a photograph in an article). Just as catalogers make decisions about whether a catalog record should be created for a whole set of volumes or for each particular volume in the set, so the metadata creator makes similar decisions. Metadata can also be used for description at any level of the information model laid out in the IFLA (International Federation of Library Associations and Institutions) Functional Requirements for Bibliographic Records (http://www.ifla.org/VII/s13/frbr/frbr.pdf): work, expression, manifestation, or item. For example, a metadata record could describe a report, a particular edition of the report, or a specific copy of that edition of the report.

Metadata can be embedded in a digital object or it can be stored separately. Metadata is often embedded in HTML documents and in the headers of image files. Storing metadata with the object it describes ensures the metadata will not be lost, obviates problems of linking between data and metadata, and helps ensure that the metadata and object will be updated together. However, it is impossible to embed metadata in some types of objects (for example, artifacts). Also, storing metadata separately can simplify the management of the metadata itself and facilitate search and retrieval. Therefore, metadata is commonly stored in database systems and linked to the objects described.

Metadata schemes (also called schema) are sets of metadata elements designed for a particular purpose, for example, to describe a particular type of information resource. The definition or meaning of the elements themselves is known as the semantics of the scheme. The values given to metadata elements are the content. Metadata schemes generally specify names of elements and their semantics. Optionally, they may specify content rules for how content must be formulated (for example, how to identify the main title) and/or representation rules for how content must be represented (for example, capitalization rules). There may also be syntax rules for how the elements and their content should be encoded.

A metadata scheme with no prescribed syntax rules is called syntax independent. Metadata can be encoded in MARC, in "keyword=value" pairs, or in any other definable syntax. Many current metadata schemes use SGML or XML. XML (Extensible Mark-up Language) is an extended form of HTML which allows for locally defined tag sets and the easy exchange of structured information. SGML (Standard Generalized Mark-up Language) is a superset of both HTML and XML and allows for the richest mark-up of a document.

## What Does Metadata Do?

An important reason for creating descriptive metadata is to facilitate discovery of relevant information. In addition to resource discovery, metadata can help organize electronic resources, facilitate interoperability and legacy resource integration, support digital identification, and support archiving and preservation.

## Metadata Element Sets

### *Resource Discovery*

Identification of information is known as resource identification. Today in the semantic web environment, information is treated as objects. In this context resource identification comes to be known as Resource Discovery.

Metadata serves the same functions in resource discovery as good cataloging does by:

- allowing resources to be found by relevant criteria;
- identifying resources;
- bringing similar resources together;
- distinguishing dissimilar resources; and
- giving location information.

### Organizing Electronic Resources

As the number of Web-based resources grows exponentially, aggregate items or portals are increasingly useful in organizing links to resources based on audience or topic. Such lists can be built as static web pages, with the names and locations of the resources "hard coded" in the HTML. However, it is more efficient and increasingly more common to build these pages dynamically from metadata stored in databases. Software tools such as ColdFusion® can be used to automatically extract and reformat the information for web applications (*http://www.allaire.com/*Products/coldfusion/).

Another method of organizing Web information is through channels. Channels are preselected Web sites that automatically "push" streams of information to a user's browser, commonly used for continuously updated information such as stock quotes and news. The dominant metadata scheme for webcasting is the *Channel Definition Format* (CDF) developed by Microsoft and its partners (*http://www.w3.org/TR/* NOTE-CDFsubmit.html, http://msdn.microsoft.com/workshop/delivery/cdf/reference/CDF.asp).

### Interoperability

Describing a resource with metadata allows it to be understood by both humans and machines in ways that promote interoperability. Interoperability is the ability of multiple systems, with different hardware and software platforms, data structures, and interfaces, to exchange data with minimal loss of content and functionality. Using defined metadata schemes, shared transfer protocols, and crosswalks between schemes, resources across the network can be searched more seamlessly.

Two approaches to interoperability are cross-system search and metadata harvesting. The Z39.50 protocol is commonly used for cross system search (*http://www.loc.gov/* z3950/agency/). Z39.50 partners do not share metadata but map their own search capabilities to a common set of search attributes. A contrasting approach taken by the Open Archives

Initiative (*http://www.openarchives.org*) is for all partners to translate their native metadata to a common core set of elements and expose this for harvesting. A search service then gathers the metadata into a consistent central index to allow cross-repository searching regardless of the metadata formats used by participating repositories.

## Digital Identification

Most metadata schemes include elements such as standard numbers to uniquely identify the work or object to which the metadata refers. The location of a digital object may also be given using a file name, URL, or some more persistent identifier such as a Persistent URL (PURL) or the *Digital Object Identifier* (DOI)

Persistent identifiers are preferred because file locations change frequently, making the URL (and therefore the metadata record) invalid. In addition to the actual elements that point to the object, the metadata can be combined to act as a set of identifying data, differentiating one object from another for validation purposes.

## Archiving and Preservation

Most current metadata efforts center around the discovery of recently created resources. However, there is a growing concern that digital resources will not survive in usable form into the future. Digital information is fragile; it can be corrupted or altered, intentionally or unintentionally. It may become unusable as storage media and hardware and software technologies change.

Format migration and perhaps emulation of current hardware and software behaviour in future hardware and software platforms are strategies for overcoming these challenges.

Metadata is the key to ensuring that resources will survive and continue to be accessible into the future. Archiving and preservation require special elements to track the lineage of a digital object (where it came from and how it has changed over time), to detail its physical characteristics, and to document its behaviour in order to emulate it on future technologies.

Many organizations internationally are working on defining metadata schemes for digital preservation, including the National Library of Australia (*http://www.nla.gov.au/padi/*topics/32.html), the British Cedars Project (CURL Exemplars in Digital Archives) (*http://www.leeds.ac.uk/* cedars/ metadata.html), and a joint Working Group of OCLC and the Research Libraries Group (RLG) (http://www.oclc.org/digitalpreservation/ presmeta_wp.pdf). Many of these initiatives are based on or compatible with the ISO Reference Model for an Open Archival Information System (OAIS) which incorporates preservation metadata along with descriptive, administrative, and rights management metadata (http://www.ccsds.org/ RP9905/RP9905.html).

### Metadata Element Sets Used in Library Environments

Many different metadata schemes are being used in library environments. A few of the most common ones are mentioned below:

- Marc 21
- Dublin Core
- Global (Government) Information Locator Service (GILS)
- Text Encoding Initiative (TEI) Header
- Encoded Archival Description
- Visual Resources Association (VRA) Core Categories

## DIGITAL LIBRARY PROJECTS

Libraries are really dynamic, growing information centers that provide access to current materials as well as archiving materials for posterity. Beehives of activity, libraries of today often sport row after row of computer workstations in addition to their book and multimedia storage. Trained professionals make themselves available to assist library users in finding materials in many formats, from print materials, to audio, to video, to Web pages. The image of the fussy librarian was never an accurate one, but it is even farther from the truth now, as librarians have become information specialists who move nearly as quickly as the technology that they've come to embrace. As technology has driven the growth of the Internet and fuelled the information explosion, it has also driven libraries' growth.

Technology has also made it possible for libraries to begin providing users with "virtual" services. Although still in the developmental stages, virtual libraries may one day offer researchers the ability to access any information they desire, anywhere in the world, at any time they need it. This will include articles from e-journals and e-newspapers as well as entire e-books, movies, recordings, and other mixed media resources.

Much of this is already happening. Academic libraries and large public libraries are already partnering with publishers to provide virtual resources to their users. It's merely a matter of time before technology is so reliable, access times so good, and stored information so exhaustive that researchers will be able to sit in their homes or offices and read, see, and hear what they want with or without the assistance of virtual librarians. The following are most of the important Digital Library Projects.

California Digital Library

*http://www.californiadigitallibrary.org/*

The California Digital Library provides a single point of access for digital collections produced or managed by the University of California. This site offers a broad range of scholarly and popular content; the digital collections reflect the diverse interests and scholarship of the University of California. This website is a first-step towards bringing together publicly accessible digital collections that are created and managed by the University of California.

Internet Public Library http://www.ipl.org/

The Internet Public Library (IPL), is a public service organization and learning/teaching environment at the University of Michigan School of Information. IPL seeks to challenge and redefine the roles and significance of libraries in an increasingly distributed and digital world.

*WWW Virtual Library http://www.vlib.org/*

Unlike commercial catalogs, the WWW Virtual Library is run by a loose confederation of volunteers, who compile pages of key links for particular areas in which they are expert; even though it isn't the biggest index of the web, the VL pages are widely recognized as being amongst the highest-quality guides to particular sections of the web.

## University Virtual Libraries

*Alexandria Digitial Library Project, University of California at Santa Barbara*
http://alexandria.sdc.ucsb.edu/

The goal of the Alexandria Digital Library Project (ADL) is to develop a globally distributed georeferenced digital library.

*Berkeley Digital Library SunSITE, University of California at Berkeley*
http://sunsite.berkeley.edu/

The Berkeley Digital Library SunSITE builds digital collections and services while providing information and support to digital library developers worldwide. SunSITE is sponsored by the U.C. Berkeley Library and Sun Microsystems, Inc.

*California Digital Library, University of California*
http://www.cdlib.org/

Harnessing technology and innovation, and leveraging the intellectual and cultural resources of the University of California, the California Digital Library (CDL) supports the assembly and creative use of the world's scholarship and knowledge for the UC libraries and the communities they serve. Established in 1997 as a UC library, the CDL has become one of the largest digital libraries in the world.

*Cornell University Library Digital Collections, Cornell University*
http://cdl.library.cornell.edu/

Cornell Library Digital Collections are open to the general public, in accordance with the terms set forth in the Guidelines for Using Text and Images from Cornell Library Digital Collections.

*DSpace, Massachusetts Institute of Technology*
http://dspace.org/

DSpace is a groundbreaking digital library system to capture, store, index, preserve, and redistribute the intellectual output of a university's research faculty in digital formats. Developed jointly by MIT Libraries and Hewlett-Packard (HP), DSpace is now freely available to research institutions world-wide as an open source system that can be customized and extended.

*Electronic Text Center, University of Virginia*
http://etext.lib.virginia.edu/

The Electronic Text Center's holdings include approximately 70,000 on- and off-line humanities texts in thirteen languages, with more than 350,000 related images (book illustrations, covers, manuscripts, newspaper pages, page images of Special Collections books, museum objects, etc.)

*Digital Library Production Service, University of Michigan*

http://www.umdl.umich.edu/

The Digital Library Production Service (DLPS) was formed in 1996 to provide infrastructure for campus digital library collections, including both access systems and digitization services. DLPS is a unit of the University Library, and is part of its Library Information Technology Division. DLPS is also responsible for the Digital Library extension Service (DLXS) and host services for other academic institutions and non-profit organizations.

*Digital Library Research Projects at Grainger Engineering Library Information Center, University of Illinois at Urbana-Champaign* http://dli.grainger.uiuc.edu/

*Digital Research Library, University of Pittsburgh*

http://digital.library.pitt.edu/

The Digital Research Library (DRL) of the University of Pittsburgh's University Library System (ULS) supports the teaching and research mission of the university and serves users through the creation and maintenance of Web-accessible digital research collections. The DRL also serves as a knowledge resource within the ULS for digital library issues and developments.

*Informedia-II Digital Video Library, Carnegie Mellon University*

http://www.informedia.cs.cmu.edu/

The overarching goal of the Informedia initiatives is to achieve machine understanding of video and film media, including all aspects of search, retrieval, visualization and summarization in both contemporaneous and archival content collections.

*Perseus Digital Library, Tufts University* http://www.perseus.tufts.edu/

Perseus is an evolving digital library, engineering interactions through time, space, and language. Their primary goal is to bring a wide range of source materials to as large an audience as possible.

*Stanford Digital Library Technologies Project*

http://www-diglib.stanford.edu/diglib/index.html

The Stanford Digital Library Technologies Project was initiated in July as part of the Federally funded Digital Library Initiative Phase 2. The goal of this Project is to design and implement the infrastructure and services needed for collaboratively creating, disseminating, sharing and managing information in a digital library context.

*UC Berkeley Digital Library Project*

http://elib.cs.berkeley.edu/

The UC Berkeley Digital Library Project is developing the tools and technologies to support highly improved models of the "scholarly information life cycle." Their goal is to facilitate the move from the current centralized, discrete publishing model, to a distributed, continuous, and self-publishing model, while still preserving the best aspects of the current model such as peer review.

### Government Virtual Libraries

*The Virtual Reference Desk Project*

http://www.vrd.org/index.shtml

The Virtual Reference Desk (VRD) is a project dedicated to the advancement of digital reference and the successful creation and operation of human-mediated, Internet-based information services. VRD is sponsored by the United States Department of Education.

*United States Library of Congress* http://lcweb.loc.gov/

The Library of Congress is the nation's oldest federal cultural institution and serves as the research arm of Congress. It is also the largest library in the world, with nearly 128 million items on approximately 530 miles of bookshelves. The collections include more than 29 million books and other printed materials, 2.7 million recordings, 12 million photographs, 4.8 million maps, and 57 million manuscripts.

*National Archives & Records Administration*

/www.archives.gov/welcome/index.html

NARA, an independent Federal agency, is America's national record keeper. NARA's mission is to ensure ready access to the essential evidence that documents the rights of American citizens, the actions of Federal officials, and the national experience. Among the treasures available online are the cornerstone documents of our Government - the Declaration of Independence, the Constitution of the United States, and the Bill of Rights, as well as many current and past exhibits.

*Smithsonian Institution* http://www.smithsonian.org/

The Smithsonian is committed to enlarging our shared understanding of the mosaic that is our national identity by providing authoritative experiences that connect us to our history and our heritage as Americans and to promoting innovation, research and discovery in science. These commitments have been central to the Smithsonian since its founding more than 155 years ago.

*Library and Archives Canada* http://www.archives.ca/

Library and Archives Canada is an innovative knowledge institution that combines the collections, services and staff expertise of the former National Library of Canada and National Archives of Canada. The objective is to provide all Canadians with easy, one-stop access to the texts, photographs and other documents that reflect their cultural, social and political development. Working closely with other archives and libraries, they will continue to acquire and preserve Canada's documentary heritage in all its forms.

### Virtual Libraries by Subject

*Asian Studies WWW Virtual Library*

http://coombs.anu.edu.au/WWWVL-AsianStudies.html

This website is a global collaborative project which provides access in bibliographic and in hypertext terms to networked scholarly documents, resources and information systems concerned with or relevant to Asian Studies.

*The World-Wide Web Virtual Library: Chemical Engineering*

http://www.che.ufl.edu/www-che/

This subject catalog lists information resources relevant to Chemical and Process Engineering.

*Links for Chemists*

http://www.liv.ac.uk/Chemistry/Links/links.html

Links for Chemists is an index of chemistry resources on the web. This site is the copyright of The University of Liverpool, Department of Chemistry.

*WWW Virtual Library: Electrical and Electronics Engineering*

http://webdiee.cem.itesm.mx/wwwvlee/

The Electrical and Electronics Engineering Virtual Library is hosted at Monterrey Tech, State of Mexico Campus, Electrical and Electronics Engineering Department. Contents include: Academic and Research Institutions, Information Resources, Journals and Magazines, Products and Services, and Standards.

*WWW Virtual Law Library* http://www.law.indiana.edu/v-lib/

One can search, browse by topical listing (Administrative Law, Business and Commercial, Law Civil and Appellate Procedure, Constitutional Law, Contracts, Criminal Law and Evidence, Environmental Law, Family Law, Foreign and International Law, Intellectual Property Law, Labour and Employment Law, Property Law, Taxation, and Torts), or browse by information source (Law Schools/Libraries, Law Firms, Law Journals, U.S. Government, State Government, Organizations, Foundations, Non-Profit Vendors, and Publishers.)

*Mathematics WWW Virtual Library*

http://www.math.fsu.edu/Virtual/index.php

This collection of Mathematics-related resources is maintained by the Florida State University Department of Mathematics as a free service to the online community. Information is categorized by subject: Addresses and Societies, Bibliographies, Department, Education, Electronic Journals, General Resources, Gophers, High School Servers, Newsgroups, Online Books, Preprints, Science and Math, Software, Specialized Fields, and TeX Archives.

*WWW Virtual Library: Microbiology & Virology*

http://www.microbiol.org/vl_micro/

This section of the Virtual Library is devoted to the science, practice, and application of microbiology and virology. Subjects covered include culture collections, databases, educational sites, journals, government and regulatory sites, images, medical microbiology, university departments, virology, protista, and references to newsgroups, Email lists, and other resources for the microbiologist.

*The World-Wide Web Virtual Library: Pharmacy*
http://www.pharmacy.org/

This website includes pharmacy related resource available on the Internet, including: Associations, Community Pharmacy Pages, Conferences, Databases on the WWW, Government WWW Sites, Hospital Pages, Jobs and Pharmacy, Journals and Books, Miscellaneous Pharmacy Pages, Pharmaceutical Companies, Pharmacy Listservs, and Pharmacy Schools on the WWW.

*WWW Virtual Library: Philosophy*
http://www.bristol.ac.uk/Depts/Philosophy/VL/

The WWW Philosophy Virtual Library is located at the University of Bristol, hosted jointly by the Department of Philosophy and the Institute for Learning and Research Technology. This Virtual Library section is now provided in collaboration with SOSIG, the Social Science Information Gateway.

*Psychology WWW Virtual Library*
http://www.clas.ufl.edu/users/gthursby/psi/

The Psychology Virtual Library keeps track of online information as part of the WWW Virtual Library. Sites are inspected and evaluated for their adequacy as information sources before they are linked to. World Wide Web

*Virtual Library: Statistics* http://www.stat.ufl.edu/vlib/statistics.html

Sections include: Data Sources; Job Announcements; Departments, Divisions, and Schools of Statistics; On-Line Educational Resources; Government Statistical Institutes; Statistical Research Groups, Institutes, and Associations; Services; Archives and Resources; Software Vendors and Software FAQs; Journals; Mailing Lists and Archives; and related News Groups.

*World Wide Web Virtual Library: Veterinary Medicine*
http://netvet.wustl.edu/vetmed.htm

The WWW Virtual Library Veterinary Medicine is a selected collection of veterinary medical Internet resources. This page began operation on December 7, 1994.

*Women's Studies Section* tp://libr.org/wss/WSSLinks/index.html

WSSLINKS was developed and is maintained by the Women's Studies Section of the Association of College & Research Libraries. The purpose of WSSLINKS is to provide access to a wide range of resources in support of Women's Studies.

## Literature Virtual Libraries

*The Online Books Page, University of Pennsylvania*
http://digital.library.upenn.edu/books/

The Online Books Page is a website hosted by the University of Pennsylvania Library, that facilitates access to books that are freely readable over the Internet. It also aims to encourage the development of such online books, for the benefit and edification of all.

*Project Gutenberg* http://www.gutenberg.org/

Project Gutenberg is the Internet's oldest producer of free electronic books (eBooks or etexts). Their present collection of more than 10,000 eBooks was produced by hundreds of volunteers. Most of the Project Gutenberg eBooks are older literary works that are in the public domain in the United States. All may be freely downloaded and read, and redistributed for non-commercial use.

*Digital Book Index* http://www.digitalbookindex.com/

Digital Book Index provides links to more than 88,000 title records from more than 1800 commercial and non-commercial publishers, universities, and various private sites. About 49,900 of these books, texts, and documents are available free, while many others are available at very modest cost.

*Humanities Text Initiative (HTI) American Verse Project*

http://www.hti.umich.edu/a/amverse/

The American Verse Project is a collaborative project between the University of Michigan Humanities Text Initiative (HTI) and the University of Michigan Press. The project is assembling an electronic archive of volumes of American poetry prior to 1920. The full text of each volume of poetry is being converted into digital form and coded in Standard Generalized Mark-up Language (SGML) using the TEI Guidelines, with various forms of access provided through the WWW.

*Romantic Circles* http://www.rc.umd.edu/editions/

Romantic Circles is a website devoted to the study of Romantic-period literature and culture, published by the University of Maryland and supported, in part, by the Maryland Institute for Technology and the Humanities (MITH). Romantic Circles' Electronic Editions collection is a searchable archive of carefully-chosen texts based on the highest scholarly standards. All contributions are peer-reviewed. Keyword searches can be conducted on the entire library or can be limited to the works of a particular author or text.

*The Victorian Women Writers Project*

http://www.indiana.edu/~letrs/vwwp/

The goal of the Victorian Women Writers Project is to produce highly accurate transcriptions of works by British women writers of the 19th century, encoded using the Standard Generalized Markup Language (SGML). The works, selected with the assistance of the Advisory Board, will include anthologies, novels, political pamphlets, religious tracts, children's books, and volumes of poetry and verse drama. The texts will be made freely available through the World Wide Web.

*E-Book Library, Electronic Text Center, University of Virginia*

http://etext.lib.virginia.edu/ebooks/ebooklist.html

1,800 publicly-available e-books including classic British and American fiction, major authors, children's literature, the Bible, Shakespeare, American history, African-American documents, and much more. Each text on this list can be accessed in HTML (web version) for online viewing, and can be downloaded as both a MS Reader E-book for the Microsoft Reader and a Palm-readable text for the Palm Reader.

*Internet Classics Archive* http://classics.mit.edu/

Select from a list of 441 works of classical literature by 59 different authors, including user-driven commentary and "reader's choice" Web sites. Mainly Greco-Roman works (some Chinese and Persian), all in English translation. Construct powerful queries to search the texts provided locally and remotely. Search by work and author, as well as the entire archive.

*Bibliomania* http://www.bibliomania.com/

Bibliomania has more than 2000 free online texts, study guides and reference resources. Contains fiction, non-fiction, and poetry sections, with a limited reference section.

## Digital Library Initiatives at Higher Education in India

Most higher education and research institutions in India are funded by the central and state governments. Those institutions have made a significant contribution to the transmission of knowledge and to research in all fields and disciplines. Universities and research institutes have played a leading role in transforming the country into a modern industrialized and technologically advanced state. The green revolution and tremendous progress in dairy development have made India a major food-producing country. Its development of space technology, the production and launching of indigenous satellites, and the development of peaceful nuclear energy have brought it into the forefront of technologically advanced nations to which a large number of developing countries look for training and guidance. Indian universities and institutes of higher learning support the needs and aspirations of Indian students and scholars. The libraries of those institutions also play a vital role in acquiring and disseminating information for academic and research activities. Digital libraries are a way of making educational and research data and information available to faculty, researchers, students, and others at the institutions and worldwide.

## Digital Library Projects in India

Libraries are the storehouse of knowledge as they maintain the book and other knowledge resource available—mostly in printed form. However, with the advent of digital technology and Internet connectivity, the library scenario is changing fast. Digital technology, Internet connectivity and physical content can be dovetailed resulting in Digital Library. Data available in physical form can be preserved digitally in Digital Library. Digital Libraries have the ability to enhance access to information and knowledge. They also Bridge barriers of time and space.

In the past initiatives have been taken by different Ministries/ Departments/organizations for digitizing and preserving data available in physical form. However, this activity has been restricted mostly in the area of the work/interest of the organization. Department of Information Technology too has in the past, supported projects in the area of Digital

Libraries. This also includes initiatives taken in collaboration with Indian Institute of Science, Bangalore and Carnegie Melon University, USA, under Million Book Universal Digital Library Programme.

### Digital Library of India

The Indian Institute of Science (IISc), Carnegie Mellon University (CMU), the International Institute of Information Technology, Hyderabad (IIITH), and many other academic, religious, and government organizations in India, a total of more than twenty "Content Creation Centres," have become partners in the Digital Library of India (DLI). The DLI seeks to preserve Indian heritage that is contained in books, manuscripts, art, and music. Each centre brings its own unique collection. This digital library is also a test-bed for Indian language research. The DLI is a leader in worldwide efforts to make knowledge free. A pilot project to scan some 10,000 books was initiated at CMU and then followed up at IISc, IIIT-H, and other organizations. All the processes involved have been perfected. The vision is to preserve all the knowledge of the human race in digital form and make that content searchable, independent of language and location, and to ensure that the cultural heritage of countries like India is not lost during the transition from paper to bits and bytes, as they were lost during a former transition of cultural content from palm leaves to paper.

So far, more than 289,000 books have been scanned, of which nearly 170,000 are in Indian languages. More than 84,000 books (25 million pages) are available on the DLI web site at the *Indian Institute of Science,* and more than 149,000 books (43 million pages) are available on the DLI web site at the *International Institute of Information Technology*. The link to other partner sites is also provided through a *commonly accessible website*.

Funding for the DLI comes from multiple sources. The Office of the Principal Scientific Advisor to the Government of India is funding the project at the Indian Institute of Science. The Ministry of Communication and Information Technology (MCIT) is funding the project at various DLI partner centres. The National Science Foundation (USA) is providing funding for scanners and software research and development through Carnegie Mellon University. The First Citizen of India, His Excellency Dr. APJ Abdul Kalam, President, who himself is one of the contributors to this vision, has personally taken a keen interest in making the Rashtrapathi Bhavan one of the major centres of the DLI.

### National Mission for Manuscript Digitization

India has one of the oldest and largest collections of manuscripts in the world. These are in different languages and scripts, and written on materials such as birch bark, palm leaf, cloth, paper, etc. They are in libraries, museums, monasteries, and in the collections of individuals. A significant portion is not archaically preserved. Experts estimate that most palm leaf manuscripts will perish due to wear and tear over the next 50 to 100 years. The National Mission for Manuscripts has taken a significant step. The

Department of Culture, and Ministry of Tourism and Culture, Government of India, launched the National Mission for Manuscripts in February 2003. The objectives of the mission are to facilitate conservation and preservation of manuscripts through training, awareness, and financial support; to document, catalogue, and promote access to Indian manuscripts and to encourage scholarship and research. In addition, the Central Secretariat Library (CSL), in the Department of Culture, has undertaken the massive task of digitizing government document resources. Expected benefits are the creation of a National Directory of Custodial Institutions and Individuals and Subject Directories; a National Manuscript Library to provide central access; raising awareness of the rich intellectual heritage of India; providing policy inputs to conserve, preserve, digitized, improve access, and save manuscripts for posterity; creating interest among scholars and institutions to for training in traditional Indian languages and subjects; and improving accessibility to all the stakeholders.

### Traditional Knowledge Digital Library (TKDL)

TKDL is a collaborative project of the National Institute of Science Communication and Information Resources (NISCAIR), the Council of Scientific and Industrial Research, the Ministry of Science & Technology and Department of AYUSH, and the Ministry of Health and Family Welfare, which this is being implemented at NISCAIR. An inter-disciplinary team of Traditional Medicine (Ayurveda, Unani, Siddha, Yoga) experts, patent examiners, IT experts, scientists, and technical officers are involved in the creation of TKDL for Indian Systems of Medicine. The project documents the public domain traditional knowledge related to Ayurveda, Unani, and Siddha, in five international languages: English, German, French, Japanese, and Spanish. Traditional Knowledge Resource Classification (TKRC), an innovative structured classification system for systematic arrangement, dissemination, and retrieval has been developed for about 10,500 sub-groups of a single International Patent Classification (IPC), i.e. AK61K35/78 for medicinal plants. TKDL is India 's effort to protect its traditional medicine from foreign pharmaceutical companies who might try to copyright such medicine. TDKL will serve not merely as a source of protection for intellectual property but also as a means by which its researchers can further study and document the scientific underpinnings of the medicines and remedies in the collection.

### Digital Library Initiative at National Library of India

The National Library of India is a permanent repository of all material produced in India and written by Indians, and also about India written by foreign authors, wherever published in any language. The library has a large collection of publications in English and other European languages, as well as Chinese, Japanese, Arabic, and Persian. There is also a rich collection of Sanskrit, Persian, Arabic, and Tamil manuscripts and rare books. One function of the National Library is to conserve the printed heritage for future generations. The library has separate divisions for physical, chemical, reprographic, and digital conservation. Rare and brittle books and other documents on are being scanned and stored on compact disc. English books and documents published before 1900 and Indian publications before 1920 are considered for digitisation. So far, 6,600 books in Indian and English languages have been scanned, with a total of over 25,00,000 pages.

### Centre for Development of Advanced Computing (C-DAC) Digital Library of Art Masterpieces

This is the first initiative of its kind in Asia and it will digitize 200 rare paintings of Rabindranath Tagore and Amrita Shergill from the National Gallery of Modern Arts (NGMA). The infrastructure to host this digital library will be located at the C-DAC Bangalore. C-DAC and Hewlett Packard launched the joint initiative "When Art Meets Technology" for digital preservation, restoration, and dissemination of art from the NGMA at Bangalore on February 4, 2003.

### Indira Gandhi National Centre for the Arts (IGNCA)—Kalasampada

IGNCA has taken up the Kalasampada Digital Library-Resource for Indian Cultural Heritage (DL-RICH) project, which is sponsored by the Ministry of Communication and Information Technology (MCIT). This project aims to develop software that will allow users to interact and explore images, audio, text, graphics, animation, and video in an integrated approach to the study of Indian art and culture. Kalasampada will facilitate access for students, scholars, artists, and the research and scientific community. The materials include several hundred thousand manuscripts, more than one hundred thousand slides, thousands of rare books, photographs, audio, and video.

### V.V. Giri National Labour Institute

The Archives of Indian Labour were created by the V.V. Giri National Labour Institute and the Association of Indian Labour Historians (AILH). The archive preserves documents, builds collections, and initiates research in labour history. The collections include documents from different organisations. Documents from labour movements are included, as well as personal accounts and memories of labour leaders and workers. The archive uses Greenstone, an open-source digital library system, to integrate text, audio, and video.

### Indian Parliament Library

This library serves members of Parliament and officers and staff of Lok Sabha Secretariat. Large databases were initially developed by the computer centre. The data are stored and available now in PARLIS (Parliament Library Information System).

### Khuda Baksh Oriental Public Library

This library has a rich collection of manuscripts in Persian, Arabic, Urdu and other languages. The descriptive catalogue is available in a 30-volume set which appeared in 1923 and was reprinted in the 1970s. Print catalogues were converted to machine-readable form by NICNET, which has undertaken the digitisation project. Some 400 thousand pages are now available. Documents are accessible as JPEG files. There is no retrieval mechanism for the text, since documents are treated as collection of image files. The catalogue is not searchable using a metadata scheme or any descriptors.

### Indira Gandhi Memorial Library, University of Hyderabad

TAs well as being the first fully automated library in India, it was the first to begin a digital library program. Since 2002 the library has digitized around 250,000 pages, primarily theses and dissertations, as well as 300 books in English and Indian languages. The library has access to about 170,000 electronic journals. The library preserves discs that accompany printed books and journals by uploading them to the CD server, which is linked to the digital library system. The library scans printed journals from Indian publishers and maintains them in the digital library as well. The library uses the open source software Space for its institutional repository.

Maintenance of a digital library includes content creation, designing and updating webpages, metadata creation, uploading and linking digital content. The digital library uses MARC-21 for metadata and PDF for digital content.

### Raman Research Institute

The Raman Research Institute Digital Repository allows the Institute community to deposit pre-prints, post-prints, and other publications and organizes these publications for retrieval. It also contains the annual reports of Institute and newspaper clippings from its archives. The Repository uses DSpace.

### National Chemical Laboratory

National Chemical Laboratory is an interdisciplinary research centre focusing on polymer science, organic chemistry, catalysis, materials chemistry, chemical engineering, biochemical sciences, and process development. It partners with industry, and some 400 graduate students are pursuing doctoral degrees. About 50 Ph.D. degrees are awarded each year. The institute has the second largest number of papers in chemical sciences (ca. 430), files the largest number of patents, both in India (60) and abroad (60) and produces the largest number of Ph.Ds. in chemical sciences in India. The repository uses DSpace. There are currently 500 theses, project reports, and journal articles available.

### National Institute of Oceanography

The digital repository of the National Institute of Oceanography collects and preserves institutional publications (journal articles, conference proceedings, technical reports, theses, dissertations, etc). Some of the completed and ongoing projects are:

Marine boundary layer characteristics during a cyclonic storm over the Bay of Bengal.
Variation of wave directional spread parameters along the Indian coast
Study of Goa and its environment from space: A report on coastal sand dune ecosystems of Goa: Siginficance, uses and anthropogenic impacts.
The coastal regulation zone of Goa: Oceanographic, environmental and societal perspectives.
Marine pollution detection through biomarkers in marine bivalves.
The repository uses Space.

### ETD and Institutional Repository

Theses and dissertations are a bedrock of graduate education. Thesis and dissertation research is guided by experts in the field and frequently funded by highly competitive scholarships and grants. Theses and dissertations are useful sources of secondary information, particularly in the humanities, where texts are important and ideas stay current longer. Most of these works languish in college and university libraries and archives. Electronically publishing of theses and dissertations brings this valuable material more prominence. An Institutional Repository (IR) is a digital archive of the intellectual output of a university. Theses and dissertations are one basic category of material for an IR.

### Vidyanidhi Projects

Vidyanidhi (which means "treasure of knowledge" in Sanskrit) is a digital archive of dissertations, as well as a set of resources for doctoral research in India. Vidyanidhi is being developed as a national repository and a consortium for electronic dissertations, through participation and partnership with universities, academic institutions, and other stakeholders. Vidyanidhi began as a pilot project in 2000 with governmental support, well as support from the Ford Foundation and Microsoft India. The Ford Foundation support is for focusing on Social and Human Sciences. The Microsoft support is for the implementation of Unicode for Indian Languages. Vidyanidhi is a member of the Networked Digital Library of Theses and Dissertations (NDLTD), and UNESCO and other efforts in this direction. UNESCO supports ETD initiatives worldwide.

### Electronic Theses and Dissertation Project of INFLIBNET Centre

INLIBNET hosts a bibliographic database 200,000 dissertations from about two hundred Indian universities going back to 1905. The Repository uses DSpace, which complies with the Open Archives Initiative (OAI) framework allowing publications to be easily indexed and searched by web search engines and other indexing services.

### Indian Institute of Astrophysics

The Indian Institute of Astrophysics has its origins in the Madras Observatory, which was created in the late 18th century. Today the Institute is a national research centre for physics and astronomy. Its repository includes dissertations from researchers associated with the Institute, as well as papers from the Bulletin of the Astronomical Society India beginning with volume 1 (1973), journal articles, and conference papers. Archival materials from the 18th, 19th, and 20th centuries have recently been added. These materials are manuscripts, photographs, annual reports, instruments and their descriptions. The repository uses DSpace.

### Indian Institute of Science, Bangalore

The Institute uses *e-Prints*, an institutional repository of research output. The archive is maintained by the National Center for Science Information (NCSI) and it supports self-archiving in various file formats (pdf, Word, html, etc.) Around 5,000 articles are available.

### Indian Institute of Technology, Bombay

The repository has bibliographic information and abstract for dissertations beginning in 1965. The masters thesis database has bibliographic information and abstract from 1999 on. More than 3,000 full text theses and Dissertations are available in the *ETD database*. The repository uses Greenstone, open source software, which complies with the Open Archives Initiative (OAI) protocol.

### Indian Institute of Management, Kozikode

The IIM-K institutional repository uses GNU E-Prints software, which was developed at the University of Southampton. The community can archive preprints, postprints, and other scholarly publications. Anyone can access the archive, but submission of documents is limited to the IIMK research community. At present around 200 full-text documents are available in the repository.

### Indian Institute of Technology, New Delhi

Digital library initiatives began in 1998 with an upgrade to a faster Internet connection. The high-speed Internet connection led to a number of digitized collections. IITs receive grants from government bodies such as AICTE (All India Council of Technical Education) and the Ministry of Human Resources Development and Management (MHRD) to develop digital libraries. Online courseware has been developed and older volumes of journals have been digitized, among other projects. More than 500 dissertations are available in the repository. The campus has facilities for submitting material to the repository. More than 25,000 pages of journals were scanned and are available on the Institute intranet.

### Indian Institute of Technology, Kharagpur

The Central Library, IIT Kharagpur, created an electronic library in 1994, which is now called a digital library. Older documents have been digitized, and it has large number of electronic resources such as *EiTech* index, *Compendex,* IEEE/IEE journals in full text, *INSPEC, Current Contents, Chemical Abstracts, Biotechnology Abstracts, Agricultural Abstracts, Library and Information Science Abstracts,* ASTM standards and ABI. The institutional repository collects, preserves, and disseminates research output. At present, access is restricted to the IIT Kharagpur campus LAN only and submission of documents to this repository is also limited to the IIT Kharagpur research community. The repository uses DSpace.

### Librarian's Digital Library

This repository is at the Documentation Research Training Centre, Indian Statistical Institute, Bangalore. It is aimed at librarians world-wide, and uses DSpace. It contains articles, theses and dissertations, presentations, multi-lingual documents, photographs, etc.

### National Institute of Technology, Calicut

"Nalanda" was initiated in 1999 and is one of the largest digital libraries in the country. It serves the campus with research and other academic information in science, engineering, and technology. The software used was developed by the institute itself. Nalanda is accessible from anywhere on campus. The repository contains theses and dissertations, course materials, articles, and annual reports.

### National Institute of Technology, Rourkela

Formerly known as Regional Engineering College (REC), this is one of the premier institutions for technical education in the country. NIT is a joint undertaking of Government of India and Government of Orissa. This Institutional Repository uses DSpace. At present around 343 documents are available in the repository.

## ELECTRONIC JOURNALS

*An electronic journal is a publication issued at regular intervals and available electronically.* Electronic journals are often called *e-journals.* There are different types of electronic journals:

*Full text*—these are e-journals where complete articles are available rather than just summaries or abstracts. Usually the whole of the journal is available online.

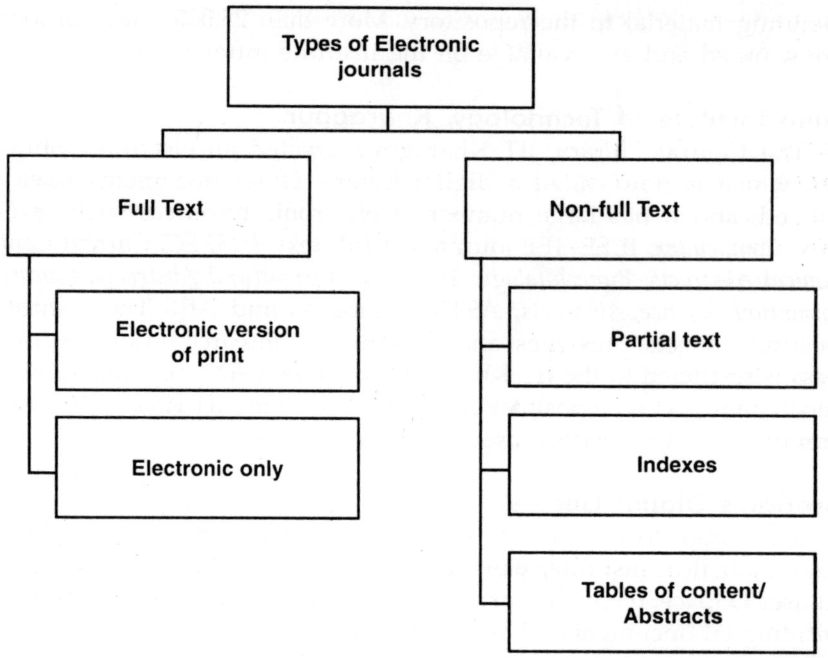


*Electronic version of print*—these are journals that are available both in print and electronically. Sometimes the electronic version may differ from the print journal e.g. articles may appear electronically before they are printed or the electronic version may have supplementary material on it.

*Electronic only*—these are journals that are only available electronically.

It should be noted that sometimes electronic journals allow you to access the full text of *particular articles or sections* of the journal, but not all the articles, e.g. Oxford Review of Economic Policy.

*Non-full text*—these are e-journals will *not* be able to access the full text of the whole journal.

*Indexes*—some e-journals may make their cumulative indexes available as well as, or instead of their tables of contents.

*Electronic tables of contents/Abstracts*—many journals allow you to access their table of contents and/or abstracts (summaries) of articles even when you cannot get the whole journal electronically.

## E-BOOK (ELECTRONIC-BOOK)

An E-Book is an *electronic* version of a traditional print book that can be read by using a personal computer or by using an E-Book reader. (An E-Book reader can be a software application for use on a computer, such as Microsoft's free *Reader* application, or a book-sized computer that is used solely as a reading device, such as Nuvomedia's Rocket E-Book.) Users can purchase an e-Book on diskette or CD, but the most popular method of getting an e-Book is to purchase a downloadable file of the e-Book (or other reading material) from a Web site (such as Barnes and Noble) to be read from the user's computer or reading device. Generally, an e-Book can be downloaded in five minutes or less.

Although it is not necessary to use a reader application or device in order to read an E-book (most books can be read as PDF files), they are popular because they enable options similar to those of a paper book—readers can bookmark pages, make notes, highlight passages, and save selected text. In addition to these familiar possibilities, e-Book readers also include built-in dictionaries, and alterable font sizes and styles. Typically, an e-Book reader hand-held device weighs from about twenty-two ounces to three or four pounds and can store from four thousand to over half a million pages of text and graphics. A popular feature is its back-lit screen (which makes reading in the dark possible).

Some e-Books can be downloaded for free or at reduced cost, however, prices for many e-Books—especially bestsellers—are similar to those of hardcover books, and are sometimes higher. Most e-Books at Barnes and Noble, for example, are comparable in price to their traditional print versions

## Advantages

- Text can be searched automatically and cross-referenced using *hyperlinks*.
- A single e-book reader containing several books is easier to carry around (less weight and volume) than the same books (or sometimes even a single book) in printed form. Even hundreds or thousands of books may be stored on the same device. Using removable media even more can be carried around easily.
- Also at a fixed place such as at home it can be an advantage that an e-book collection requires very little space.
- Mobile availability of e-books may be provided for users with a mobile data connection, so that these e-books need not be carried around.
- E-books can allow non-permanent highlighting and annotation.
- Font size and font face can be adjusted.
- An e-book can be offered indefinitely, without ever going "out of print".
- Depending on possible digital rights management, it may be easy and cheap to produce a back-up for the case that the e-book is lost or damaged, and/or it may be possible to get a free new copy if that happens.
- It is easier for authors to self-publish e-books.
- A free e-book can stimulate the sales of the printed version.
- The production of e-books does not consume *paper, ink,* etc.

- E-books may allow animated images or multimedia clips to be embedded.
- E-books allow for greater fidelity in colour reproduction compared to *CMYK* colour printing (although some e-book readers have only monochrome displays).
- Depending on the device an e-book may be readable in low light or even total darkness. For devices for which this applies, energy consumption for reading without daylight is less than that of a lamp needed for reading a printed book.
- An e-book can automatically open at the last read page.
- While an e-book reader costs much more than one book, the electronic texts are generally cheaper. Moreover, a great share of books are available for free, without any charge at all. For example, all fiction from before the year 1900 is in the *public domain*.
- *Text-to-speech software* can be used to convert e-books to *audio books* automatically.

## E-Book Formats

The major problem with e-books is the many formats competing for prime time, including Adobe PDF, which is very popular, as well as Microsoft Reader, e-Reader, Mobipocket Reader, OPS and Open Reader.

Although it would seem a no-brainer, most formats do not support dictionaries and encyclopedias all that well. They have a search capability, but not a direct lookup, which means if a person looks up the term "network", all the definitions that contain the word "network" will be retrieved rather than the single definition of that term. The results are akin to the mountain of results retrieved by a search engine.

# Glossary of Terms

**Accuracy**—One of the considerations in determining sample validity: the degree to which bias is absent from the sample—the under estimators and the over estimators are balanced among members of the sample (i.e. no systematic variance).

**Alternative hypothesis**—That a difference exists between the sample parameter and the population statistic to which it is compared; the logical opposite of the null hypothesis used in significance testing (notation: HA ).

**Ambiguous questions**—Questions that are not clearly worded and likely to be interpreted by respondents in different ways.

**Analytical study**—A study that tries to explain why or how certain variables influence the dependent variable of interest to the researcher.

**Applied research**—Research conducted in a particular setting with the specific objective of solving an existing problem in the situation.

**Arbitrary scales**—Universal practice of ad hoc scale development used by instrument designers to create scales that are highly specific to the practice or object being studied.

**Area charts**—A statistical presentation technique used for time series and frequency distributions over time; a.k.a. stratum or surface charts.

**Area sampling**—A type of cluster sampling usually applied to a population with well-defined political or natural boundaries but without a detailed sample frame; population is divided into homogeneous clusters from which a single-stage or multistage sample is drawn.

**Association**—The process used to recognize and understand patterns in data, then used to understand and exploit natural patterns.

**Attitudinal factors**—Peoples' feelings, dispositions, and reactions toward the organisation and factors in the work environment such as the work itself, the co-workers, or supervision.

**Audience**—The intended reader of the secondary source; one of the five factors used to evaluate the value of a secondary source.

**Authority**—The credibility of a secondary source as indicated by the credentials of the author and publisher; one of five factors used to evaluate the value of a secondary source.

**Bar charts**—A statistical presentation technique that represents frequency data as horizontal or vertical bars, vertical bars are most often used for time series and quantitative classifications (histograms, stacked bar, and multiple variable charts are specialized bar charts).

**Bar code**—Technology used to simplify the researcher's role as a data recorder, involving a label reading device that scans electronically read codes on product labels and service documents.

**Basic research**—Research conducted to generate knowledge and understanding of **phenobmena** (in the work setting) that would add to the existing body of **knowledge** (about organisations and management theory)

**Bayesian statistics**—An approach that goes beyond sampling data for making decisions by including all available data—specifically subjective probability estimates based on general experience rather than on specific data collected (see Appendix B).

**Behavioural factors**—Actual behaviour of employees on the job, such as being late, working hard, remaining absent, or quitting work.

**Bias**—Any error that creeps into the data. Biases can be introduced by the researcher, the respondent, the measuring instrument, the sample, and so on.

**Bibliography**—A listing of books, articles, and other relevant materials, alphabetized according to the last name of the authors, referencing the titles of their works, and indicating where they can be located.

**Bivariate correlation analysis**—Measures of correlation that use non-continuous variables and that distinguish between independent and dependent variables.

**Bivariate normal distribution**—An assumption of correlation analysis, that data are from a random sample of a population where the two variables are normally distributed in a joint manner.

**Branched questions**—A type of measurement question that determines the respondent's path (question sequencing) in a study; the answer to one question assumes other questions have been asked or answered, and directs the respondent to answer specific questions that follow and skip other questions.

**Briefings**—An oral presentation technique made to a small group of interested managers, where statistics constitute an important portion of the topic and which lasts from 20 minutes to an hour.

**Broad problem area**—A situation where one senses a possible need for research and problem solving, even though the specific problem is not clear.

**Buffer question**—A type of neutral measurement question designed chiefly to establish rapport with the respondent (usually nominal data).

**Callbacks**—Procedure involving repeated attempts to make contact with a targeted respondent to ensure that the targeted respondent is reached and motivated to participate in the study.

**Case study**—The documented history of noteworthy events that have taken place in a given institution.

**Category scale**—A scale that uses multiple items to seek a single response.

**Causal analysis**—Analysis done to detect cause-and-effect relationships between two or among more variables.

**Causal hypothesis**—Statement that describes a relationship between two variables with respect to some cases, one variable leads to an effect on the other variable (a.k.a. explanatory hypothesis).

**Causal study**—Attempts to reveal the relationship between variables; a.k.a. causation (A produces B or causes B to occur).

**Cells**—In a cross-tabulation, a sub-group of the data created by the value intersection of two (or more) variables, where each cell contains the count of cases as well as the percentage of the joint classification.

**Census**—A count of all the elements in a population.

**Central tendency**—A measure of location, most commonly the mean, median, and mode.

**Checklist**—A measurement question that poses numerous alternatives and encourages multiple responses, but where relative order of those responses is not important (nominal data).

**Chi-square test**—A non-parametric test of significance used for nominal measurements.

**Classification data**—Personal information or demographic details of the respondents such as age, marital status, and educational level.

**Classification question**—A type of measurement question that provides sociological-demographic variables for use in grouping respondent's answers nominal, ordinal, interval or ratio data).

**Closed questions**—Questions with a clearly delineated set of alternatives that confine the respondents' choice to one of them.

**Cluster analysis**—A technique that identifies homogeneous sub-groups or clusters of study objects or people, then displays the relevant clusters in a diagram (dendogram); viewing the data by segmented or groups of data cases.

**Cluster sampling**—A sampling plan that involves dividing the population into clusters or sub-groups, then drawing a sample from each sub-group in a single-stage or multi-stage design.

**Coding**—Assigning numbers or other symbols to answers to that responses can be tallied and grouped into a limited number of classes or categories.

**Comparative scale**—A scale that provides a benchmark or point of reference to assess attitudes, opinions and the like.

**Comparative study**—A study conducted by collecting data from several settings or organisations.

**Complex probability sampling**—Several probability sampling designs (such as systematic and stratified random), which offer an alternative to the cumbersome, simple random sampling design.

**Computer-assisted telephone interviews**—(CATI)—Interviews in which questions are prompted onto a PC monitor that is networked into the telephone system, to which respondents provide their answers.

**Computer-administered telephone survey**—A study conducted wholly by computer contact between respondent and interviewer, where questions are voice-synthesized and data are tallied continuously.

**Computer-assisted personal interviewing (CAPI)**—A personal, face-to-face interview where the researcher may be guided by computer-sequenced questions, where data may be entered as responses are given, or where visualization techniques may be provided digitally to each participant.

**Computer-assisted telephone interviewing (CATI)**—A study conducted wholly by telephone contact between respondent and interviewer where interview is software-driven, usually in a central location with interviewers in acoustically isolated interviewing carrels; data are tallied, as they are collected.

**Concept**—A bundle of meanings or characteristics associated with certain events, objects, conditions, or situations.

**Concurrent validity**—Relates to criterion-related validity, which is established at the same time the test is administered.

**Confidence**—The probability estimate of how much reliance can be placed on the findings; the usual accepted level of confidence in social science research is 95%.

**Consensus scale**—A scale developed through consensus or the unanimous agreement of a panel of judges as to the items that measure a concept.

**Constant sum rating scale**—A scale where the respondents distribute a fixed number of points across several items.

**Construct validity**—Testifies to how well the results obtained from the use of the measure fit the theories around which the test was designed.

**Content analysis**—A flexible, widely applicable tool for measuring the semantic content of a communication—including counts, categorizations, associations, interpretations, etc. (e.g. used to study the content of speeches, ads, newspaper and magazine editorials, etc.); contains four types of items: syntactical, referential, propositional, and thematic.

**Content validity**—Establishes the representative sampling of a whole set of items that measures a concept, and reflects how well the dimensions and elements thereof are delineated.

**Contingency tables**—A cross-tabulation table constructed for statistical testing, with the test determining whether the classification variables are independent.

**Control group**—The group that is not exposed to any treatment in an experiment.

**Controlled variable**—Any exogenous or extraneous variable that could contaminate the cause-and-effect relationship, but the effects of which can be controlled through the process either of matching or randomization.

**Control—**The ability to replicate a scenario and dictate a particular outcome;

**Convenience samples**—A low-cost but less reliable non-probability sample where element selection is unrestricted or left to those elements easily accessible by the researcher.

**Convergent validity**—That which is established when the scores obtained by two different instruments measuring the same concepts, or by measuring the concept by two different methods, are highly correlated.

**Correlation analysis**—Analysis done to trace the mutual influence of variables on one another.

**Correlation matrix**—A table used to display coefficients for more than two variables.

**Correlation study**—A research study conducted to identify the important factors associated with the variables of interest.

**Correlational hypothesis—**Variables occur together in some specified manner without implying that one causes the other.

**Creativity session**—Qualitative technique in child research where an individual activity session is followed by a sharing session, where children build on each other's creative ideas.

**Criterion variable**—Variable of primary interest to the study, also known as the dependent variable.

**Critical value**—The dividing point(s) between the region of acceptance and the region of rejection; these values can be computed in terms of the standardized random variable due to the normal distribution of sample means.

**Cross cultural research**—Studies done across two or more cultures to understand, describe, analyse, or predict phenomena.

**Cross-sectional study**—A research study for shich data are gathered just once (stretched through it may be over a period of days, weeks, or months) to answer the research question.

**Cross-tabulation**—A technique for comparing two classification variables (usually nominal data variables).

**Cumulative scaling**—A scale development technique in which scale items are tested based on a scoring system, where agreement with one extreme scale item results also in endorsement of all other items that take a less extreme position.

**Data mining**—Helps to trace patterns and relationships in the data stored in the data warehouse.

**Data**—Facts (attitudes, behaviour, motivations, etc.) collected from respondents or observations (mechanical or direct) plus published information; categorized as primary and secondary.

**Decision variable**—A quantifiable characteristic, attribute, or outcome on which a choice decision will be made.

**Deduction**—The process of arriving at conclusions based on the interpretation of the meaning of the results of data analysis.

**Dependency techniques**—Those techniques where criterion or dependent variables and predictor or independent variables are present (e.g. multiple regression, MANOVA, discriminant analysis, etc.)

**Dependent variable (DV)**—The variable measured, predicted, or otherwise monitored by the researcher, expected to be affected by a manipulation of the independent variable.

**Depth interview**—An extensive one-on-one objective-driven and orchestrated conversation with a participant, usually lasting 1 or more hours.

**Descriptive hypothesis**—States the existence, size, form or distribution of some variable.

**Descriptive statistics**—Display characteristics of the location, spread, and shape of an array of data.

**Descriptive study**—Attempts to describe or define a subject, often by creating a profile of a group of problems, people or events, through the collection of data and the tabulation of the frequencies on research variables or their interaction; the study reveals who, what, when, where, or how much; the study concerns a univariate question or hypothesis in which the research asks about or states something about the size, form, distribution, or existence of a variable.

**Dichotomous scale**—Scale used to elicit a Yes/No response, or an answer to two different aspects of concepts.

**Dictionary**—Secondary sources that define words, terms or jargon unique to a discipline; may include information on people, events, or organizations that shape the discipline; an excellent source of acronyms.

**Direct observation**—When the observer is physically present and personally monitors and records the behaviour of the subject.

**Directional hypothesis**—An Educated conjecture as to the direction of the relationship, or differences among variables, which could be positive or negative, or more or less, respectively.

**Discriminant analysis**—The joining of a nominal dependent variable with one or more independent internal or ratio variables into an equation that is used to predict the classification of a new observation.

**Discriminant validity**—That which is established when two variables are theorized to be uncorrelated, and the scores obtained by measuring them are indeed empirically found to be so.

**Disguised question**—A measurement question designed to conceal the questions and study's true purpose.

**Distribution (of data)**—The array of value counts from lowest to highest value, resulting from the tabulation of incidence for each variable by value.

**Don't know (DK) responses**—A response provided by respondents when they have insufficient knowledge to answer the question, when the instrument fails to provide an understandable operational definition for a construct, when the respondents have not formed a judgment on an issue, are reluctant to provide an answer, or feel the issue is too unimportant to formulate an answer.

**Double blind (study)**—A condition that exists when neither the researchers nor the subjects know when a subject is being exposed to the experimental treatment (IV).

**Double sampling**—A procedure for selecting a subsample from a sample for further study; a.k.a. sequential sampling or multi-phase sampling.

**Double-barreled question**—A type of multiple questions that includes two or more questions in one that the respondent might need to answer differently to preserve the accuracy of the data.

**Dummy variable**—Nominal variable used in multiple regression and coded 0, 1 as all other variables must be interval or ratio measures.

**Editing data**—The process of going over the data and ensuring that they are complete and acceptable for data analysis.

**Editing**—A customary first step in analysis for detecting errors and data omissions, correcting them when possible, and certifying that minimum data quality standards are achieved.

**Efficiency in sampling**—Attained when the sampling design chosen either results in a cost reduction to the researcher or offers a greater degree of accuracy in terms of the sample size.

**Electronic questionnaire**—Online questionnaire administered when the microcomputer is hooked up to computer networks.

**Element**—A single member of the population.

**Ex post facto design**—Studying subjects who have already been exposed to a stimulus and comparing them to those not so exposed, so as to establish cause-and-effect relationships (in contrast to establishing cause-and-effect relationships by manipulating an independent variable in a lab or a field setting).

**Executive summary (final report)**—This document is written as the last element of a research report and is either a concise summary of the major findings, conclusions and recommendations or can be a report-in-miniature covering all aspects in abbreviated form.

**Executive summary**—An informative abstract providing the essentials of the proposal without the details.

**Exogenous variable**—A variable that exerts an influence on the cause-and-effect relationship between two variables in some way, and needs to be controlled.

**Experience survey**—An exploratory technique where knowledgeable experts share their ideas about important issues or aspects of the subject and relate what is important across the subject's range of experience; usually involves a personal or phone interview.

**Experimental design**—A study design in which the researcher might create an artificial setting, control some variables, and manipulate the independent variable to establish cause-and-effect relationships.

**Experimental group**—The group exposed to a treatment in an experimental design.

**Experimental treatment**—The manipulated independent variable.

**Experiments**—Studies involving intervention (manipulation of one or more variables) by the researcher beyond that required for measurement to determine the effect on another variable.

**Explanatory hypothesis**—Statement that describes a relationship between two variables with respect to some case, one variable leads to an effect on the other variable (a.k.a. causal hypothesis).

**Exploration**—The process of collecting information to formulate research, investigative, or measurement questions; loosely structured studies that discover future research tasks, including developing concepts, establishing priorities, developing operational definitions, and improving research design; a phase of a research project where the researcher expands understanding of the management dilemma.

**Exploratory data analysis**—A process whereby the actual data patterns guide the data analysis or suggest revisions to the preliminary data analysis plan

**Exploratory research**—Research undertaken to expand understanding of the research dilemma, identify alternative ways to address a problem.

**Exploratory study**—A research study where very little knowledge or information is available on the subject under investigation.

**Extemporaneous presentation**—An oral presentation technique made from minimal notes or an outline, with a more conversational style.

**External validity**—When an observed causal relationship can be generalized across persons, settings, and times.

**Extraneous variable**—Variables to assume (because they have little affected, or their impact is randomized) or exclude from a research study; notation: EV.

**F ratio**—The result of an F test, done to compare measurements of k independent samples.

**Face validity**—An aspect of validity examining whether the item on the scale, on he face of it, reads as if it indeed measures that it is supposed to measure.

**Faces scale**—A particular representation of the graphic scale, depicting faces with expressions that range from smiling to sad.

**Factor analysis**—Techniques for discovering patterns among the variables to determine if an underlying combination of the original variables (a factor) can summarize the original set.

**Factor scales**—Types of scales that deal with multidimensional content and underlying dimensions, such as factor, and cluster analyses, and metric and non-metric Multi-dimensional scaling.

**Factor**—Denotes an independent variable (IV) in an experiment; these are divided into treatment levels for the experiment.

**Factorial validity**—That which indicates through the use of factor analytic techniques whether a test is a pure measure of some specific factor or dimension.

**Factors**—In principal components analysis, the result of a transformation of a set of variables into a new set of composite variables (factors) that are linear and not correlated with each other.

**Field conditions**—The actual environmental conditions where the dependent variable occurs.

**Field experiment**—An experiment done to detect cause-and-effect relationship in the natural environment in which events normally occur.

**Filter question**—A question used to qualify the respondent's knowledge about the target questions of interest.

**Findings non-disclosure**—A type of confidentiality, when the sponsor restricts the researcher from discussing the findings of the research project.

**Five-number summary**—The median, upper and lower quartiles, and the largest and smallest observations of a variable's distribution.

**Fixed sum**—A scale where the respondent assigns 100 points to continuous scale or discrete categories (2-100) (generates interval data).

**Focus group**—An information collection approach widely used in exploratory studies involving a panel of subjects led by a trained moderator that meets for 90 minutes to two hours; the moderator uses group dynamics to explore ideas, feelings, and experiences on a specific topic; can be conducted in person or via phone.

**Forced choice**—Elicits the ranking of objects relative to one another.

**Formal study**—Begins with a hypothesis or research question and involves precise procedures and data source specifications; tests the hypothesis or answers the research questions posed.

**Format**—How the information is presented and how easy it is to find a specific piece of information within a secondary source; one of five factors used to evaluate the value of a secondary source.

**Free-response question**—A type of measurement question in which the respondent provides the answer to without the aid of an interviewer (either in phone, personal interview or self-administered surveys); a.k.a. open-ended question (nominal, ordinal or ratio data).

**Frequencies**—The number of times various sub-categories of a phenomenon occur, from which the percentage and cumulative percentage of any occurrence can be calculated.

**Goodness of fit**—A measure of how well the regression model is able to predict Y.

**Graphic rating scale**—A scale that graphically illustrates the responses that can be provided, rather than specifying any discrete response categories.

**Graphic rating scale**—A scale where the rater places his or her response along a line or continuum; the score or measurement is its distance in millimeters from either end point.

**Halo effect (error)**—A systematic bias that the rater introduces by carrying over a generalized impression of the subject from one rating to another.

**Handbook**—A secondary source used to identify key terms, people, or events relevant to the management dilemma or management question.

**Histogram**—A bar chart data display technique that groups data values into equal intervals; especially useful for revealing skewness, kurtosis, and modal pattern.

**Hypothesis testing**—A means of testing if the if-then statements generated from the theoretical framework hold true when subjected to rigorous examination.

**Hypothesis**—A proposition formulated for empirical testing; a tentative or conjectural declarative belief or statement that describes the relationship between two or more variables.

**Independent variable (IV)**—The variable manipulated by the researcher, which causes an effect or change on the dependent variable.

**In-depth interview**—A type of interview, usually unstructured and in an unconstrained environment, that encourages the respondent to talk extensively, sharing as much information as possible.

**Index**—Secondary data source that helps identify and locate a single book, journal article, author, etc. from among a large set.

**Indirect observation**—When the recording of data is done by mechanical, photographic, or electronic means.

**Induction**—To draw a conclusion from one or more particular facts or pieces of evidence; the conclusion explains the facts.

**Internal validity**—The ability of a research instrument to measure what it is purported to measure; when the conclusion(s) drawn about a demonstrated experimental relationship truly implies cause.

**Internal validly of experiments**—Attests to the confidence that can be placed in the cause-and-effect relationship found in experimental designs.

**Internet**—A vast network of computers connecting people and information worldwide.

**Interval scale**—A multipoint scale that taps the differences, the order, and the equality of the magnitude of the differences in the responses.

**Intervening variable**—A variable that surfaces the function of an independent variable and helps in explaining the influence of independent variable on the dependent variable.

**Interview schedule**—An alternative term for the questionnaire used in an interview (phone or in-person communication approaches to collecting data).

**Interviewer error**—Error that results £Tom interviewer influence of the respondent.

**Interviewing**—A data collection method in which the researcher asks for the information verbally from the respondents.

**Intranet**—A company's proprietary computer network.

**Investigative questions**—Questions the researcher must answer to satisfactorily arrive at a conclusion about the research question.

**Item analysis scaling**—Scale development where instrument designers develop instrument items and test them with a group of respondents; individual items are analyzed to determine those which highly discriminate between persons or objects; e.g. Likert scale and summated scale.

**Judgment sampling** —It is a non-probability sample design in which the sample subject is chosen on the basis of the individual's ability to provide the type of special information needed by the researcher.

**Lab experiment**—An experimental design set-up in an artificial setting where the controls and manipulations are introduced to establish cause-and-effect relationship among variables.

**Leading questions** —The questions asked in such a way which leads the respondents to give the answers that the researcher would like to obtain.

**Leniency (error)**—An error that results when the respondent is consistently an easy rater.

**Letter of transmittal**—An element of the final report, this letter refers to the authorization for the project and any specific instructions or limitations placed on the study and states the purpose and scope of the study; not necessary for internal projects.

**Level of significance**—The probability of rejecting a true null hypothesis.

**Likert scale**—A variation of the summated rating scale, this scale asks a rater to agree or disagree with statements that express either favorable or unfavorable attitudes toward the object.

**Literature review**—The documentation of a comprehensive review of the published work from secondary sources of data.

**Loaded questions**—Questions that would elicit highly biased emotional responses from subjects.

**Local area network**—Computers in close proximity connected together, enabling people to share information and files.

**Longitudinal study**—A research study for which data are gathered at several points in time to answer a research question.

**Management information system**—A generic term for information within an enterprise, facilitated by software and technology.

**Management question**—The management dilemma restated in question format; categorized as "choice of objectives", "generation and evaluation of solutions", or "trouble-shooting or control of a situation".

**Management report**—A report written for the non-technically-oriented manager or client.

**Manipulation**—How the researcher exposes the subjects to the independent variable to determine cause-and-effect relationship in experimental design.

**Mean**—The average of a set of figures.

**Moderating variable**—A variable on which the relationship between two other variables in contingent. That is, if the moderating variable is present, the relationship between the two variables will hold good, not otherwise.

**Mortality**—The loss of research subject during the course of the experiment, which confounds the cause-and-effect relationship.

**Motivational research**—It is a data gathering technique directed towards surfacing information ideas, and thoughts that are not easily verbalized.

**Multidimensional scaling (MSD)**—A scaling technique for objects or people where the instrument scale seeks to measure more than one attribute of the respondents or object; results are usually mapped.

**Multiple choice-multiple response scale**—A scale that offers respondent multiple options and solicits one or more answers (nominal or ordinal data); a.k.a. checklist.

**Multiple choice-single response scale**—A measurement question that poses more than two responses but seeks a single answer, or one that seeks a single rating from a gradation of preference, interest or agreement (nominal or ordinal data) a.k.a multiple choice question.

**Multiple regression analysis**—A statistical technique used to predict the variance in the dependent variable by regressing the independent variable against it.

**Multiple regression**—A descriptive tool used to (1) develop a self-weighting estimating equation by which to predict values for a dependent variable from the values of independent variables, (2) control confounding variables to better evaluate the contribution of other variables, or (3) test and explain a causal theory.

**Multistage cluster sampling**—A probability sampling design that is a stratified sampling of clusters.

**Nominal scale**—A scale that classifies individuals or objects into mutually exclusive and collectively exhaustive group and offer basic information on the variables of interest.

**Non-contrived setting**—Research conducted in the natural environment where activities take place in the normal manner.

**Non-directional hypothesis**—An educated conjecture of a relationship between two variables, the directionality of which cannot be guessed.

**Non-parametric statistics**—Statistics used to test hypothesis, when the population from which the sample is drawn cannot be assumed to be normally distributed.

**Non-probability sampling**—A sampling design in which the elements in the population do not have a known or predetermined chance of being selected as sample subjects.

**Non-participant observer**—A researcher who collects observations data without becoming an integral part of the system.

**Nuisance variable**—A variable that contaminates the cause-and-effect relationship.

**Null hypothesis**—The conjecture that postulates no differences or no relationship between or among variables.

**Numerical scale**—A scale with bipolar attributes with five points or seven points indicated on the scale.

**Objectivity**—Interpretation of the results, on the basis of the results of the data analysis as opposed to emotional interpretations.

**Objects**—Concepts of ordinary experience, like people, books, autos, genes, or peer-group pressures.

**Observational survey**—Collection of data by observing people or events in the work environment and regarding the information.

**Observation**—The full range of monitoring behavioural and non-behavioural activities and conditions (including record analysis, physical condition analysis, physical process analysis, non-verbal analysis, linguistic analysis, extra linguistic analysis, and spatial analysis).

**Open-ended question**—A type of measurement question in which the respondent provides the answer without the aid of an interviewer.

**Operational definition**—A definition for a variable stated in terms of specific testing criteria or operations, specifying what must be counted, measured, or gathered through our senses.

**Operations research**—A quantitative approach taken to analyze and solve problems of complex nature.

**Ordinal scale**—A scale that not only categorizes the qualitative differences in the variables but also allows for the rand ordering of these categories in a meaningful way.

**Paired comparison**—Respondents choose between two objects at a time, with the process repeated with a small number of objects.

**Paired-interviews**—In this 45-60 minute interview, two children, either friendship-pairs or straight-pairs (children who don't know each other ahead of time), interact a moderator.

**Panels**—A technique for longitudinal survey work using the same respondents repeatedly over time, using personal, phone, and computer interviewing as well as self-administered survey techniques; the use of mail-delivered diaries is common.

**Participant observation**—When the observer acts as both observer and participant with the subject; the observer can be known or concealed.

**Participant**—A term used to describe the respondent, subject, or sample element in a research study.

**Path analysis**—The use of regression to describe an entire structure of linkages that have been advanced by a causal theory.

**Path diagram**—A diagram that presents predictive and associative relationships among constructs and indicators in a structural model.

**Pearson correlation coefficient**—The r symbolizes the estimate of linear association based on sampling data and varies over a range of + 1 to –1; the prefix (+, -) indicates the direction of the relationship (positive or inverse), while the number represents the strength of relationship (closer to 1, the stronger the relationship; 0 = no relationship); and the p represents the population correlation.

**Personal interview**—A face-to-face, two-way communication initiated by an interviewer to obtain information from a respondent.

**Pie charts**—A statistical presentation technique that uses sections of a circle (slices of a pie) to represent 100% of a frequency distribution of the subject being graphed.

**Pilot test**—A trail collection of data to detect weaknesses in design and instrumentation and provide proxy data for selection of a probability sample.

**Population**—The entire group of people, events, or things of that the researcher desires to investigate.

**Population frame**—A listing of all the elements in the population from which the sample is drawn.

**Pretest** —A test given to subjects to measure the dependent variable before exposing them to a treatment.

**Pretesting survey questions**—Test of the understandability and appropriateness of the questions planned to be included in a regular survey, using a small number of respondents.

**Primary data**—Data collected firsthand for subsequent analysis to find solutions to the problem researched.

**Primary sources**—Original works of research or raw data without interpretation or pronouncements that represent an official opinion or position; include memos, letters, complete interviews or speeches, laws, regulations, court decisions and most government data, including census, economic and labour data; the most authoritative of all sources.

**Probability sampling**—The sampling design in which the elements of the population have some known chance or probability of being selected as sample subjects.

**Problem definition**—A precise, succinct statement of the question or issue that is to be investigated.

**Pure research**—Research that aims to solve perplexing questions of a theoretical nature, with little direct influence on actions, performance, or policy decisions (a.k.a. basic research).

**Purpose**—What the author (or in the case of many Internet sites, the collective authors in an institution) is trying to accomplish with the secondary source; one of five factors in secondary source evaluation.

**Purposive sampling**—A nonprobability sampling design in which the required information is gathered from special or specific targets or groups of people on some rational basis.

**Purposiveness in research** —The situation in which research is focused on solving a well-identified and defined problem, rather than aimlessly looking for answers to vague questions.

**Qualitative study**—Research involving analysis of data / information that are descriptive in nature and not readily quantifiable.

**Qualitative techniques**—A fundamental approach of exploration, including in-depth interviews, participant observation, videotaping of subjects, projective techniques and psychological testing, case studies, elite interviewing and document analysis.

**Quantitative data** —Data that are not immediately quantifiable unless they are coded and categorized in some way.

**Questionnaire**—A preformulated written set of questions to which the respondent records the answers, usually within rather closely delineated alternatives.

**Quota sampling**—A type of purposive sampling in which relevant characteristics are used to stratify the sample in an attempt to improve the representativeness of the sample.

**Random assignment**—A process that uses a randomized sample frame for assigning subjects to experimental and control groups in an attempt to assure that the groups are as comparable as possible with respect to the dv; each subject must have an equal chance for exposure to each level of the independent variable; a.k.a. Randomization.

**Random dialing procedures**—A procedure for bypassing out-of-date phone directories that requires choosing phone exchanges or exchange blocks and then generating random numbers within these blocks for calling

**Random error**—Error that occurs erratically, without pattern; see also sampling error.

**Range**—The spread in a set of numbers indicated by the difference in the two extreme values in the observations.

**Ranking question**—A measurement question that asks the respondent to compare and order two or more objects or properties using a numeric scale.

**Rating question**—A measurement question that asks the respondent to position each property or object on a companion verbal, numeric, or graphic scale.

**Rating scale**—A measurement approach that asks the respondent to score an object or property without making a direct comparison to another object and thus position each factor on a companion scale, either verbal, numeric, or graphic (ordinal or interval data); see also rating question.

**Recall dependant questions**—Questions that elicit from the respondents information that involves recall of experiences from the past that may be hazy in their memory.

**Reliability**—A characteristic of measurement concerned with accuracy, precision, and consistency; a necessary but not sufficient condition for validity (if the measure is not reliable, it cannot be valid).

**Replicability**— The repeatability of similar results when identical research is conducted at different times or in different organizational settings.

**Representativeness of sample**—The extent to which the sample that is selected possesses the same characteristics as the population from which it is drawn.

**Research**—An organized, systematic, critical, scientific inquiry or investigation into a specific problem, undertaken with the objective of finding answers or solutions thereto.

**Research design**—The blueprint for fulfilling research objectives and answering questions.

**Research interference**—The extent to which the person conducting the research interferes with the normal course of work at the study site.

**Research process**—Various decision stages involved in a research project, and the relationship between those stages.

**Research proposal**—A document that sets out the purpose of the study and the research design details of the investigation to be carried out by the researcher.

**Research question(s)**—The choice hypothesis that best states the objective of the research; the answer to this question would provide the manage with the desired information necessary to make a decision with respect to the management dilemma.

**Research variable**—An event, act, or characteristic measured by research.

**Sample**—A subset or sub-group of the population.

**Sample size**—The actual number of subjects chosen as a sample to represent the population characteristics.

**Sample statistics**—Descriptors of the relevant variables computed from sample data.

**Sampling**—The process of selecting items from the population so that the sample characteristics can be generalized to the population. Sampling involves both design choice and sample size decisions.

**Sampling error**—A reflection of the influences of chance in drawing the sample from the population the error not accounted for by systematic variance

**Sampling frame**—A list of elements in the population from which the sample is actually drawn

**Scale**—A tool or mechanism by which individuals, events, or objects are distinguished on the variables of interest in the same meaningful way.

**Scaling**—The assignment of numbers or symbols to an indicant of a property of objects to impart some of the characteristics of the numbers to the property

**Secondary data**—Data that have already been gathered by researchers, data published in statistical and other journals, and information available from any published or unpublished source available either within or outside the organisation, all of which might be useful to the researcher.

**Secondary sources**—Interpretations of primary data generally without new research.

**Selection effects**—The threat to internal validity that is a function of improper or unmatched selection of subjects for the experimental and control groups.

**Self-administered questionnaire**—A survey delivered to the respondent via personal (intercept) or non-personal (computer-delivered, mail delivered) means that is completed by the respondent without additional contact with an interviewer.

**Semantic differential scale**—A scale that measures the psychological meanings of an attitude object and produces interval data uses bipolar nouns, noun phrases, adjectives, or non-verbal stimuli such as visual sketches.

**Simple random sampling**—A probability sampling design in which every single element in the population has a known and equal chance of being selected as a subject.

**Simulation**—A model building technique for assessing the possible effects changes that might be introduced in a system.

**Software**—Technology that is capable of designing programmes to meet the different needs of individuals and companies.

**Standard deviation**—A measure of dispersion for parametric data; the square root of the variance.

**Staple scale**—A scale that measures both the direction and intensity of the attributes of a concept.

**Statistical regression**—The threat to internal validity that results when various groups in the study have been selected on the basis of their extreme scores on some important variables.

**Statistical significance**—The quality of the difference between a sample value and its population value the difference is statistical significance if it is unlikely to have occurred by chance (represent random sampling fluctuations).

**Statistical study**—A study that attempts to capture a population's characteristics by making inferences from a sample's characteristics; involves hypothesis testing and is more comprehensive than a case study.

**Stratified randam sampling**—A probability sampling design that divides the population into meaningful subsets and then randomly chooses the subjects from each subject.

**Structural variables—**Factors related to a form and design of the organisation such as the role and positions, communication channel, control systems, reward systems and span of control.

**Structured interviews**—Interviews conducted by the researcher with a predetermined list of questions to be asked to the respondents.

**Structured observational studies—**Studies in which the researcher observes and notes specific activities and behaviour that are important factors for observation, before the commencement of the study.

**Subject**—A single member of the sample.

**Survey**—A means of questioning a respondent via a collection of questions and instructions for both the respondent and the interviewer; a.k.a questionnaire, instrument, or interview schedule.

**Synopsis**—A brief summary of the research study.

**Systematic observation**—Data collection through observation that employs standardized procedures, trained observers, schedules for recording and other devices for the observer that mirror the scientific procedures of other primary data methods.

**Systematic sampling**—A complex probability sampling technique in which the population (N) is divided by the desired sample (n) to obtain a skip pattern (k). Using a random start between 1 - k, each kth element is chosen from the sample frame; usually treated as a simple random sample but statistically more efficient.

**Technical report**—A report written for an audience of researchers on technical aspects

**Technology**—Any mechanism that transforms inputs to outputs.

**Telephone interview**—The information gathering method by which the interviewer asks the interviewee over the telephone, rather that face-to-face, for information needed for the research.

**Tertiary sources**—Finding aids to discover primary or secondary sources, such as indexes, bibliographies, and Internet search engines; also may be an interpretation of a secondary source.

**Test unit**—An alternative term for a subject within an experiment; it can be a person, an animal, a machine, a geographic entity, etc.

**Theoretical framework**—A logically developed, described and explained network of associations among variables.

**Theory**—A set of systematically integrated concepts, definitions and propositions that are advanced to explain a phenomena (facts).

**Time sampling**—The process of selecting some time points or intervals to observe elements, acts, or conditions from a population of observable behaviour or conditions to represent the population as a whole; three types include time-point samples, time-interval samples or continuous real-time samples.

**T-test**—A parametric test to determine the statistical significance between a sample distribution mean and a population parameter, when the population standard deviation is unknown and the sample standard deviation is used as a proxy.

**Type I error**—A type of hypothesis testing error when a true null hypothesis (there is no difference) is rejected; the alpha (D) value called the level of significance is the probability of rejecting the true null hypothesis.

**Type II error**—A type of hypothesis testing error when a false null hypothesis (there is no difference) is rejected; the beta (D) value is the probability of incorrectly rejecting the false null hypothesis; the power of the test = 1 – 0, and is the probability that we will correctly reject the false null hypothesis.

**Unbalance rating scale**—An even numbered scale that has no neutral point.

**Unbiased questions**—Questions posed in accordance with the principles of wording and measurement, and the right questioning technique so as to get the least biased responses.

**Unstructured observational studies**—Studies in which the researcher observes and makes notes of all activities and behaviour that occurs in the situation without pre-determining what particular variable will be of specific interest.

**Unstructured question**—A type of measurement question in which the respondent provides the answer to without the aid of an interviewer (either in phone, personal interview or self-administered surveys); see also open-ended question or free response question (nominal, ordinal or ratio data).

**Validity content**—The degree to which a research instrument provides adequate coverage of the topic under study.

**Validity**—A characteristic of measurement concerned that a test measures what the researcher actually wishes to measure; that differences found with a measurement tool reflect true differences among respondents drawn from a population.

**Validity-construct**—The degree to which a research instrument is able to measure or infer the presence of an abstract property.

**Variable**—A characteristic, trait, or attribute that is measured; a synonym for a construct or the property being studied; a symbol to which values are assigned; includes several different types: continuous, control, decision, dependent, dichotomous, discrete, dummy, extraneous, independent, intervening, and moderating variables; see also research variable.

**Variable**—Anything that can take on differing or varying values.

**Web site**—Site accessible on the Internet created by individuals and organisations for the purpose of sharing information.

# Bibliography

Aderson, T.W., Introduction to Multivariate Statistical Analysis, New York : John Wiley & Sons, 1958.

Arthur, Maurice, Philosophy of Scientific Investigation, Baltimore : John Hopkins University Press, 1943.

Ballou, Stephen, V., A. Model for Theses and Research Papers, Boson : Houghton Mifflin, 1970.

Barzeen, Jackques, and Graff, Henry F., The Modern Researcher, New York: Harcourt, Brace & World, 1970.

Campbell, William Giles and Stephen Vaughan Ballou, Form and Style : Theses, Reports, Term Papers, Boston : Houghton Mifflin Co., 1974.

Doby, John T., (ed.), An Introduction Social Research, Harrisburg, Pa : Stack Pole Co., 1954.

Edwards, Allen L., Experimendal Design in Psychological Research, New York : Hold Rinehart and Winston, 1972.

Janda, Kenneth, Data Processing, Evanston, 111. : North-Western University Press, 1965.

Johnson, Janet Buttolph and Joslyn, Richard A., Political Sciene Research Methods, New Delhi : Prentice Hall of India, 1989.

Komidar, Joseph, S., "Use of the Library", in Goode, William, J. and Hatt, Paul K., Methods in Social Research, New York : McGraw Hill Book Company, 1952.

Kahn, Robert, I., and Cannell Charles, F., The Dynamics of Interviewing, New York : John Wiley and Sons, 1957.

Kapp, R.O., The Presentation of Technical Information, London: Constable, 1946.

Levin, Richard, I. Statistics for Management, New Delhi : Prentice-Hall of India Pvt. Ltd., 1986.

Mueller, John H., Schuessler Karl, F., and Costner, Herbert, L., Statistical Reasoning in Sociology, Boston : Houghton Mifflin, 1970.

Murdick, Robert, G., Business Research Concept and Practice, Scranton, Pa: International Text Book, 1969.

Niol, Norman H.L., *et al.*, Statitical package for the Social Sciences, New York : McGraw Hill Book Co., 1975.

O.R. Krishnaswami, Methodology of research in social sciences, New Delhi: Himalaya Publishing House, 2006.

Parsons, C.J., Theses and Project Work, London : George Allen and Unwin, 1973.

Richardson, S.A., Dohrenwend, B.S., and Klerin, D., Interviewing : Its Forms and Functions, New York: 1965.

Sehmid, Calvin F., Handbook of Graphic Presentation, New York : Ronald Press, 1954.

Tyler, Leona E., Tests and Measurements Englewood, Cliffs N.J., Prentice Hall, 1963.

William, G. Zigmund, Business research methods, Bangalore: Thomson Learning, 2005.

# Index